# THE SECRET LIFE OF A SATANIST

## The Authorized Biography of Anton LaVey

# THE SECRET LIFE OF A SATANIST

## The Authorized Biography of Anton LaVey

**By Blanche Barton**

**Compleat with Bibliography, Glossary, &
Texts by Anton Szandor LaVey**

𝕱𝖊𝖗𝖆𝖑 𝕳𝖔𝖚𝖘𝖊
𝕷𝖔𝖘 𝕬𝖓𝖌𝖊𝖑𝖊𝖘

The Secret Life of a Satanist © 1990, 1992 by Blanche Barton

ISBN: 0-922915-12-1

9 8 7 6

For a free catalogue of Feral House books, send SASE to:

Feral House
2532 Lincoln Blvd. #359
Venice, CA   90291


Acknowledgements:

     Many thanks are due Burton Wolfe for blazing the trail in his *Devil's Avenger.*
     I would also like to thank Bill Densley and Velora MacKenzie for their support and encouragement, on this and many previous projects. They knew it all along.
     — Blanche Barton

Mail meant for the Church of Satan should be sent to:

Church of Satan
PO Box 210082
San Francisco, CA  94121

This book is dedicated to Anton Szandor LaVey — a harsh critic, demanding teacher and, to my death, a tantalizing mystery.

# Contents

## V. Appendices

## VI. Texts by Anton LaVey

The Secret Life of a Satanist

"World-historical individuals ... may all be called Heroes, inasmuch as they have derived their purposes and their vocation not from the calm regular course of things, sanctioned by the existing order; but from a concealed fount, from that inner Spirit, still hidden beneath the surface, which impinges on the outer world as on a shell and bursts it into pieces.

"They were practical, political men. But at the same time they were thinking men, who had an insight into the requirements of the time — what was ripe for development. This was the very Truth for their age, for their world.... It was theirs to know this nascent principle, the necessary, directly sequent step in progress, which their world was to take; to make this their aim, and to expend their energy in promoting it. World-historical men — the Heroes of an epoch — must therefore be recognized as its clear-sighted ones; *their* deeds, *their* words are the best of the time."

— Georg Wilhelm Hegel, *Philosophy of History*.

"The word 'hero' never seems to fit the noir protagonist, for his world is devoid of the moral framework necessary to produce the traditional hero. He has been wrenched from familiar moorings, and is a hero only in the modern sense in which that word has been progressively redefined to fit the existential bias of contemporary fiction. For the past fifty years we have groped for some term that would more aptly describe such a protagonist: the Hemingway hero; the anti-hero; the rebel hero; the non-hero."

— Robert G. Porfirio, "No Way Out: Existential Motifs in the Film Noir," *International Film Quarterly,* Autumn, 1976.

"People write fictional characters because the real thing doesn't exist."

— Anton LaVey, conversation with author.

# What Manner of Man is This?

One couldn't dream of a more diabolical-looking man. With his head shaven in the tradition of carnival strong men, and a black, Mephistophelean beard tracing up thinly around his lips, Anton LaVey's appearance is decidedly barbaric. His amber eyes look more leonine than human. The small gold ring in his left ear conjures childhood images of gypsies and pirates. Many would see him as their nightmarish vision of the Devil himself.

My impression of Anton LaVey matured slowly, over a period of some 10 years before I ever met him. My father (a dyed-in-the-wool Satanist if ever there was one, though he emphatically denies any theistic label) raised me on generous portions of Kipling and London, with enough Robert Louis Stevenson thrown in to instill me with an early fascination with the hidden and the fantastic. By the age of 13, I was already a jaded occult connoisseur. I pored over all available magical texts ancient and modern, from *Albertus Magnus* to *Diary of a Witch,* and could feel only disdain at their flaccid meanderings.

It's not surprising then that for a long time I resisted reading *The Satanic Bible,* saving myself from certain frustration. During my sexually and intellectually seething adolescence, I had my own ideas about Satan — thoughts that surely no living soul could understand but me. I was wrong. When I finally cracked open LaVey's now-infamous book, I felt a thrill of satisfaction. There were others like me out there, and they called themselves Satanists.

I read Burton Wolfe's *The Devil's Avenger* to find out whether this strange, bald-headed man wasn't just posturing — mouthing-off from a cloistered tower, play-acting his cynicism. But knowing more about LaVey only made me more curious for answers to my questions.

The High Priest of the Church of Satan doesn't look much different than he did in 1967, when he burst into international prominence by performing the world's first public Satanic wedding. With so few new photographs released during LaVey's ten-year media hiatus (roughly from 1976-1986), I can be forgiven for expecting to see a paunchy, balding, good-natured fellow by the time we finally met. LaVey is not paunchy, nor is he good-natured. The intervening years have served to accentuate the angles of his face, making him look more severe than ever. He is also more cynical, bitterly misanthropic, and violently determined in his role as founder of the Church of Satan.

This book attempts to peek into the soul of a heretic. Not a cardboard devil or the comfortably menacing fiction that religionists have, for centuries, earned their living denouncing from every pulpit. If LaVey were a cooperative scapegoat, he would be an inarticulate, posturing dilettante who could be trotted out on talk shows, righteously set upon and vanquished. He has not obliged. Nor is he a pretentious self-proclaimed *evocateur* who can be safely snickered at for spouting what he claims to be the Dark Prince's given word.

Anton LaVey is a complex, and in many ways a frighteningly deceptive man. "No one in the world is more justified in being cynical and bitter than me," says LaVey. "Everyday I think less and less of what others are going to think." It's this "justifiable bitterness" that spurs expressions of LaVey's darkest nature. As Wolfe projected in the conclusion to his first biography, LaVey has become increasingly reclusive and fiercely protective of what he has achieved. He prefers to limit companionship to that of his daughters, a few close, Cerberean friends and professional associates.

After finally being granted an initial interview with LaVey in 1984, it became clear to me that if I wanted to more thoroughly explore this Black Magician's heart and mind, I would have to become woven into the fabric of his everyday life. And so I did. He needed a Girl Friday and seemed satisfied with my enthusiastic determination. Over time, it became my role to arrange interviews with reporters, students and members; iron out travel itineraries; generate informational literature; handle correspondence; straw boss; and generally keep complications to as dull a roar as possible. Along the way, I watched, I listened. To stories, jokes, long-neglected tunes, movies that contained the germs of LaVeyan Satanism. And, as unobtrusively as possible, I began to take notes.

Upon first meeting Anton LaVey, many are disarmed by his good-natured wit, extraordinary talent and almost self-deprecating manner. Those who have the opportunity to be around him for any length of time eventually see a seething, brutal side to LaVey. There is, at times, an almost unbearable oppressiveness to his intolerance and anger. Here is a man who can spend hours delighting in playing forgotten songs, or playing with an animal, yet will become monstrously callous when he feels the need. LaVey is idealistically against hunting and would be the first person to stop to help an injured animal along the road, yet put a nickel in him and he will enthusiastically advocate putting a bounty on selected humans. He speaks with such fervor one doesn't need to question his sincerity.

LaVey can appear infirm one minute and possessed of a madman's supernatural strength the next. Well-trained in firearms and judo, I've seen him deal swiftly and savagely with rowdies who have dared to approach him. On the pistol range, I once made the mistake of bringing up a subject I knew produced a violent reaction in LaVey. Answering my question with barely controlled rage, he hit a perfect bull's eye 200 feet away. He prefers to work his 14-foot bullwhip to siphon off pent-up aggressions, snapping the end off a cigarette just as skillfully as he did when he learned fancy whip cracking from Col. Tim McCoy 40 years ago. With all the elements of daring, mystery and intrigue, Anton LaVey seems less like the neurotic, cramped contemporary than an imposing, complex fictional character out of the pages of Jack London or Somerset Maugham.

The idea behind starting the Church of Satan was not to gain millions of dependent souls who needed activities and organized weekly meetings to keep them involved. LaVey started an organization for non-joiners, the alienated few who felt disenfranchised because of their independence, and who pridefully adopted Satan, the original rebel, as their patron. LaVey wanted to make Christianity, which he sees as fostering stupidity and dull complacency, obsolete. The gulf between our social evolution and our scientific and technological advances was getting dangerously vast. LaVey wanted to give us tools for a revolution against artificial "morality" before the intellectual cramping became fatal for us all. In Satanism, Anton LaVey provided Christianity's *coup de grace*.

Yet despite his influence, LaVey, for the most part, has been ignored by the avatars of our media-centric culture. Visit the "New Age" section of your nearest bookstore. You'll see the entrepreneurs who have taken up LaVeyan ideas, slapping a more palatable name on them to their critical and financial profit. Even the scholars who investigate "evil," "demonic" or even literally "Satanic" influences in the modern world, plainly drawing from LaVey's philosophy, routinely give not so much credit as a notation in their bibliography. And then there are the Johnny-come-lately pseudo-Satanic groups, some claiming to have "taken over where the Church of Satan left off," but most, as LaVey says, still afraid of the dreaded "S" word.

You can't avoid seeing, on book racks or on talk show panels, an impressive range of Satanic "experts" (usually claiming affiliations with law enforcement, academia, or counseling centers) who adroitly spin their heads around avoiding confrontations with *real* Satanism. Christian alarmists tremblingly hold aloft tattered copies of *The Satanic Bible* into the eyes of television cameras while muttering inane and unsupported balderdash about bloody sacrifices and unspeakable crimes against children. Knowing Anton LaVey as long as I have, my mind whispers a question: is the patent absurdity of the Christian hysteria part of a diabolical plan to create a pro-Satanic backlash? At these times I get the idea Anton LaVey must be the most dangerous man in the world.

The outsider, the alien, will always receive a meager amount of credit. LaVey knows that's an inevitable consequence of being an accuser — people don't like to hear what you have to say. Still, maybe we're due for a renaissance of the brutal, principled *film noir* anti-hero. In this new Satanic world of his own making — expect that the Devil will get his due.

# Chapter One

# Satanists Are Born, Not Made

If the gods have any sense of the dramatic, it should have been a dark and stormy night on April 11th, 1930 — the night Anton Szandor LaVey was born. Somewhat prophetically assigned by birth the sign of Aries (symbolized by the horned ram), Anton LaVey is a mixture of French, Alsatian, German, Russian and Rumanian stock. Even at birth, his overabundance of silky black hair and strange amber eyes hinted at his Mongolian heritage and his Gypsy blood. Throughout his life he has been mistaken for a Latino, Prussian, even an Oriental, because of this unusual blending. Though born in Chicago in the shadow of where the black, trapezoidal-shaped John Hancock Building now stands, his parents relocated to the San Francisco Bay Area soon after his birth. Tony, as he would be known in his younger years, spent much of his boyhood in adjacent towns, where he had the freedom to explore the ranging, undeveloped swamplands that have since been developed into tract homes and shopping malls.

Augusta LaVey and her husband Joe, a liquor distributor, raised Tony as they would any other bright, even-tempered boy, attempting to instill useful middle-class values without pressing any particular religious dictates on him. By the time he was seven, he grew absorbed with tales of the supernatural and occult which would obsess him for the rest of his life. Unable to fully understand what he read because of his young age, he consulted his maternal grandmother, Luba Kolton (born Lupescu-Primakov, from a Gypsy father and a Jewish mother), who regaled Tony with the mysteries of her Transylvanian homeland — superstitions passed from generation to generation and incorporated in the greatest vampire legend of all, *Dracula*. Dogs baying when their masters died, fears that having your picture taken would rob you of your soul, what it meant when a bird flew into a house — all these were night-fears that threaded through Grandma

Kolton's stories. Accounts of bloody battles fought against Turkish and Russian invaders, between Hungary and Rumania over the rights to rule, spurred Tony's imagination. His grandmother also digressed about the eccentrics in his own family — her late husband, Boris Kolton, a Trotskyite and lifelong iconoclast from the ancient Togarma Tribe in Georgia (from whom Togare, the famous Eurasian wild animal trainer, took his name), and her brother who traveled with carnivals and circuses from the Black Sea to Hungary as a bear trainer. Young Tony soon allied himself much more with the personalities he read and heard about than with any of the boys who were expected to be his peers.

Not entirely satisfied by his grandmother's stories, Tony started exploring the foundations of the apocryphal tales she told him. Spared a highly religious, superstitious background, Tony began an autodidactic tour through the darkest realms of occultism. He avidly read anything he could find on the subject — classic ghost and horror stories, Bram Stoker's *Dracula*, Mary Shelley's *Frankenstein*, and the most popular expression of the dark side of its time, *Weird Tales* magazine. By the age of 12, Tony had already skimmed, and been disappointed by widely-circulated grimoires like the *Albertus Magnus* and *Sixth and Seventh Books of Moses*. He found Montague Summers' and Arthur Waite's magical treatises laden with useless obfuscation and concentrated on the real magic of hypnotism and stage effects. After devouring Dr. William Wesley Cook's *Practical Lessons in Hypnotism*, Tony was quickly able to apply its methods with great success. Looking back on his childhood explorations, LaVey recalls, "I looked through all the grimoires and all I saw was junk. Casting a circle to protect yourself! When I started devising my own rituals, out of frustration with all I'd seen, I shaped a glowing pentacle to attract these forces. Then I found [William] Mortensen [photographer who wrote *The Command to Look*]. And I realized this is magic. This is what I've been looking for. But it can't be. This is just a little book on photographic techniques. I went through squabblings within myself. But finally realized this was real magic. I relied more on fiction for magical truth. Lovecraft, Hodgeson's *Carnacki*, Long's *Hounds of Tindalos* — that's where I found food for thought that I couldn't find in the so-called 'dangerous' dark books of magic.

"Hadn't anyone called forth the demons before as their friends? I thought surely they had. It makes one believe that people probably were doing it on a carefully guarded underground level — and maybe they didn't let it out because they were getting results."

It became increasingly clear that Tony's interests were not the same as the average boy's. He was never much for sports, which stigmatized him as "unhealthy." But he never had any trouble making friends and his home was always full of kids expecting Tony to devise some interesting activities for the day. He organized mock military orders and secret societies but got disgusted because the other boys broke character or lost interest too easily. More often than not, his interactions with other boys parasitically drained LaVey. "They'd come over to my place, enthused as hell about what I was doing, bust up my stuff and then go home." LaVey didn't find his inability to fit in particularly distressing. "I never was a 'rebel' because I was never a part of anything to rebel against. I was never accepted by groups in the first place."

Nor did Tony have a need to be particularly rebellious toward his parents, though he never felt either of them had the capacity to understand him. "My mother was sort of a flibbertigibbet type —always had to be rearranging the furniture, or worse, had to move us to another house for some petty reason or another. I hated being moved around so much but my father was not the kind of man to kick up any fuss. People called him a real prince. To me, they both seemed rather indecisive people, who never had many opinions about anything. From a young age, they followed my advice on things like what kind of cars to buy, anything that involved an aesthetic eye. They pretty much let me do what I wanted, except my mother always cautioned me not to hurt my hands — you know, 'play nize, don't fight' — because of my music. Of course, as I got older, I didn't tell them much about what I was doing because I didn't want them to worry."

From the time LaVey began school, complications began. School was a place for Tony to escape from. He was never happy being "one of the guys" and found he was much more intensive in his studies whenever he cut school so he could study the things that interested him most. While most boys looked forward to summer, Tony didn't. It would mean an intrusion on his long, liquid days alone. The streets would again be filled with loud-mouthed kids who would expect him to join in their baseball and football games. He waited for the days to grow short again, when they would return to their confining classrooms and he could resume his studies elsewhere. He was delighted with his solitude, and the few friends he accepted into his world were, like him, outcasts.

Huey Long, Rasputin, Sir Basil Zaharoff, Milton, London, Nietzsche, Capone and other "de facto Satanists" who practiced or wrote of rational self-interest, became LaVey's primary teachers. As LaVey later taught in his pre-Church of Satan seminars, nascent imagery is often all one needs for a strong influence. "You don't need to know all about their lives, be a scholar about everything they ever wrote or did. Fictional characters, like Ming the Merciless, weren't nearly as important to me as a person who actually lived. If I appeared different it's because I *was* different. My first expression of that ingredient surfaced in an image of existing outlawry. I was derisively labeled a pachuco or hood because I wore a hat and zoot-style clothes because they were the only clothes I felt comfortable wearing. I wasn't trying to be different — just doing what came naturally."

*He recalls an incident with another boy and a bird in his backyard when he was 11 years old. Impulsively shot the boy in the back with a b.b. gun as boy was about to fire his own gun at a bird sitting on a branch all of ten inches away. The intrepid hunter dropped his gun with a howl of pain. This was Tony's first lesson in "Good Sportsmanship." He got hauled down to the police station for a big lecture on how only a coward shoots another boy in the back, and after all, "it was only a bird."*

There were plenty of adventures available to a boy during the thirties. When the Golden Gate Bridge opened as the engineering marvel of the century in 1937, LaVey was one of the first to stroll from one end to the other, when pedestrians were allowed free rein before opening it to cars. LaVey recalls, "It was a thrill to be one of the first people across the Golden Gate Bridge. Of course, there were a lot fewer people then so it was fun to be on this wide expanse where cars were supposed to be. Not like it was when they closed the bridge to cars for a few hours during the 50th anniversary celebration in 1987. The planners didn't anticipate the crowds. 800,000 people packed on there — so thick you couldn't see the roadway. They flattened the natural arch of the span. It would have been quite a celebration if it had collapsed." Since he was there when it opened, Anton appropriately drove his '37 Cord across the Bridge on its 25th Anniversary celebration and in the early morning of its 50th.

Tony's musical training began early. After entering a music store when he was five and plucking out a tune on the harp (!), his parents recognized his talent and left musical avenues open for him. From the time he was young, LaVey learned to play musical instruments that required specific techniques. He learned the difference between playing a trombone and a clarinet, a plucked instrument or one you play with a bow. Consequently, he had a hunger to play orchestral arrangements, encompassing several instruments blending the way he heard them in his head.

Drawn to the keyboard because of its scope and versatility, Tony learned to play a piano simulating the inflections of other instruments. He toyed with many instruments to know how they should sound, and today can pick up most any instrument and play it. "Especially with modern synthesizers, you should know how to play acoustical instruments first," says LaVey, "to get the technique right, so you can evoke and translate them to a keyboard instrument." Even on the violin as a kid, Tony was lucky enough to have a teacher who took the time to write out orchestral arrangements for him. "I remember him writing out an entire arrangement for Tchaikovsky's 'Marche Slave' so I could play it on the violin." Having prodigiously played bass drum (the cannon part) for the 1812 Overture when he was nine years old, LaVey went on to become second oboist with the San Francisco Ballet Symphony Orchestra when he was 15. "I just liked the sound of the instrument." He spent a short time teaching accordion door to door when it was a very popular instrument for parents to "encourage" young boys to learn. Though he barely knew the instrument when he began, LaVey kept one week ahead of his students while he learned it. "When I applied for the job, this guy handed me an accordion and miraculously I fumbled my way through 'Sorrento' — which happened to be his favorite number. By lesson number six, I was ripping through 'The Sabre Dance' and shaking the bellows for 'Lady of Spain.' Almost like Dick Contino."

From his childhood, LaVey admits much of his success comes from simply being in the right place at the right time. Already having visited the 1933-34 Chicago "Century of Progress" World's Fair when he was only a few years old, his parents took him to the World's Exposition in San Diego. The buildings and zoo built for the 1935 event are still standing as one of that city's major tourist attractions. Tony also visited the New York World's Fair in 1939, though he wasn't as impressed with its famous trilon and perisphere as he was by the beautifully-colored lights playing on San Francisco Bay at the other less publicized World's Fair that same year on Treasure Island.

Tony discovered new fascinations at the 1939-40 World's Fair on San Francisco's man-made Treasure Island, constructed from fill specially for the event. Though he was just a schoolboy, he dressed in adult-looking hats and jackets — no one questioned why he was allowed to roam about the fair alone. In Sally Rand's Nude Ranch on the "Gayway" fun zone, he stood watching the topless cowgirls spin lariats and pitch horseshoes for at least twenty minutes before anyone showed him the door. "I guess they thought I was a midget. A slightly older friend pulled the same thing and got away with it, but unexpectedly spied his bare-ass Sunday School teacher among the girls. To this day he claims that moment as his Christian disillusionment and Satanic epiphany."

Being naturally fascinated with places where other people didn't go, Tony wandered to the outer edges of the island, on the windward side. His explorations paid off. He found a life-size model of a tenement set up in the Federal Building, one of several examples of the work the government had accomplished through agencies like the WPA, CCC, NRA, TVA, etc. This peculiarly evocative exhibit was supposed to show the horrendous squalor of tenement living, and how slum clearance was changing all that for the betterment of society as a whole. The actual exhibit was preceeded by a screening of *One Third of a Nation*, an early-30's movie showing the deplorable conditions which a large portion of Americans were faced with at that time. After the film, the visitor was ushered past a detailed stage set graphically showing those very conditions described in the movie. The rooms were crummy and unkempt, with dirty laundry piled in a basket, flowered wallpaper stained and peeling, and half-broken furniture cluttering the dimly-lit flat. Sounds of an elevated railway and someone coughing consumptively from an imagined next room played over the loudspeakers. Tony experienced a thrill of voyeuristic pleasure, like legally breaking into someone's house.

Entranced by the total environment before him, he learned an important method of magic and evocation. Not every part of a cold water flat could possibly be included in the small amount of space available, but it evoked all that wasn't there nonetheless. Tony discovered that the entire object does not have to be included but enough of the right cues must be presented so that the viewer's (or participant's) mind can be allowed to fill in the rest. He was so entranced by a scaled-down replica of Chicago that it inspired him to build a miniature city in his bedroom. This early practical knowledge of experiential evocation combined with techniques of sensory projection he refined through the years led Tony to develop androids, and rituals for the Church of Satan.

As World War II began, LaVey acquired an interest in military weapons, logistics, and uniforms. He spent hours at the library, poring over texts on navies, ordnances and armies. LaVey gathered information on airships — the Hindenburg, Graf Zeppelin, the Shenandoah, the Akron, the Macon. (Many years later, LaVey would contribute to Michael Mooney's book and subsequent film, *The Hindenburg.) Jane's Fighting Ships,* the naval munitions catalogue began in 1897 by Fred T. Jane, was a primary sourcebook. It contained advertisements for cannons, torpedoes — anything a country needed to wage war — from the world's leading munitions-makers like Krupp and Vickers. Tony decided he must have a copy and began saving any spare change to put toward the $20 purchase price.

"It seems that if you want to start a war," LaVey thought, "you can buy an army or navy to do it. Look, here's this guy, Francis Bannerman, who buys an island along the Hudson River and stocks a castle with enough weapons for the annihilation of the whole world. If there's a conflagration somewhere he supplies whichever side has the money to buy his stocks of armaments. It's so cut and dried. The warlords order enough equipment for an army or navy from Bannerman's Arsenal, and just like that gain control over the destinies of millions of people. For these munitions-makers it's just a commercial proposition. Whole populations are engaged in wars on the assumption that there's one side against another side. Yet here are these arms-outfitters, right in the middle of it all, even in places where people are fighting on behalf of an ideology, and they're selling armies and navies over the counter to the enemies trying to overthrow the very countries in which they, the arms-people, are living."

In high school, Tony decided, though he had a consuming interest in many things military, he definitely didn't want to participate in the required gym classes or ROTC courses. In honor of the French Foreign Legion, he donned a French kepi (straight from Bannerman's catalogue), which he alternated with a leather flying jacket and white silk scarf, or an Afrika Korps hat. He had no patience for his less-dramatically oriented school chums. When he rode the school bus, LaVey has said he felt he was imprisoned with "a cage of barbary apes." When Tony was made to go to gym class, despite his vehement protests, he learned to feel only contempt for the towel-snapping, fun-loving young jocks he was expected to jostle and joke with. As with many young men who find themselves unusually well-endowed, Tony felt self-conscious undressing in front of other boys. He grew to detest the "latent homosexuals and gung-ho types" he had to rub bodies with in gym. Their nudge-nudge stares and chiding asides only reinforced Tony's awareness of his "difference." Though he was deemed a freak by his classmates, Tony considered himself "an island of sanity surrounded by the noise and savagery of cretin-like teenagers constantly charged up with energy repressed at home." He hated team sports and felt running around a track was a colossal waste of time that no animal would subject itself to. But then, thought Tony, animals have better sense.

Tony wanted to study judo but there were no such classes offered. Instead, LaVey convinced a doctor to write him a note to excuse him from gym, so he spent his ROTC and gym periods in a special room resting with other non-athletic boys. Luckily there was a young, well-built school nurse to keep LaVey occupied. Apparently she had a penchant for looking at young boys' privates. If he complained of an ailment, he was instructed to take off his pants, no matter what the problem seemed to be. "I don't know if she did it to other boys; I was too embarrassed to ask anybody else." She would turn around discreetly, to preserve his privacy, but LaVey noticed her always sneaking peeks in her purse mirror while pretending to inspect her lipstick.

*Had tail removed. Extra vertebra removed near the end of Tony's spine which formed prehensile tail, a caudal appendage, which seems to occur about one in every 100,000 births. Never gave him much pain until puberty. "Started giving me a lot of trouble around 11 years old or 12. Had it drained a couple of times. I had to learn to sit sideways." Then it became re-inflamed, terribly painful. "They took me in to the emergency room one night — they had to drain it again. There was a cold snap on. It was dur-*

*ing the war and no rooms were available at the hospital. The doctors didn't want to risk a general anaesthetic and send me home in the cold, so they only gave me a local. I bit through the rubber pad I was laying on and bent the steel bar on the side of the gurney."*

Young LaVey's major male role models were his uncles. Masculine archetypes of the 30's and 40's, Tony was inspired and encouraged by each. Through one uncle who had a ship which was recruited for Coast Guard Reserve submarine patrol during the war, Tony enhanced his love of the sea. LaVey remembers being fascinated by submarines, considering himself singularly blessed when he watched the U.S.'s largest submarine surface practically underneath him. And the China Clipper, the legendary Pan Am aircraft which took off from San Francisco Bay made Pacific runs, one of which LaVey was able to go on.

When one of LaVey's uncles was hired, in the spring of 1945, as a civilian engineer to rebuild air strips for the Army in Germany, Tony went with him. The uncle had been recently divorced and so had been issued a family visa to accommodate his wife. Young LaVey was provided an opportunity to accompany him in her absence. It was during this trip he saw confiscated Nazi *schauerfilmen* (horror films) at a command post in Berlin. The German interpreter explained that the films were more than fictional accounts but rather symbolic or thinly disguised portrayals of an occultic Nazi mindset. Rumors of a Black Order of Satan worshippers as an integral element of the Third Reich could not help but fuel LaVey's interest. Tony was impressed by the cinematographic techniques of Weimar and Nazi period films as *The Cabinet of Dr. Caligari, M, Hitlerjunge Quex, Morganrot,* and the *Mabuse* films. The brooding lighting and strange, haunting angles had a dramatic impact on LaVey. Decades later, he would reproduce those elements in the rituals of the Church of Satan. The obtuse angles employed in the expressionistic films planted the seeds in LaVey for what he would eventually develop into his "Law of the Trapezoid." Equally thrilling to young LaVey was an opportunity to play the cinema organ at the dome in Brighton. In North Africa on VE Day, he even had a chance to visit Legion headquarters at Sidi bel Abbis in Morocco — "not to mention picking up a Legion kepi and an Afrika Korps cap firsthand."

In his eclectic reading, Tony discovered three men he considered were truly applying the Devil's tools to their benefit: Rasputin, Cagliostro and Sir Basil Zaharoff.

Rasputin was born Gregory Efimovitch in 1871, in Petronovskoye, Siberia. When he joined a religious sect in 1904 called the "Khlysty," he adopted the philosophy shared by the Marquis de Sade: "Sin that you may be forgiven." At night in the woods outside his village, he would gather young girls around the fires with him, telling them, "A particle of the Supreme Being is incarnated in me. Only through me can you hope to be saved; and the manner of your salvation is this: you must be united with me in soul and body." Speaking such ideas, burning incense and further heightening his witches to a fever pitch, he would lead orgiastic revelries until dawn. He eventually drew the attention of the czar's court, which he utilized by casting his Svengali-spell over the czarina. She became convinced Rasputin (whose name was either a play on *rasputny*, Russian for "debauched," or *rasputi*, which meant "crossroads" — a term applied to the village from which he came, and its inhabitants) was the only one capable of curing her afflicted child. Thus, from meager beginnings, Rasputin was able to become the most influential man in pre-Bolshevik Russia.

Count Alexander Cagliostro claimed to be 5,557 years old — a friend to the Queen of Sheba, Cleopatra, and a score of other powerful women of history. This 18th Century magician said he had learned powerful secrets of performing miracles, curing ailments, and prolonging life through these intimate associations from his past. The denizens of the royal courts he visited couldn't buy his potions fast enough. Cagliostro was everyone's darling, his attentions curried by emperors, Cardinals, queens and even the Pope until he was finally discovered to be nothing more than a common back-country Italian, uneducated and swindling. Those who had been taken in by him, enraged by their own naivete, convicted Cagliostro of heresy and left him to die unmourned in prison four years after his imprisonment.

But it was Sir Basil Zaharoff that became a main focus in LaVey's life, so much so that, many years later, he opened *The Satanic Witch* with an homage to Zaharoff as one who knew how to use the power of women to his advantage. LaVey's grandson, born in 1978, was named "Stanton Zaharoff" in his honor. He was the most successful and cynical arms merchant of all time, supplying weapons for the Boer War, the Russo-Japanese

War, the Balkan Wars, and World War I. Again, though born in poverty, Zaharoff grew to influence kings and parliaments, and eventually became a Knight of the British Empire. Yet, in McCormick's biography, *Peddler of Death*, Zaharoff summarized his philosophy thus: "I made wars so that I could sell arms to both sides ... I sold armaments to anyone who would buy them. I was a Russian when in Russia, a Greek in Greece, a Frenchman in Paris."

Zaharoff used any nefarious tactics he could devise to orchestrate his desired ends. He used bribes and tricks to beat out rival war merchants. He planted rumors to set friend against friend, and used the charms of beautiful women to tempt or defeat those he wished. Planting news stories to inflame people to a war-like pitch, assassinating opposing officials when necessary, Zaharoff manipulated battles once the wars began. To insure that the battles raged and more money was spent for armaments, millions of young men's lives could be lost. LaVey's respect for Zaharoff grew even stronger when he discovered that, even after Zaharoff's death, those who tried to expose his manipulations or criticize him lost their jobs, suffered ill health and even death, as if Zaharoff were reaching out from his grave to exert his continuing influence on the earthly plane. From all descriptions, Sir Basil looked a lot like LaVey in his youth. At Zaharoff's estate in the south of France, Chateau Balincourt, he had a black-draped Satanic chapel hidden within its walls. A blue twilit grotto far beneath the castle, where swan boats could float in under the castle by way of a disguised tunnel, was used as a trysting place. These were true black magicians to LaVey — not the supposed "evil ones" who were tortured and burned at the stake. Zaharoff, Rasputin, and Cagliostro were Satanists LaVey could respect and emulate.

As Tony became more and more involved in the lives of magicians and the literature of the occult, the farther he felt from other boys his age, and the more irrelevant his required schoolwork became. Following in Zaharoff's footsteps, LaVey wished to combine gentility and ruthlessness in the same young man. He studied judo at the Duke Moore Studio in San Francisco, earning several degrees by the end of 1946. He found judo much more satisfying than the established American ideal of "scientific boxing." When overly-aggressive young boys were laid flat by Tony's perplexing maneuvers, he was called a "sneaky Jap" and accused of not fighting fair. LaVey began to revel in confusing people's narrow notions. The same year he became second oboist for the San Francisco Ballet Orchestra, Tony dropped out of his junior year of high school. He let his hair grow longer, began wearing leather jackets and zoot suits, and hung around disreputable poolhalls, finding camaraderie in gamblers, pimps, prostitutes, hustlers and pool sharks. "They told me that a proficiency at billiards was indicative of a misspent youth." Tony delighted in the incongruities: painting, studying magic and philosophy, playing classical music, yet acting, looking and thinking like a common hood.

During time spent on the East Coast, young Tony had a chance to make regular trips to Steeplechase Park where he got a taste of earning money from understanding human foibles. He noticed many of the men would gather around what came to be called the "Blowhole Theater," a spot where unsuspecting girls walked across a hidden puff of wind where their skirts would blow up over their heads, exposing their legs and underwear (or lack of same). A row of seats were set up so the men could get a good view without standing all day. One day a man leaned over to Tony with a rather distressed look on his face and offered him a quarter to sit in his seat while the man was gone to the bathroom. LaVey happily complied. After that Tony made his pocket money by looking available whenever one of the "audience" members started looking nervously around. He'd step up and offer, "Save your seat for a quarter, mister?"

Tony learned new lessons from the underworld "businessmen" in newly established Las Vegas when he accompanied and assisted his father's brother, Bill LaVey's business there after the war. The emerging gambling capital was just a tiny oasis in the middle of the desert. Bill had provided good raw alcohol to Al Capone's distillers during Prohibition in Chicago and renewed old ties after the war, having enjoyed a prosperous wartime business manufacturing aircraft landing gear and patrol boats. Bill became involved with Bugsy Siegel in developing the Flamingo for Meyer Lansky. As Tony sat with his uncle in gambling joints and nightclubs, Siegel lieutenants like Al Greenberg and Moe Sedway had their own interests to advocate to an impressionable LaVey — how everyone is on the take, no matter what high or low position they may hold. "Everything is a racket, including the church. The superior man recognizes these facts and lives accordingly. The fool continues to go straight for God and country. The crafty man figures out how to work the rackets himself so he doesn't wind up a slave to the crooked politicians and bosses. He refuses the life of the millions of people in offices and factories tied to the routine of going to work at eight o'clock every morning, stagnating at a deadly dull job, having lunch at the time they are told, coming home at five every evening, and for all this drawing a wage that is only enough to sustain their humdrum existence."

LaVey was impressed by these outlaws who survived outside the system by exploiting men's natural foibles and vices. He considered them rough-hewn versions of Zaharoff, with philosophy and conviction behind their actions. Tony understood, also, that these men often killed each other, and that the only ones who were really remembered by the general public were the ones who died a death gory enough to hit the papers. But Tony wasn't disillusioned by that, nor by his uncle finally serving a sentence for tax evasion in the federal penitentiary at McNeil Island. They were still surviving in the way they chose; that was the most important thing. Had circumstances been only slightly different, Tony might well have become involved in the rackets himself. As LaVey has grown older, his admiration for these Satanic practitioners has not faltered. Rather he has found the most discouraging aspect of forming friendships with these jaded older men was that most of them died in the 1950's and 60's. Left alone, LaVey had to create/discover new compatriots.

"Not many people were born in the same year I was, so it's hard for me to find people with my orientation or knowledge, as far as music, movies, memories — all those things that make up a person's past. I guess that's why I seemed to gravitate to companions who were older than I was when I was a young man — I was hungry for this past that I'd missed. Or, on the other end of the spectrum, I've gravitated to people much younger than myself, who are attracted to this lost knowledge *I* now carry. My world was that of the late 30's and early 40's. My crystallization came during the *film noir* period right after the war — that weird twilight era. Is it any wonder I am the way I am? Saturn was predominant during the period during which I achieved my maturity. My memories stretch back to that Antediluvian world before the war. All those memories of my childhood and young adulthood are reflected in who I am, what I am, what I've begun. The movies that portrayed my role models were American *film noir*, with the hard-boiled anti-heroes that actually had deeper feelings and loyalties than the acceptable people." LaVey still concentrates on playing and promoting his kind of music — "Gal in Calico," "For Sentimental Reasons," "Nature Boy," "All Through the Day," "Either It's Love Or It Isn't," "The More I See You," "In Love In Vain," "I Wonder," "Temptation," "Prisoner of Love," "Golden Earrings," "I Remember You." As LaVey's revived influence spreads, more early, straight recordings are being resurrected of what he likes to label "bombastic music."

By the time LaVey was 16, he was forming definite ideas about women as well as magic and true power. His sexual explorations stretched back to when he was about five years old when he remembers a little girl coaxing him back into her bedroom at her birthday party. Her mother came back and scolded her for leaving her guests and the distraught dear peed her panties. LaVey admits the experience was enough to have started him off on a distinctly fetishistic sexual path. Matters got worse when he was about 11, earning extra change picking up empty bottles around an outdoor dance pavilion. One day while reaching far back under the structure, he discovered a hole fortuitously positioned right underneath the ladies' restroom. It was actually a gap between the floor and the front of the commode through which an observant boy could get a front-row peek at any girl who happened to sit down there. Tony made sure he was front and center whenever he spied an interesting woman going to relieve herself. LaVey had already established his own ideas of sexiness and developed a fixation for actress Iris Adrian, the archetype of the plump, blonde, gum-snapping, B-movie chorine. He decided that Hollywood was all backwards because the prettiest girls were always cast as walk-ons. (LaVey was to subsequently number Miss Adrian among his personal friends.)

Unfortunately, because LaVey was already developing a decidedly sinister look, most girls he went out with had to meet him "around the corner" so her parents wouldn't see the kind of boys their daughter was keeping company with. LaVey found his earliest romantic experience a bitterly painful one and, feeling betrayed and doomed because of his differentness, he decided he would either join the Foreign Legion or the circus. Somewhere he would find or make a place where he would fit in. Recognizing his increasing stigma, LaVey left home in search of adventure and soon found the perfect showcase for his marginal attributes.

## Chapter Two

# Never Help a Midget Move an Elephant Tub

After talking to a young man in a pool hall who had worked for the Clyde Beatty Circus, Tony LaVey became intrigued with the lifestyle and possibilities. In the spring of 1947, he signed on as a circus roustabout and cage boy, responsible for feeding and watering the big cats. He developed an immediate rapport with the lions and tigers, discovering he usually felt more comfortable and relaxed around the big cats than he did walking down city streets or any place where humans gather.

It wasn't long before Beatty, increasingly aware of LaVey's affinity for the big cats, began to confer the tricks of his trade. Tony was soon following in his great uncle Lazlo's footsteps (who had traveled with a circus in Russia and Hungary). He learned the motions and mechanics of Beatty's act — the use of the whip, stick, revolver and chair (which is used to imitate an open mouth; anything open will work, like a hat shoved into a lion's face to make it back off). Tony was able to put a cat through a hoop, do rollovers — and after a short time, 17-year old LaVey was handling eight Nubian lions and four Bengal tigers in the cage at once to the musical strains of Beatty's ubiquitous "Paso dobles." "You never teach cats 'tricks'" says LaVey, "you just find what they like to do then build an act around that. Cats love to go through hoops, get on their 'personal' pedestal, all that stuff they use in standard acts. That's why the word 'trainer' is more appropriate than 'tamer.' You work *with* the cats, rather than trying to break their spirit or tame them." When Beatty scheduled a "double date performance" (a Saturday children's matinee or a charity performance preceding the usual nighttime show), LaVey often performed alone with the cats in the big cage.

"When I was under canvas," LaVey remembers, "I let my hair get pretty shaggy. I wore black pants with full-cut red shirts and black leather boots —

actually the show's uniform colors. Audiences must have figured me out as some kind of Mongolian tribesman. I felt right with the image and took pride in it. It seemed to work with both the cats and the audience. Once people see an image like that, they don't forget. It was the only way circus people remembered or recognized me when I went back to visit now and again, up into the 1960's."

Somewhere there are films floating around of Anton LaVey working the cage. Says LaVey, "A guy named Tom Upton was around then. He spent most of his time filming all the circuses. All the circus people knew him; he was welcome on any lot in the country. All you had to do was look in his direction and he'd regale you with films and stories. Always wanted to get people together to watch his movies. The performers loved him. He'd set up his projector backstage and run it for the performers. He was a short fellow, rather round and had a spheroid little wife named Crystal. Must have shot thousands of reels between the late 30's and mid-'60's. Some of our early members who were around got to see some of his stuff. He brought them over and showed them to us a few times. Sure enough, there I was, leaping and jumping around the cage with my Mongolian hair flying.

In order to help the lions and tigers feel more comfortable around him, reducing the risk of injury, Tony began initiating an intimacy level beyond friendship, so the big cats would accept him more as a part of their very existence. When he fed them, Tony put his own hamburger down on the ground beside their food, mimicking their growling noises as he ate. When practicing with the cats in the cage, he'd crawl through the sawdust behind them. LaVey even began sleeping in their cages with them once in awhile. "I really miss having a big cat around, after 20 years of my life spent in intimate contact with them — from 17 to 37, when Togare went to the zoo. There's nothing like it. Once you've established a rapport with a cat, they'll never forget you. A young black leopard I worked with on the Beatty show named Zombie remembered me 13 years later when I happened to see him in a little traveling circus. When I moved toward the cage, this (by that time) old, moth-eaten leopard lifted his head and started making these friendly chirruping noises of recognition. I looked closer and sure enough it was the same cat I'd worked with long before."

As friendly as LaVey got with the cats, though, he admits he's gathered his share of close calls and has scars on his hand and chest to remind him that nothing can protect you from unintentional mishaps or an overexuberant lion. "I've caught a claw or been knocked to the ground. It happens to every trainer once in a while. Lions are incredibly powerful creatures. All they have to do is brush you while they're running through their paces; that's enough to knock any man down. They're fantastically fast, too. The instant you hit the ground, one of them is on top of you, and there you are on your back in the sawdust with the lion hovering over you, breathing hot breath down your throat and as you look up, the jaws staring you in the face seem to be as big as a whale's."

What possessed LaVey to risk his life, not only during the circus performances but when sleeping and eating with the tigers and lions, and later choosing to live with a leopard, then a lion in his home, risking an attack every day? "I learned so much in the cage," explains LaVey. "Even getting knocked down taught me great lessons. That's when you really learn power and magic, even how to play God: when you're lying in the sawdust with a lion breathing in your face. You know that the natural instinct of the beast is to sink its teeth into the playful fellow creature on the ground, not realizing that its skin is tender and its bones can be crushed — that it can't withstand clawing and biting like another lion. So, lying there knocked down, you have just one defense left: willpower. Any good cat trainer has to learn how to use it, how to charge himself full of adrenaline, to send out gamma rays that penetrate the brain of the cat, so that it will hold off chewing or clawing you while you grope around for your stick. Then, when you get your hands on it, you've got about one second to whip it across the lion's nose and jump to your feet while the lion is distracted. And if you can't reach the stick, you have to do it by giving the cat a solid punch on the nose."[1]

After a while, Tony's creative drive led him in other directions within the circus community. As LaVey explains, "There's always something to do in a circus — people 'double in brass,' usually having two or more alternate jobs to do, unless they have a real speciality act." Animal training was thrilling, but Tony knew he could never find complete fulfillment working an animal act all his life. It seems inevitable that Tony's extensive musical talents would not go unnoticed, or not utilized, by the other circus performers — and indeed they weren't.

Tony had taught himself piano over the years by listening to a song on the radio or phonograph and diligently picking out the notes and chords until he could play it with ease. While he was on the road with the Beatty show, Tony asked the circus calliope player, an alcoholic who leaned on the keys more than he actually played them, if he could practice for half an hour, just to keep from getting rusty. ("Fred had callouses on his elbows from playing so hard.") The calliope player refused, and LaVey, angered by the boozer's petty power trip, cursed him. A few nights later, he had fallen ill and couldn't be revived for the evening's performance. Tony volunteered to play, though he wasn't at all sure he could even play the calliope. But, never one for taking a cringing approach, LaVey started right off with the galloping Lone Ranger theme from Rossini's "William Tell Overture."

LaVey was an immediate success with both the audience and the other circus performers. Beatty gave the drunk "professor" a sabbatical and made

### ☞ PRESENTING ☜

## Professor Anton Szandor LaVey

### THE
### GREAT SZANDOR

#### PLAYER OF THE
## CALLIOPE
### BOTH STEAM AND AIR

### AND ARTIST AND MANIPULATOR
### OF THE
### AEOLIAN BAND ORGAN
### ORCHESTMELOCHOR
### APOLLONICON
### MOSCOW CHIMES
### ORIENTAL MUSIC CAR
### CAMPBELLICAN PIPES
### UNI-FON

### AND THE
### WURLITZER UNIT ORCHESTRA

☞ WHOSE... Music will brighten the hearts
of children of all ages - - - AND Stir or soothe the
most ferocious beasts of the jungle!

Tony the regular calliope player. When the Beatty show entered the next town, LaVey was at the calliope which was perched on a flatbed truck, acting as Pied Piper to lure adults and children to the circus grounds. Wherever Tony went, flamboyant handbills advertised him in the most extravagant terms possible (pictured page 34).

While many of the fantastic-sounding instruments on LaVey's handbill were nearly extinct, Anton (as he asked friends to now call him instead of his childhood nickname) mastered each of them, or an equivalent. True to his own hype, LaVey learned that he could indeed stir or soothe both humans and animals with his music. Through experimentation, he found the magical effects of music — how certain chords and cadences would effect the audience, the animals and the performers. Anton found that the jungle cats performed best to dominant chords and barbaric beats. The big cats liked minor chords emphasized but LaVey varied the chords, appropriately alternating majors and minors. Elephants liked a predominance of dominant majors with a ponderous beat which best matched their slower gait and metabolisms. Seals and dogs (which are, according to LaVey, very much alike), seemed to respond best to major chords with no minors thrown in. When LaVey stuck to the bright dominant major chords, the dogs and seals were easiest to work with. The other performers in the circus were grateful and perplexed by LaVey's unusual abilities to add special life to their acts with his music.

In addition to working with bandmasters like Vic Robbins, Merle Evans, and Henry Keys, Anton would subsequently perform mood-setting, emotionally-charged music to accompany some of the world's most famous circus acts: the Hannefords' riding team, the Concellos, Harold Alzana, the flying Wallendas, the Cristianis, and others. Through the years, LaVey has been gratified to receive supportive letters and membership inquiries from the children, grandchildren, nieces, and nephews of these performers, who had heard of LaVey from their illustrious relatives telling tales about him over the dinner table. One of Anton's favorite circus characters was Hugo Zachinni, known as the Human Cannonball. Though his actual billing read, "The Human Projectile," common parlance seemed to like the sound of "Cannonball" better and that is what stuck. Zachinni was once a devout Catholic but had become disenchanted, eventually becoming such a militant atheist, he would take any opportunity to talk about what a racket organized religion was. "Whenever anyone would ask about the cannon, he'd launch into a tirade about the crooks that run the churches whenever he'd gather a good tip. Then his wife would come running out and accuse him of having 'too much-a wine.'" Zachinni was pleased he and his brother, Edmundo, had found a way to capitalize on the public's lust for violence by inventing and patenting a device for shooting a man out of the barrel of a cannon, which earned them a small fortune. Actually a rather eclectic fellow, Zachinni was a fine painter and taught fine arts classes until his death. Many of his paintings wound up in major collections. LaVey also recalls Zachinni's dismay over the consistent mispronouncing of his name. "People used to come up to him and say, 'Oh, Mr. Zuchinni...'. He'd say, 'Yesterday I'm-a Zachinni, today I'm-a zuchinni, pretty soon I'm-a gonna be squash.'"

*Anton had a run-in with a midget on the Beatty show. Instructed to run across the lot for a spike, he saw a midget under a semi-trailer, struggling with a big elephant tub — the decorated hollow pedestals elephants perform on. LaVey tried to help him and the midget cussed him out and kicked him in the shins. He found out later that it wasn't a good idea to try to help a midget do anything physical because you might get kicked in the balls.*

Among the other interesting people LaVey met during his time in the circus, was *Weird Tales* writer Robert Barbour Johnson ("Rubberbubber Johnson" as he introduced himself). He and LaVey struck up a friendship that would last until many years after the Church of Satan was officially formed. At the time, along with a writing contract with Blue Book magazine (five circus stories a year), Johnson was working as an animal trainer himself. Johnson was always fascinated by the magic and synchronicity found in mundane life, yet took the wildly outrageous in his stride. Though never publicly known as an artist, the paintings Johnson did of circus and carnival scenes, with its unusual use of lighting and texture using the minutest specks of paint, will hopefully be exhibited one day. LaVey has many memories of their years together, and loves to recount stories of their expeditions. Then at one point, LaVey simply didn't hear from him anymore. "Johnson always wanted to disappear, just walk off the edge of the earth somewhere, like Ambrose Bierce or B. Traven. I guess that's what he finally did."

*Not long before Clyde Beatty died of stomach cancer, he came in and listened to LaVey play the theater pipe organ at the Lost Weekend, a nightclub where he was working in San Francisco in the early 60's. He nursed a 7-Up, just listening. It was one of those drizzly winter off-nights when only a handful of regular customers made him appear even more a stranger in their midst. Anton played the act: "The Jungle Queen," "Espana Cani," Ravel's "Bolero" — all the rest, ending with the ominous closing chords of Puccini's* La Boheme. *No one else besides Anton knew who the stranger was, but one of the owners who was tending bar discreetly caught on. After about an hour and a half, the great Clyde Beatty quietly said his goodbye, got up and walked out into the foggy night.*

## Chapter Three

# Mister, I Was Made For It

*"Here they are, the creatures of the night, body snatchers, Dracula's pets. Come in and see the fiendish animals. Bone-gnawing, horrible creatures on the inside. Captured just four miles from Dr. Frankenstein's castle and brought here alive and breathing. Grave robbers. The devil's disciples of the animal world. Creeping, crawling graveyard pests, a menace to the peace of the dead. Alive on the inside in a well-lighted arena for you to see and study. Battlefield pests, feed on dead and dying soldiers..."* — suggested spiel for grind show exhibition of an armadillo, Don Boles, *The Midway Showman*.[2]

After traveling with the Beatty show through California, Oregon, Washington, Nevada, Arizona, and New Mexico, the circus season ended in October, 1947, and Anton was ready to move on. Life as a lion trainer and circus musician was lively enough, but he suspected there were still horizons to explore, seamier ways of making a living.

He'd heard from his circus cronies about the differences between working the carnival circuits and working in a circus. Circus people considered what they did real art, dazzling family entertainment compared with the cheap tricks and "mitt camp" aspects of the carnival. Circus people think carnies are sociopaths, drifters, marginals trying to run away from the law or some nefarious activity or other — trying to get lost. Carnies think circus people are wage slaves and prima donnas, that they only need skills not street smarts, that they're just performers, and have no need for real mental acuity.

This was enough to encourage Anton to get off-season work with various west coast amusement facilities such as The Pike Amusement Park in

Long Beach, California, where he played the steam calliope across from Professor Theobald's flea circus. Professor Theobald was a rather eccentric German gentleman who enjoyed rolling up his sleeves and letting his fleas feast on his arms for their dinner. He blustered against LaVey's noisy calliope, complaining that the music upset his tiny performers: "Please! It disturbing my fleas; they will not performing right." "He'd plead with me to play more softly. You can't play a calliope softly; it's either loud or not at all. I could never get through to him, much as I sympathized."

There were plenty of interesting characters for LaVey to meet on the carny circuit: Francisco Lentini made something positive out of having three legs, using his third leg for a stool when he went fishing and always dancing with the prettiest girls on any dance floor, inventing a unique waltz that made them the center of attraction. "He was the only person I ever saw who danced in 5/4 time — Tchaikovsky could've written some great stuff for him." Though Lentini didn't mind being born with three legs, he was rather self-conscious about a little finger-like appendage that grew out of his third leg and always wore extra long socks to cover it. Anton also liked the Human Ostrich, Jacob Heilberger, who had mastered his stomach reflexes so well that he could regurgitate objects at will. He was a highly cultured Jewish engineer, educated at Berlin University, who had fled Germany when the Nazis came to power. Disguising his brains and education, Heilberger horrified audiences by swallowing live mice, golf balls, and eggs that hatched into live chicks, jumping out of his mouth.

Of course, there was the sex show which was presented in the guise of an educational hygiene lecture to avoid getting harassed by the local clergy or shut down by the cops. Dr. Hart played the sex doctor (later to become "Dr. Elliot Forbes"), assisted by pulchritudinous girls in scanty nurses' uniforms who pointed out various parts of the anatomy on oversized charts. Usually there were Kroger Babb films or Army training films on the dangers of V.D. shown, complete with decaying noses of men in the advanced stages of syphilis, which Anton delighted in accompanying by playing "Claire de Lune" and other classical pieces. By the time the film was over, many of the men who had been suckered into buying a ticket had already slunk out the side of the tent, leaving their snow cones and popcorn uneaten beneath the seats and swearing off sex forever.

Anton went on to work the biggest traveling shows on the Pacific Coast, carnivals like Craft's 20 Big Shows, West Coast Shows and Foley & Burke. They'd set up next to circuses in big cities like L.A. (in smaller cities, some carnies would show up to be part of the midway independently), at county fairs, on rodeo lots, dirt lots, football fields ... they mostly brought sparkle and excitement to thriving farm communities like Modesto, Turlock, and Redding, and rustic backwater towns with names like Crow's Landing, Ceres, Atwater.

LaVey played either a calliope, Wurlitzer band organ or Hammond along every midway, providing music to keep people moving among the various attractions; his beloved "shit-kicker," "aircraft plant," "shipyard" music — "Roly Poly," "Detour," "Sunflower," "No Vacancy," "Dear Okie" — in addition to more mainstream standards. LaVey experimented with the various sound effects built in to the band organ, for use on the midway or merry-go-round: drums, gong, trolley bell, tambourines, bird whistles, horses' hooves, horns ... all add that jangling, off-rhythmic quality to the music associated most with the combined midway smells of popcorn, sawdust and cotton candy. The bally platform, sporting exaggerated paintings of what could be seen and experienced inside the tent flaps, provided an excellent viewing place from which Anton could witness yet another side of human nature. Though the carnivals were small, the gaudy canvases, impelling music, and grotesque exhibits combined to draw hundreds of curious folks from the surrounding countryside. They all came, dressed up in their Sunday best, hoping to see something spicy, hoping to win something special, hoping to see something they would never forget.

LaVey was also recruited to play for the traveling tent show revival meetings on Sunday. "Circuses and carnivals used to be considered the work of the Devil in the 19th century, when shows traveled in wagons and disapproving clergymen had real power. Then evangelists wised up that they could take advantage of carnival organists and crowds gathered by the entertainments, they began to tolerate us in true Christian modification." Burton Wolfe's introduction to *The Satanic Bible* quotes LaVey on his telling observations of these one-day-a-week Christians: "On Saturday night I would see men lusting after half-naked girls dancing at the carnival, and on Sunday morning when I was playing the organ for tent-show evangelists at the other end of the carnival lot, I would see these same men sitting in the pews with their wives and children, asking God to forgive them and purge them of carnal desires. And the next Saturday night they'd be back at the carnival or some other place of indulgence. I knew then that the Christian Church thrives on hypocrisy, and that man's carnal nature will out!"

The midway runs in an oval all around the carnival, with rides, games, concessions and food stands on either side and the "shows" way at the other end of the oval, opposite the gate. The carnival backlot is where the real action is — the Mitt Camp, the girl show, the 10-in-1 (freaks), the crime show, the pickled punks exhibit (ordered direct from Tate's Curiosity Shop — Devil babies, $75; mummified bodies, $50...). Inside the show tents, Anton played Hammond organ for the hootchy-kootchy girls and hula-hula dancers.

There were always plenty of girls around the carnival, both working and coming to see the show. "Several carny acts used girls for flash. The girlie shows and sex shows, though, were for different purposes. The girlie shows were like traveling strip joints. The girls would come out on the bally platform to flaunt their stuff then the talkers got the gentlemen inside for the strip. It was usually a 50¢ blow-off. Then, once inside, they would give either a soft or hard core show, depending on how solid the canvasmen had been able to fix it with the law.

"The sex show was another thing altogether. It was a doctor and naughty nurse set-up, where the blow-off would most likely be a 'Secrets of Hygiene' demonstration, following a 'Miracle of Life' grind show. That's where they left swearing they'd never look at a sexy woman again." LaVey explains that none of the carnies had affairs with the female carny performers — that it would be regarded as something akin to incest. With discretion, it was expected that relationships would occur with the girls who came for the glitter and excitement of the carnival. Blatant "chasers," however, were poison to carnival operators, classified with "drunks" and "agitators," with most job offers posted in The Billboard (the weekly newspaper covering the outdoor amusement industry) instructing such types to "stay where you are." Anton had liaisons with girl towners who paraded around the midway, all dressed up to see the closest thing they'd ever get to glamor, or local girls who got a bug in them to be movie stars and their first step was joining the carnival as a "dancer." They usually would only get as far as the next small town then give up.

*If the show played a town where a "Midnight Spook Show" happened to be playing at the local theater, LaVey endeavored to assist the likes of "Dr. Zomb", "Dr. Doom", and "Dr. Tomb" by throwing spaghetti and grapes with shouts of "Worms!" and "Eyeballs!" from the balconies of pitch dark small-town theaters into the laps of the audience below.*

Sometimes Anton worked the rides or, when the funhouse blow-hole operator needed to be relieved, LaVey was his enthusiastic stand-in. There was also the Ten-in-One, where all the freaks and sideshow performers were featured: the Sword Swallower, the Pinhead, the India Rubber Man, the Glass Eater, the Alligator Boy; Grace McDaniels, the mule-faced woman, and Johnny Eck, the incredible half-man. As always, LaVey found friends among those which society in general would consider outcasts. "Freaks were the royalty of the carnival world — they got validation they never would have gotten on the outside. The human oddities, natural freaks, were in a much more esteemed position than sword-walkers or fire-eaters, or even tattooed people, who all had to learn their freakish talents or, in the case of tattoos, modify their bodies to make themselves distinguished. The natural freaks literally had a special birthright."

More than any of the other shows, LaVey enjoyed working the Mitt Camp where all the mystics, fortune-tellers, Gypsy palm readers, hypnotists, and magicians were gathered. There, Anton learned all the secrets of the "Romany trade" he could glean. Joe Calgary taught LaVey the magic of billet-reading — describing, while blindfolded, what is written on a paper concealed inside a sealed envelope. Johnny Starr, a flashy carny pitchman, taught Anton how to play swami by sitting behind a table in a turban while a pretty girl collected folded messages from audience members, brought them onto the platform and dropped them into a clouded crystal bowl. When the messages would fall directly through the bowl, down a chute to the eager hands of LaVey under the stage, Anton would open the papers up, shine a flashlight on them and display them through a magnifying lens for the swami Starr to see onstage. The turbaned showman would miraculously recite exactly what the audience members had written, to their stupified delight and wild applause. "Johnny wore the turban (or some other kind of hat) not originally as an affectation, but to cover a tantalum plate in his head, the result of a war injury."

LaVey watched and listened attentively, learning everything he could: phrenology, palmistry, astrology, and magic tricks. He worked up an impressive act for himself as a hypnotist in the Ten-in-One, with the high point coming when he made a girl as stiff as a board, stretching her across two chairs and letting someone sit on her. By this time LaVey's image had become stereotypical carny: flashy sports coats, hand-painted ties, pencil-thin moustache. He was getting more than a college education could ever teach him — a confidence man's education in hustling, exploiting man's carnal nature — and enjoyed looking the part. The scar on his cheek he'd received in a knife fight with a friend only added a sinister, jaded quality to his features.

Through his carny experiences, he learned how much people would demand, and pay, to be fooled — how ghouls looked for always ghastlier thrills; how voyeurs wanted newer, more prurient treats; how the lonely and the sick wanted miracles — and how they only hate *you* when they're not fooled enough. The carny magician knows there aren't any miracles—there is only what you make happen in life yourself. Yet people will always be willing to throw away their money for just a chance to win "flash" — rhinestone bracelets, cheap wristwatches, giant plush animals, or "slum" — worthless token prizes.

*Monster Midway* and *Step Right Up!*, two of the few bread-and-butter books on carnivals, were written by a couple of LaVey's cronies, William Lindsay Gresham and Daniel P. Mannix. Though Gresham's association was cut short by his tragic death, LaVey, as of this writing, still maintains friendly correspondence with Dan Mannix. LaVey memorialized his friendship with Gresham in the names of his daughter and grandson — Zeena and Stanton — named after characters in Gresham's other famous carnival novel, *Nightmare Alley. The Midway Showman* is another fine book covering the subject, in which author Don Boles writes, "The ability to treat ordinary subjects in a grand manner, to invent tinseled lies about them, and the gall to sell tickets to their exhibition qualify a man for the showman's trade ... Here, humbuggery is comparable to magic: carnival showmen feel it is permissible to fool people so long as you give them their money's worth in entertainment."

LaVey has been put down on many occasions for being from a "circus and carnival background," as if it were proof that he's really a charlatan. But as LaVey himself explains, the subculture of the carnival has its own standards, its own principles. "In the carny, we knew who was a fake and who was the genuine article. Traveling tent-show evangelists hung around carnivals like 'lot lice'. No one liked them. They'd always come around where there was a good tip worked up. All of them admitted they were in the 'Jesus racket' and just took advantage of the tip that the carnival gathered. At least, in those days, not many of them pretended to really believe any of the bullshit they were selling. They just figured they were taking advantage of the rubes, like any of the other traveling shows. Like undertakers, they would joke and crack wise about what they were doing when they were out of Aunt Minnie's earshot. More than a few of them eventually ended up in Folsom or San Quentin if they happened to fleece the wrong person. But if they were at least honest, you could have some respect for them. That's carny law."

*"Laura the Pitiful, come in and see the devil's child. See her alive on the inside. Better shorten her chain, boys, she's getting restless. Listen to her scream! What's she doing now? Throw her another chicken, she might be hungry. Watch her jump. Listen to her howl. Abandoned as a child to be reared among wild animals. Grunts, growls, screams, and howls. But poor Laura can't speak a word. See her now. See how low a human being can go. Once seen, never forgotten..."*[3]

# Chapter Four

# Nights With Marilyn Monroe

*It's 1948, a sultry Los Angeles night. Step through the doors of an old-time burlesque house, escaping the raucous, insistent voice of the barker outside. Scents from the lobby — popcorn, cigar smoke, disinfectant, cola — mingle with the moldy aroma of old theater carpet. Pass through the musty curtains into the theater itself and smell the stale muscatel bottles fallen from hands of slumbering drunks in the back row, always clattering to the floor and rolling forward when the girl on stage is performing her most captivating moves.*

*Grab a seat near the front, along the runway thrusting into the seating area. From here, you can get the best view of the stage. Ease back, put your hat in your lap and wait for the curtain to rise.*

*Sitting through the candy-butcher's pitch, your attention is diverted when you see a pale, dark-haired young man slip through the side curtain carrying some sheet music, his actions not quick but directed, practiced. He spreads the pencilled manuscript paper out before him, and has time to peer over his cigarette at the sheet as the candy-butcher shuffles back up the aisle. The young man strikes the first jubilant chords bringing on the chorus girls. His expression changes to a faint, prideful smile as the next girl peeks through the curtain ready to go into her act. The lights dim and a single blue spot is thrown on the stage.*

*A fleshy young blonde begins her slow strip as the organist segues into "Hymn a L'Amour." Her movements are at once girlishly innocent and irresistibly sensual. You notice the two of them, dancer and musician, your gaze shifting from her undulating flesh to his Svengali gaze, watching her, his hands moving with her across the keys, controlling her from the darkness.*

Every couple of weeks the theme changed at the Mayan Burlesque Theater. This performance centered on Paris, so the organist played a bootlegged, handwritten arrangement of "Hymn a L'Amour," just composed by Edith Piaf's accompanist, not yet released in this country. The dancer? — Marilyn Monroe.

Carnival season ends roughly when the cold winter wind drives people indoors, leaving the chilly midway deserted. Those who can, take on other jobs until the troupe is reunited in the spring for another tour. Tony LaVey had earned a reputation as a flamboyant personality (and reliable musician) with burlesque theater owners, and so had little trouble finding jobs on the stripper circuit in Los Angeles. He did stints at the Mayan and the Burbank, two of the more popular theaters, as well as Zucca's, a legendary Culver City night spot. Marilyn Monroe (alternately "Marilyn Marlowe," "Noreen Mortensen" and "Mona Monroe") had recently been cancelled by Columbia, and had accepted the theater manager's offer "until something better came along." She needed the money to keep her room at the Hollywood Studio Club, an apartment complex full of other starlets and hopefuls, within earshot of Central Casting.

Anton was 18 years old, claiming to be 25. "Marilyn said she was 22 but I didn't believe her. It seemed like every girl I'd meet or work with was '22 years old.' The 16-year-olds chose '22' because they thought nobody'd believe them if they said '21' — and the 28-year-olds figured they were still youthful enough to get away with it." Having already posed for dozens of girlie magazines and doing a couple of bit parts in the movies, Marilyn's first featured part (as a stripper in *Ladies of the Chorus)* was released, and Marilyn and Anton went to see it together. "She seemed more interested in listening to people's comments as they left the theater than watching what she looked like up there. It was hard for her to realize that person on the screen was her."

As a burlesque dancer, "... she was what the other girls called a 'chain-dragger,' which meant she was slow to take her clothes off," says Anton. "The polite term was 'exotic' — an orgasmic act as opposed to the more frenetic, fast-stepping routines. Most of the men liked it — some fell asleep but most liked the tease. For the girls who wanted to be *artistes*, that meant being a chain-dragger."

*"I always bring out the nastiness and naughtiness in women. Even when they think they are proper and acceptable and clean, I bring out the naughtiness in them. It's because I'm supposed to be so evil and wicked myself that they feel they can act nastier around me than they ever would around another man."*

She had some trouble with the stage manager. She'd planned to open her act with "It's Magic," made popular by Doris Day. "Nature Boy," a hauntingly beautiful song by Eden Ahbez, would follow. But the stage manager worried that it would put the customers to sleep. He substituted "Slow Boat to China" for "Nature Boy." *"The greatest thing, you'll ever learn, is just to love and be loved in return."* It was his job to make sure the girls varied their numbers enough to keep it lively, mix it up. Marilyn felt better with the slow stuff like "Deep Night." Anton agreed with her choice of music. "She wasn't suited for the fast-paced routines like 'Ragtime Cowboy Joe' — which were, strangely enough, just the kind of things she did later in movies ... things like 'Heat Wave' and 'Running Wild.' But her real appeal was in her soft features and almost sickly, exaggerated pasty flesh. She needed music that would accentuate those characteristics."

It was just that unusually white skin tone that attracted Anton to Marilyn in the first place. "She was really the awakening of this fascination I have for that translucent skin quality. I never had much interest in blondes in particular before I met Marilyn. But, I can think back to a party that some cronies of mine and I went to when I was about 16 years old. When we walked in the room, a bunch of the kids were wrestling, and had this girl pinned down with her dress pulled way up over her ass. I saw those thin panties stretched across her white, plump thighs ... she was blonde, with that same kind of skin. She was just another schoolgirl — I never had any love interest in her. I didn't think much of it, turned away and went about my business. It just shows you can never tell how E.C.I. is going to happen. It's not something you can plan for — it just happens."

*E.C.I. (Erotic Crystallization Inertia): The point at which a sexual archetype/fetish is fixed.*

"Then the first time I saw Marilyn on stage, she turned around and had that pale, marshmallowy flesh with little bruises down the backs of her thighs — that erotic feeling went through me that I hadn't really felt since that party a couple of years earlier. It was the awakening of a lust object, I must admit, more than an actual love object. Love only comes after lust, if it's going to come at all. Now when I think of Marilyn, I don't see her as she is in all the posters or movies — I see those wonderfully plump, white thighs."

*Incidents last forever. "The only thing I have is memories — the only thing we can be sure of. Anyone who tries to rob me of my memories attacks me in a very real way. Everything is memory and aesthetics. Those are really the only things that matter."*

Marilyn was quite taken with Anton as a musician. "It was during her 'musician phase,' when she was nursing a stifled romance with Fred Karger, Columbia's musical director." Between performances that first night, Anton approached Marilyn with some suggestions for songs to add to her routine. As the third set began, Anton interjected a couple of choruses of "Dream Lover" and "Deep Night." Marilyn responded, grateful for his skill in drawing out the most from each piece of music. Although she stripped only to her g-string and pasties, her movements had the crowd in her power. As she finished her dance, they both knew they would be lovers.

Though their time together was brief, they were inseparable and intense, as young lovers often are. LaVey moved into a motel on Washington Boulevard with Marilyn. "It was a typical fleabag auto court, like you'd expect in that area of town, but it was cheap and had a bed." Economics played a part in his move. She made $12 a day as a stripper ... $2 more than Anton.

Occasionally after leaving the theater they would drive along the Speedway from Ocean Park in Marilyn's Pontiac. The Speedway was an ineptly named long strip of narrow, pot-holed, two-lane road running along the ocean. Oil derricks bobbed up and down in the darkness to either side of the sand-blown lane.

"One night Marilyn's car broke down about a mile out and we had to walk all the way back. We made it to the P.E. Inter-Urban Train stop in Venice and waited forever. Those 'Red Cars' only came along about once an hour — they ran all the way from the Venice Pier through Hollywood along Venice Boulevard.

"Those trains got going pretty fast — some said they used to get up to 60 miles an hour at night when there wasn't any traffic. When they got going that fast, the train would start swaying — rolling and rocking. With the wheels grinding beneath you it felt almost like being on a rollercoaster. Those were the days when streetcars had wicker seats with that indigenous odor from sweaty asses sticking to them all day."

They went all the way to the back car of the train. Practically the only other person on the train was the motorman at that time of night and even he didn't come all the way to the back. There were two drunks, that's all. While the rhythmic motion of the train lulled the other passengers to sleep, Marilyn grew passionate. She clung to Anton, pressing tightly against him. Then she stood up, hiked up her tight dress and sat on his lap. "We made love back there — it was all the more stimulating because there was always the chance that the drunks might wake up and see us. She liked an element of danger. We would make love in places where there was some chance of being discovered, like in a cemetery, the back seat of her car, an abandoned building ... she liked the thrill.

"Our motel was near Redondo, so when we got off the train we took a shortcut through seven or eight vacant lots. There were big, overgrown lots all through Los Angeles at that time — that's how the Black Dahlia's body could have been dumped in one without being discovered 'til morning. It was dawn by the time we finally got back to the motel. We had to go out the next morning and get the car towed in. The tow truck driver was going to charge us $25 or something, but Marilyn got him to tow it back for nothing. Women can do that."

While Marilyn had no trouble charming men, she didn't have as much luck with her automobile. "She was a terrible driver," Anton confirms. "She hit a minister, you know. Rear-ended him when he was waiting at a stoplight. Of course, he couldn't cuss but you could see he was visibly agitated. Some people have read a lot of significance into that incident. Maybe there was. She had totally soured on religion just before I met her. She'd been told all her life that she was no good and sinful and bad. The final straw came just about two weeks before she hit that minister. She went into a Christian Science Reading Room and really tried to read that stuff. Finally she came out and decided you couldn't read it — it didn't make any sense."

Anton supposed that was one reason why they got along so well — their mutual disdain for religion.

Marilyn was fascinated with Anton's stories of his life in the carnival and his ever-deepening study of the Black Arts. While they drove along the night-misted streets of L.A., she always wanted to hear more about occultism, about death — to explore the provinces of the strange and bizarre that Anton was becoming more and more familiar with.

LaVey and Marilyn shared a cultural hunger as well. Paul Valentine (aka "Val Valentino") was an exceptionally fine dancer and choreographer at the Mayan. He was at that time married to legendary stripper Lili St. Cyr, whose act Anton had played for at Zucca's. "Paul Valentine thought I was a weird kid. Marilyn and I used to go up to the balcony together when they were running arty filler movies like *Amok* and *Omoo, Omoo, the Shark God*. One time I heard Valentine say to the straight man, 'I think they actually watch the movies up there.' We did. We were hungry. We wanted to learn — listen to the Bizet score or examine the sets." It was soon after that time that Valentine appeared, strangely enough, in the Marx Brothers' *Love Happy,* in which Marilyn was to taunt Groucho in her most famous walk-on."

One favorite parking spot was near the Ennis House on Glendower, high above Los Angeles. Built by Frank Lloyd Wright to incorporate trapezoidal shapes (as did many of Wright's projects), it has been referred to as the "Mayan Temple" because of its haunting resemblance to the ancient buildings of Central America. Many have said it is haunted — quite a checkered past. It is in a direct line with the Mayan theater.

"We got along well together for the most part. I can only remember having one fight with her. It was over this long, white WWII Air Corps scarf I had had since about '43. We couldn't find it and I was convinced she had squirreled it away somewhere and didn't want to give it back to me. I became unreasonable with her and she got petulant. I went through every carton in the trunk of her car. Eventually we found it — it was tucked all the way down at the bottom of the bed, under the covers. I still suspect she just wanted to keep it. I was pretty young about certain things — I didn't realize then how women like to keep things like that.

"People now like to talk about everyone's involvement with Marilyn, from presidents to bellhops, how she granted them sexual favors for everything she got. Like Joe Schenck — I was there at the time and I know she did go up to his place for dinner a couple of times. He would give her money to help out — that's about as far as it went. People have quoted her as saying, 'That's the last cock I'll ever have to suck.' She never said that; she never talked that way. I think of the scene in *The Producers* where Kenneth Mars is appalled at Dick Shawn's hip portrayal of Hitler: 'Der Fuhrer never said "Baby!"' She didn't do that. It just wasn't the fad that it is now. *Deep Throat* made that popular. She told me she'd 'just let him use his hands and do a lot of looking.'"

Anton LaVey is uniquely qualified to speak of that part of Marilyn's life which has generally been conceded as the "lost" period. She was drifting around, distressed about her recent dismissal from Columbia, living with part of her belongings strewn about a motel room in boxes and part in the trunk of her car — all the while retaining her coveted room at the Hollywood Studio Club. "She was a very confused girl at that time — very depressed in many ways. It was probably the lowest point in her life until the time she died."

The interlude with Marilyn lasted only a few weeks. Anton soon became involved with the daughter of an influential Los Angeles businessman. Here was an opportunity to acquire material possessions, to move forward and prosper. Even though he would gain some of what he'd hoped for, the intellectual and sexual aspects of his new affair would be limiting. He would soon long for the compatibility he had taken for granted in his relationship with Marilyn. But it was too late. She had moved on, beginning her much-chronicled meteoric rise to fulfill her dreams and consequent nightmares. While they would correspond for another decade, they would never meet again.

*"People don't realize how long forever is when they say they want to live forever. All the settings would blend together — the emotions would remain strong but the individual scene wouldn't stand out in your memory. There would be so much blending and melding in your past. Better to live a shorter time and let each instance, each setting stand out in your mind as strong as the emotions themselves."*

Though they were physically together only a short time, they established images for each other that would recur with chilling regularity throughout both their lives. Again and again, their worlds have touched in myriad ways, just as certain themes are repeated in an opera. Anton may have actualized a recurrent physical type of man for Marilyn. While the men in her life do not look the same, they do have certain characteristics in common — a leanness rather than paunchiness, dark haired, quiet, a feral rather than cherubic quality. The same reversion to type can be seen in Anton's life. Diane LaVey looks remarkably like Marilyn, and has many of the same characteristics. Anton's first wife, Carole, was often described as a "miniature Jayne Mansfield," another blonde sex symbol of the twentieth century (with whom Anton had a close association later on). And it seems today if you want to sell newspapers or magazines, just make sure there are enough headlines with either "Marilyn Monroe" or "Satan" in them.

Looking over some of his memorabilia of Marilyn (including an inscribed copy of the famous nude calender shot that not only catapulted her to fame but almost lost her a studio contract), Anton remembers. "At the time, you don't know. My relationship with her was no big deal. People have affairs, then they move away from each other. It's not that important. There were a lot of girls around who could have gone on to fame, who had similar prerequisites: who had gone to modeling school, had photos taken, even had a bit part in some movie. We didn't know what was ahead for both of us. We just enjoyed each other. As I've said, I'm a pushover for a woman who is very fair and thin-skinned. When the chips are down, that vulnerability is all that matters.

"But, of course, you get what you see — that's important to remember, considering Marilyn's life. If she looks vulnerable, she will always see to it that she will fail or do something to remain vulnerable. What you see is what you get. You *can* tell a book by its cover."

And what does the Black Pope know about Marilyn's death? He hesitates when pressed for comment. "I know of people who have disappeared for having incontrovertible evidence." His reticence is understandable, however he admits, "People come to me with things they wouldn't show anyone else. You can tell the Devil anything." That combined with his knowledge of a "lost" time in her life puts Anton in a unique position to gather bits of information about her suicide from diverse sources that others might overlook or discount.

In 1973 LaVey wrote in a *Cloven Hoof* article that Marilyn Monroe will become the Satanic "Madonna" of the 21st century. In a sense this has already happened. Since her death, she has been fashioned into a goddess. Immortal and deified, people are fascinated by the child born of a mad mother and an unknown father. She came to the public eye with no background and disappeared too soon back into the unknowing blackness from whence she came. Like so many women closely involved with Anton, she remains forever young in our minds since she never had a chance to grow old. Suspended in time, she was spared the furor of the Women's Movement, so we never had to see her change. We hold her now almost like an icon, a talisman, reminding us constantly of a mystifying past. Marilyn Monroe is not a goddess pure and sexless, but Satanically just the opposite — a fleshly goddess: passionate, flawed, enticing, beautiful. If Anton LaVey is right, and the things he is shaping come to pass, our fascination for her has helped usher in a renewed femininity.

Newspaper advertisement for burlesque show where
Anton played organ to Marilyn Monroe's "chain-dragging" act.

# Chapter Five

# Things That Go Bump in the Night

After his diversion with Marilyn in Los Angeles, Anton felt more list-less and alone than ever before. He continued to play at strip joints along Ocean Park pier, and picked up odd jobs playing for nightclubs, lodge hall smokers and stag parties. But Los Angeles had lost its appeal. Apart from a brief camaraderie with one of Lucky Luciano's Sicilian strongarms, there was nothing holding him there any longer. He decided to return to San Francisco. Even though he didn't know yet how he would earn a living, he knew the prospects could be no better or worse than in L.A.

Anton had no trouble finding work. He easily established a reputation as a reliable player for lodge hall strip shows. "Little Caesar" Granelli, a local promoter and caterer, arranged for Anton to play organ at various stag parties he sponsored at the Avalon Ballroom and the Beach Chalet. At the same time, Anton was also able to apply his talents as a photographer: he landed a job with Paramount Photo Sales (not affiliated with the movie studio) taking pictures of women in various stages of undress. He enjoyed his work — whether it was playing for women taking their clothes off or photographing women exposing themselves in more indirect ways.

When the Korean War started, Anton was faced with the possibility of getting drafted. In those days a young man didn't run to Canada to avoid the draft, but he could enroll in college. Even though Anton had never bothered to finish high school, he didn't let that stand in his way. That wasn't a hindrance to someone who had wisely learned the tricks of a carny instead. In September, 1949, he enrolled in San Francisco City College as a Criminology major and set about establishing himself as a respectable student. After classes, Anton made money the best way he knew — playing music.

Through friends, he became involved with militant Israeli groups, some of which were running guns to the newly emerged nation — organizations with names like Betar, Hashimer Hatzair, Poale Zion, the Stern Gang, and Irgun — some of which had already been likened to the Nazis due to their ferocious tactics. Paradoxically, at this same time LaVey was playing piano for reunions of the Veterans of the Abraham Lincoln Brigade, those Americans whose idealism led them to Spain in the 30's to fight for what they thought right, though irrevocably branded as leftist. It was here Anton met men like Dalton Trumbo and Alvah Bessie, two of the most notorious members of the "Hollywood Ten." Bessie worked lights at the gatherings, unable to find work anywhere else. Anton's knowledge that he was being filmed by the F.B.I. as he walked into the meeting halls didn't seem to deter him.

Anton saw that the "Red Scare" was not far removed from the Church-induced hysteria which had caused thousands to be burned at the stake as witches and sorcerers, simply because they threatened the wrong people. His sympathy for groups labeled "Commies" by prevailing conditions was undisguised. Anton's receptive manner was invigorating to the rejected patriots. He listened to disenchanted men sing songs about Madrid, Jarama, Brunete.... With little more input than a scratchy old recording, Anton would bring new life to their music. They trusted Anton, were rejuvenated by his willingness to learn and the fervor of his playing. The outcasts Anton played for appreciated his enthusiasm and regaled him with stories of the partisans who fought in the International Brigades, hoping that some bit of them would survive through him.

LaVey recalls, "The whole thing was very much like the escapades in old movies like *The Woman on Pier 13*. There were two main rendezvous spots in San Francisco, a Jewish Community Center and a Workers' Collective downtown, where fellows would come in off the boat and went right down to meet contacts in the library of one of these places. I would be hired to play for a fashion show or variety show, then I'd get through and go right down to the docks where crates of guns were being loaded onto ships to Israel. Many of the guns were ones that had been 'liberated' during the war by American soldiers and were slated as DEWAT [deactivated war trophies]. But before they had a chance to be officially deactivated they were cosmolined up and sent to Israel. They'd wind up in a crate marked 'menorahs' or something — mostly German MP 40's and P-38's, but even

Japanese Nambus, anything they could get their hands on. Afterwards, I'd get letters of praise from the fashion show organizers saying how much I'd added to their presentation; little did they know what I'd been doing after their show.

"Those Zionist gunrunners could best be called ideological mercenaries. They had a sense of, 'Well, what I'm doing may not make a hell of a lot of difference, but at least I'm doing what I know best.' Many seemed more concerned about refining and perfecting innovative weapons technology they were experimenting with than who their new relay or explosive was blowing up, though. I met Zionists that were right out of European prisons — not Nazi concentration camps, other prisons — that had lines of bullet scars up the backs of their legs from machine gun fire. By that time they were sort of ambivalent about the Nazis. Many of them had been decorated in World War I on the side of Germany, then fought in Spain *against* Germany, only to form dubious alliances with Nazis against the British in Palestine, then were fighting to affirm the new state of Israel. There was always a lot of that — more than people have, until recently, even wanted to hear. There's a book called *Zionism in the Age of the Dictators* that confirms many of my suspicions about exactly what was going on between Zionism and Nazi Germany.

"I felt a culmination of that whole episode in my life many years later, shortly after *The Satanic Bible* came out. I met with Assaf Dayan, actor son of Israel's legendary Defense Minister Moshe Dayan, and he was glowing about the book, agreed with everything in it. He said it was exactly the philosophy they practiced, were forced to practice, in modern Israel. He extended an invitation for me to stay at his family home in Tel Aviv whenever I wished."

As Anton's earnings from the carnival grew slimmer, he picked up jobs at burlesque houses, playing for headlining strippers like Lili St. Cyr, Zorita, Tempest Storm, and Evelyn West. (At Oakland's El Rey Theater, where he worked, an ex-Army photographer named Russ Meyer was about to begin a new career as a legendary nudie film maker.) Anton noticed the same phenomenon he saw in the carnival and at other strip shows he had worked. No matter how mesmerizing the woman performing onstage could be, invariably men would be distracted by a pretty girl in the audience who might "accidentally" show a little more bare leg above her stocking top than was proper. If she did it with enough apparent innocence, every eye would be focused on her rather than on the girl undulating in front of them. It was this type of prurient interest he had seen evoked at the blowhole in carnival funhouses.

A formula began to shape itself in Anton's mind which he eventually refined into the "Law of the Forbidden." This law describes the very human phenomenon of being more compelled to the forbidden than by the allowed. In the burlesque theater, the pretty patron revealing more than she realizes is far more pruriently enticing than the stripper on stage, who takes off much more. At the blowhole, the woman who is violated by the air blast will really show more than is intended to be seen — dirty underwear, no underwear perhaps! The viewer is seeing what is absolutely not intended to be seen. It then becomes nasty, and therefore, irresistible. A competent witch learns these principles and discovers ways to apply them to her advantage. (Anton outlined these techniques in *The Compleat Witch*, reissued as *The Satanic Witch* some years later.)

San Francisco's Playland at the Beach was one of America's great seaside amusement parks. Some of Anton's carny friends had off-season jobs there, and his affinity for midways drew him to the place. (Up on the cliffs sprawled the legendary Sutro Baths, a "haunted" place if ever there was one.) It was here, one night, that Anton met his first wife, Carole Lansing, the daughter of a Wells Fargo bank executive. He was immediately charmed by the five-foot-two, baby doll blonde. Carole would be described by friends as "a miniature Jayne Mansfield" many years before Anton actually became involved with Jayne. When Anton mentioned this to her, Jayne responded without hesitation, "Why settle for a miniature when you can have the real thing?"

Since Carole was underage, it was necessary for the couple to get her parents' permission before they could marry. While supportive of their daughter, her parents were suspicious of Carole's involvement with this menacing, "older man." Anton found that his looks did not find favor with most parents. While his hardened, sinister appearance was strangely compelling to girls, he had to meet his dates around the corner from their homes.

At the time he met Carole, Anton was all the more alarming because of a deep scar on his right cheek. He received it in a row with a friend when he was 16, just before he left home to join the circus. The fight started over a snide remark about the morals of the girl Anton was dating at the time. Anton became enraged. When the fight grew quite violent, the other boy pulled out a knife and sliced Anton's cheek. "He really had no choice. I was throttling him, and I had lost all consciousness of anything but the fact that he had insulted the girl. The sad thing is that he was right."

Some time after the altercation, the boy who cut Anton was hauled down to the police station on an unrelated charge. While in a holding cell, he hooked his belt around a pipe overhead, wrapped the other end around his neck, and hung himself. *Anton's first experience of unintentional retribution.*

Carole's parents were eventually charmed by Anton's reserved nature, musical talents, and commitment to their daughter. Seeing Carole's unshakable devotion, they could do nothing but accept their new son-in-law for all that he was. Anton, in turn, made efforts to settle into marital responsibilities. He combined his education in Criminology with his talents in photography in a job with the San Francisco Police Department as a police photographer. Once again, he was faced with the worst side of human nature on a daily basis. On call 24 hours a day, he would race across town to photograph a murder site, suicide, auto accident, explosion — anything that required an investigation because of the gravity of the situation.

There were enough bloody scenes to make Anton's mind seethe: children spattered on the sidewalk by hit and run drivers, young women brutally slain by jealous husbands, bloated bodies fished out of San Francisco Bay, men shot by their brothers or best friends, little girls raped and ravaged. How was he to believe that there was some plan to such senseless carnage, that God was in his heaven watching over all these people? What possible reason could there be for giving such pain and suffering to innocent souls? There could be no God. People must be made to answer to other men rather than depend on some supreme deity to dole out justice — no such God existed.

*"There is no God. There is no supreme, all-powerful deity in the heavens that cares about the lives of human beings. There is nobody up*

*there who gives a shit. Man is the only god. Man must be taught to answer to himself and other men for his actions."*[5]

Anton saw there must be a new representative of justice — not some oppressive, patriarchal, white-bearded God but a new human advocate. Someone who was not removed from us and shrouded in "divinity," but one who understood the torments of being human, who shared our own passions and foibles but was somehow wiser and stronger. Anton began to realize that most of our progress in science and philosophy had been achieved by those who rebelled against "God" and the Church, or the dictates of conventional society. We needed a representative for that revolutionary, creative, irrepressible spirit within us — not a Holy Father but perhaps a rebellious brother.

Anton already knew the single figure who fit the bill. A deity whose rebellious, passionate nature had been described from the dark beginnings of time, either in awe or fear, or both. Satan, by one name or another, haunted mankind, tempting him with sweet delights, and enlightening him with blinding secrets intended only for gods. Satan's worshippers addressed him not as "Our Father" but as a compatriot who concerned himself directly with the affairs of men and women on earth. He was one who could be petitioned for powers of retribution and who gave deserved rewards which a divine "God" would never understand. Instead of creating sins to insure guilty compliance, Satan encouraged indulgence. He was the single deity who could really understand us.

Since Anton had to keep his camera loaded and ready at all times, it encouraged him to indulge in snapping human interest shots when he saw something particularly striking. His photos from that time show the strong influence of Arthur Fellig, known as Weegee, who worked as a New York police/crime photographer in the 40's. Anton's studies have the quality of such sharp realism they border on the macabre, an early compatriot to the work of Diane Arbus.

During the years he worked for the department, his photos attracted a fair amount of attention. He exhibited some of his work, sold a few photos to magazines, and won honors in a number of competitions. People were not necessarily pleased with Anton's photos of a murder site, the mangled wreckage of a car crash, or his no less disturbing perspective on a family outing at the beach, but they were compelled to look nevertheless. Anton, however, found the camera to be too limiting, too mechanical.

Anton had already been painting for some time, experimenting, among other things, with techniques he gleaned from the works of Ivan Albright, who did the lurid painting for the color sequence in the film version of *The Portrait of Dorian Gray*. One such painting that Anton exhibited was a hideous portrait of a man in a state of semi-putrefaction — his own "portrait in the attic" accomplished at the age of 21. The painting was placed in a gallery window to attract customers, but it was too disturbing — so many people complained that it was removed.

As early as 1951, Anton's attitudes had been formulated enough to try to seek out a group of "official" devil worshippers. He visited a chapter of the Order of Thelema in Berkeley; followers of Aleister Crowley, who prided himself on being "The Wickedest Man in the World" and supposedly in touch with the darker elements. Anton was disappointed to find the Berkeley bunch mystically-minded card readers who emphasized the study of Eastern philosophy, Oriental languages, stars and contemplation to reach the spiritual Nirvana of Oneness. A few years earlier, Anton had ordered Crowley's books from Jack Parsons in Pasadena — *Equinox of the Gods, Magic Without Tears, Moonchild, Diary of a Dope Fiend, Sword and Song, Tannhaeuser, The Book of Lies, Yoga For Yahoos,* and *The Book of the Law*. When John Symonds' biography of Crowley, *The Great Beast*, came out in 1952, Anton concluded that the Thelemites' founder was a druggy poseur whose greatest achievements were as a poet and mountain climber. Despite hysterical tales of the wild Satanic orgies he was said to preside over and the blasphemous insights his writings were said to contain, Crowley's followers were rather innocuous — much more ethereal than Anton expected. It occurred to Anton that people seemed compelled to manufacture fantasies about supposed Devil-worshipping cults, no matter how bland the group might actually be.

In 1952, Anton's first daughter, Karla Maritza, was born. Her dark, curly hair and quick mind echoed her father's, forming a magical link between them from her birth. The following year, responsibilities with the police department expanded when Anton was assigned, through no request of his own, all the "repeater 800" calls that came through various bureaus.

This was the code number for "nut calls": reports of ghosts, glowing shapes floating across the back yard, weird noises, UFO sightings, mysterious rays, all things that go bump in the night. Work was becoming more interesting. No one else on the force wanted the assignments — not out of fear of ridicule, as the term "nut call" would imply, but rather because of an implicit fear of getting involved with anything "spooky."

Anton was delighted. As a ghosthunter, he employed a Theremin, an early electronic musical instrument, as an intrusion detector. Set at a fixed frequency, fluctuations in its pitch and intensity could be monitored, should any presence present itself. (Hollywood utilized the Theremin as standard equipment for spooky background music in haunted house movies.) He set traps for "ghosts": a camera loaded with infrared film had a sensitive trigger to record any ectoplasmic activity; a tape recorder was employed to record any ghastly sounds such beings might make as they passed. He spent more than one night in a sleeping bag laying in wait for the unsuspecting spectre. Anton was indeed one of America's first "ghostbusters."

*"The modern ghost hunters are the ones who know something about human nature. That is truly the paranormal of our day — the hidden secrets of the human psyche. The new Carnackis, John Silences and Jules de Grandins don't go around brandishing Tibetan thunderbolts and standing in protective pentacles anymore, banishing the old kinds of demons and monsters.*

*"The delver who would now confront malevolent forces on their own turf, the way they did in the old pulp magazines, would look the unsuspecting in the eyes and say, 'You're not happy, are you? You turn up your stereo full blast, listen to the incessant beat and let the music whip you. Driving down the freeway you roll your windows up tight and savor the sensation. You're a new slave, the walking dead, a pod person, and don't even know it. I know what you need even though you don't. Galley slaves you might have been, oarsmen pulling in time to the driver's drum beats.*

*"Here in my hand I hold a bullwhip that will vanquish you, or liberate you, depending on your predisposition. You cannot fool me. You may be able to fool these men of letters but you aren't fooling me. I know what you need.' The modern ghost hunters are the experts of the supernatural — Freudian concepts now lost in dusty hidden texts. They discover the mean-*

*ings behind meanings. Their Jehovah can't do it anymore — never could properly. It takes a Devil — always has. If they want Hell, I'll give them Hell."*

Of course, most of Anton's experiments proved to be unnecessary, except to satisfy his own scientific curiosity. On his regular assignments, Anton was learning still more about the mysteries of the human animal. The scenario might run something like this: Anton would report to a house to find a harried couple frightened out of their sleep by unearthly moans coming from the locked attic. Crawling through the cobwebs and searching under the eaves of the house, Anton would discover the source of the "unearthly moans": a rusty can whistling in the wind, or a poor, half-starved cat who had fallen through a broken skylight and then had no way out.

But when Anton would present the overwrought residents with the simple cause of their problems, their disappointment would be only too obvious. "Was that all it was?" Anton learned to spice it up a bit: "Well, of course, there *was* more to it than that," he would all but wink. "But I took care of that for you too." A much more satisfying answer — some sort of exorcism had been performed on their behalf and Anton could leave them considerably relieved that their cherished fears remained intact. Again, he saw that regardless of evidence, people would insist on believing what they wished to believe. His reputation as a ghosthunter grew stronger and others began contacting him for investigations and "exorcisms." Anton learned the fine art of providing remedies and maintaining mystery at the same time. Though most of the "800" cases made Anton cringe because of their foolishness and blind insistence on the supernatural, his reputation outside of the police department grew.

Within a few short years, Anton had developed a steady clientele doing the work he most enjoyed. People would pay good money to have their houses "cleaned" of spirits, or to be hypnotized to help them stop smoking, lose weight or muster up the courage to ask for the raise they needed. Eventually, clients asked Anton's advice on how to make simple charms or cast spells of love or vengeance. Surely someone who knew so much about the spirit world would be able to help them get their boyfriends back. And so he did. By 1955, he was ready to quit the police department and concentrate all his energy on further explorations into the Black Arts.

To supplement his income as an exorcist and hypnotist, Anton returned to playing the organ, this time at a former speakeasy and house of ill-repute called Mori's Point, located along the beach about 15 miles south of San Francisco. Anton had moved his family to a flat near Sutro Heights overlooking Playland at the Beach, where 3-year-old Karla was serenaded nightly by the shrieks and laughter from the midway below.

She wasn't apt to get bored, either, by a lack of house pets. One of Anton's associates, writer Junius Adams, knowing of his love and history with big cats, had smuggled a ten-week old black leopard through Burma and then Israel to give to Anton. The cat, named Zoltan, had the run of the house and took great delight in laying in wait at the top of the stairs when-ever anyone entered the place from the floor below. When the unsuspect-ing guest reached a certain point on the stairs, Zoltan would fly full force at him and try to send his quarry tumbling back down the stairs with him. Some wary friends learned to call up to Anton before mounting the stairs to make sure he had his charge under control.

Anton also recalls how Zoltan liked to climb into Karla's crib with her to sleep when she was a tiny girl. He and Carole would awaken to the slight creak of the crib as Zoltan jumped up and balanced on the sidebar, fol-lowed by a muffled "plonk!" as he landed beside Karla, trying to be as quiet about it as he could. In the morning, Anton would find his daughter sleep-ing soundly, face pressed against the bars and leg dangling, while Zoltan snoozed contentedly, taking up three quarters of the crib.

When the cold ocean winds blew the fog over the cliffs near Anton's flat, into the tree-lined park that was once the grounds of Adolph Sutro's mansion, Anton would drape himself in his black overcoat and take Zoltan out to prowl beside him through the mist. Late-night strollers or people waiting for the bus would take one look at the ominous pair and run. At least one would-be attacker was shocked to discover that the "dog" at the end of the gleaming steel chain was no dog. Anton reveled in the reaction and felt he was discovering a formula for himself. He needed larger quarters where he would be free to exercise his eccentricities.

Already Anton was getting local press because of his odd practices and unusual house pets. Many of his cronies from the circus and carnival days had maintained friendships, blending well with the unusual personalities drawn to Anton's Sutro Heights flat as murmured rumors spread. He saw he needed a place with many rooms, separate from prying neighbors, a unique place he could decorate in his own fashion — one more suited to his growing reputation as ghost-hunter, hypnotist, and magician. He needed time to be able to apply some of the magical formulas that were coming to a boil in his mind. His life was forming itself, echoing patterns that had followed him from his boyhood. There could be no denying the sinister directions which tempted him relentlessly onward.

# Chapter Six

# Walpurgisnacht, 1966

*The men that walk with Satan, their years are as a day;*
*They know each generation as a dream that drifts away.*
*And they bid mankind make merry and revel while they may.*
— "The Men That Walk With Satan" by Robert E. Howard

Without the pressure to look "respectable" as a police photographer, Anton regrew the Mephistophelean beard and moustache. His blue-black hair almost reached the leonine proportions it had when he worked with the big cats in the circus — still unacceptably long by 1956 standards. He had to be neat and trim while working as a cop, but not as a hypnotist.

Anton described the house he had in mind and his real estate agent lined up some places for him to see. On an outing to see a house near the exclusive Sea Cliff area a few blocks from the Golden Gate Bridge, Anton was immediately intrigued by a weathered, slate-grey, Victorian across the street. He was not discouraged by the "Sold" sign in front, nor by the real estate agent who insisted it was not the kind of place he was looking for. Anton knew it was.

*LaVey takes well-deserved pride in what he has acquired as "white elephants" — often rare and increasingly valuable, but always unusual. He gets these items for their intrinsic value to him rather than monetary speculation then, because of his acquisitive nature, he holds on to them. Cars, for example, he has purchased at one time or another: 1934 Duesenberg ($175), 1937 Cord ($265), 1941 Hollywood Graham ($150)....*

His agent asked to see the inside and, cautioning Anton that the house was already on consignment with his real estate agency, he introduced Anton to the residents as an historian interested in interior design. The owner happened to be there, arranging for the sale of the house. Surprised at Anton's enthusiasm, she proudly gave him the grand tour.

As she slowly led Anton through each of the 13 rooms, the woman's conversation revealed that the house had been used at various times as a speakeasy, spiritualists' parlor, and house of ill-repute. She tactfully alluded to the many eccentricities that had been added over the years: secret panels, trapdoors, and hidden rooms. Mary Ellen Pleasant, better known as "Mammy Pleasant," San Francisco's most notorious madam during the Barbary Coast days, bought the place for the then young mulatto owner to operate for her. Most closets in the house contained hidden panels that were used to rob the customers while they were being "entertained." With secret passages webbing the entire place, it is possible to move throughout the house without once being seen. Various devices were strategically placed to produce rappings and other eerie effects during seances.

Anton was enchanted, and after he told the owner he planned to practice magic in the house, she was equally determined he should be the one to own it. She was glad to find someone who could really appreciate its illustrious history and who seemed destined to add a little history of his own. Anton was, in fact, offering a little more money than the real estate agency — that was enough of an excuse for her to get out of any commitment she had with them and sell the house to Anton instead.

The first thing Anton did after he moved in was to paint the house black. After an unproductive search, he concluded that black house paint was not being manufactured. Anton found some black surplus submarine paint, rented some scaffolding, and went to work. There were a few minor changes to be made on the inside, wallpaper to hang, tiles to replace, and a few coats of paint to add, but by Halloween, the LaVeys were ready to show off their new home in grand style. Their midnight party was a glittering success. It was obvious to Anton that there should be many more such events. The house seemed to thrive on gatherings for magical purposes and it would be a shame to limit his magical explorations here to only one participant.

Anton's new neighbors were keeping an eye on all the activity around the strange house, made to look even stranger by its new occupants. There were already rumors flying around the neighborhood of the mysterious man with the lovely wife and daughter, walking up the front stairs trailing a black panther on a leash behind them. At the time, Anton had a black 1949 Citroen which he parked in front — a low, sinister car which added to the looming effect of the house. Eventually, some of the older people got curious enough to talk to Anton, which gave him the opportunity to find out even more about his new home. They were glad to tell him the legends surrounding the place, knowing they would be appreciated by this odd young man.

*"There I was up there on the scaffolding, concentrating on the trim around the windows when I heard a cackling voice behind me: 'I used to buy my liquor here.' I turned around and there stood this old duffer who spent the next half hour regaling me with his stories of the all-night parties that used to go on here during Prohibition."*

The house was originally built in 1887 by a Scottish sea captain on timbers brought around Cape Horn as ship's ballast. The captain presumably spent some happy time in the house but after six years of marriage, his wife disappeared under mysterious circumstances. The captain went off and was never heard from again.

After the great San Francisco earthquake of 1906, a grand fireplace was constructed in the front parlor from large paving stones that had been dislodged in the waterfront area. The iron-colored, chiseled stones had originally come from Roman ruins in England, were carried around Cape Horn on sailing ships as ballast, then used as paving stones and fill along the waterfront in San Francisco. Incredibly hard, rough-hewn, dark — they look like the kind of stones one would associate with ancient Druid sacrificial altars. After the earthquake, the stones were piled as rubble and the owner of the house got a mason to haul cartfuls to her home for the fireplace.

An unusually large construction resulted which would have been considered grotesquely impractical by anyone but Anton. Eventually this parlor became the main ritual chamber for the Church of Satan. The oversized mantle was large enough for a nude woman to recline comfortably during their Satanic ceremonies, photographs of which appeared in periodicals around the world. Anton felt it was a particularly magical connection that the first public Satanic altar was made from stones traced directly to the

Roman Empire. It seems the house was designed for Anton, as if he conjured it out of his dreams.

As LaVey has said, he never had to go looking for publicity, no matter what his detractors would claim — publicity has always had a way of finding him. Within a few months of inaugurating his "black house," Herb Caen, San Francisco's most widely read columnist, got wind of Anton's unusual occupations, and equally unusual home, complete with a jungle cat and a tarantula meandering through the secret passageways. It made excellent copy.

Anton had recently begun performing on the mighty Wurlitzer theatre organ at the Lost Weekend cocktail lounge. The only instrument of its kind played every night of the week, the Wurlitzer drew aficionados from across the country to hear it. At San Francisco's Civic Auditorium, he was hired to play the largest pipe organ west of Chicago — an Austin concert model originally built for the 1915 Panama-Pacific World's Fair. Its five keyboards, eight thousand pipes and unwieldy installation had intimidated the most experienced players. Anton launched into the job without a thought, concentrating on the skills of crowd-pleasing he had developed along the midway. Taken aback by the nonchalance of the new organist, the auditorium's managers offered Anton an ongoing position. Soon he was to become San Francisco's city organist, playing for cultural events, conventions and games.

A crowd of influential and eccentric people were gathering around Anton, at ease in the surroundings of his home and pleased for the opportunity to share iconoclastic interests and hobbies. Before the Age of Video, it was common practice for people of like mind to form somewhat informal social circles for parties, soirees, dinners, and the like. This extraordinary group of people who came to hobnob at the Black House Anton came to call "The Magic Circle."

At first, there was no set itinerary, and conversations flowed freely over cocktails, accompanied by Anton or another member of the group playing Hammond or piano in the corner. The LaVeys hosted four major parties a year, at New Year's, Midsummer's Eve, Walpurgisnacht and Halloween. Elaborate costume parties were held year-round, often following outlandish themes. Blending together LaVey's old carny and circus chums, his friends from the police department, and newer additions — wealthy eccentrics and literary iconoclasts — who gathered around LaVey because of his growing reputation as San Francisco's Black Magician, proved quite a potent brew. Idle chatter about the occult evolved to speculations about the efficacy of magic and spells, spurring on Anton to organize nights of actual ritual for his eager guests. It wasn't until much later that LaVey actually opened his doors to the public and began formalized seminars, charging a moderate fee at the door for lectures on the subjects Anton had come to know so well.

Among those first members of what would eventually evolve into the Church of Satan, was "the Baroness," Carin de Plessen, who grew up in the Royal Palace of Denmark. She lived in an isolated mountaintop home in Marin County with several Great Danes, and never missed one of Anton's events. Another member was the heir to the Vickers munitions estate who had known Basil Zaharoff and told Anton tales of the strange black chapel Zaharoff had at his chateau.

LaVey's gatherings have never been ordinary. Those who attended Anton's soirees have always comprised an array of professions and pursuits. There were artists, attorneys, doctors, writers, and law enforcement officers. City Assessor Russell Wolden might share the room with Donald Werby, one of San Francisco's most influential property owners; anthropologist Michael Harner with writer Shana Alexander. A ship's purser might be seated next to a deep-sea diver, a dildo manufacturer next to a plastic surgeon. A famous tattoo artist, the grandson of a U.S. president, the owner of one of the world's largest collections of Faberge artifacts all were seen at LaVey's get-togethers. The field of fantasy and science fiction personages alone yielded the likes of Anthony Boucher, August Derleth, Robert Barbour Johnson, Reginald Bretnor, Emil Petaja, Stuart Palmer, Clark Ashton Smith, Forrest J. Ackerman, Fritz Leiber, Jr., to name a few, into LaVey's circle of magical compatriots.

Through San Francisco socialite Brooks Hunt, Anton was introduced to a man who would have a profound influence on him: Dr. Cecil E. Nixon. Mr. Hunt enjoyed Anton's musicianship and knew of his involvement with hypnosis and magic. He suggested Anton meet Dr. Nixon since their interests seemed to run on the same lines.

Dr. Nixon looked like he stepped from the pages of a Victorian novel, with his wing-tipped collars, high-button shoes, and gold pince-nez perched on his nose. The angles of his face were strong, though now grown gaunt over the years, his nose was long and fine, with a thick moustache and hair parted sharply in the middle. He looked like exactly what he was: an eccentric who was secretive about most details of his life, self-educated in stage magic, mind reading, ventriloquism and hypnotism. Though Dr. Nixon graduated from medical school, he worked in the circus as a hand for some years instead of establishing himself as a doctor. After futilely falling deeply in love with a bareback rider, he left the circus to eventually set up a dental practice. Mostly retired by the time Anton met him, he still had a small office set up in his home for clients who refused to go to anyone else.

*"I've always had an appreciation for characters — because of their exclusivity. They are unique. Perhaps it was because of my abiding respect for characters that I had to create something like the Church of Satan. There are a lot of things I could have settled on in my life. I felt competent enough in my abilities as a musician, animal trainer, hypnotist, photographer, or painter. Perhaps with enough practice and patience, I might have flourished as any of these things. But I never would have been unique, I never would have been the only one doing it. Constantly being critiqued by my peers, I would have entered a fraternity, so to speak. So I did something no one had ever done before — but not by design. Rather as a synthesis of all that had gone before. Something that, for good or ill, better or worse, would remove me from any grouping."*

Dr. Nixon's large home on Broadway Street was his bastion of gentility. He had carved or obtained intricate embellishments and laid them into the ceilings and walls. He filled the house with rococco furnishings, fine statues, unusual art pieces, musical instruments, and antiques he had collected from around the world. There was also a flavor of a carnival funhouse with several of Dr. Nixon's inventions hidden throughout the house, triggered to operate on various cues. Besides the music he had constantly piped to every room of the house, there was a mechanical bird hidden in the living room wall, which flew out every twenty minutes, and chirped. His doorbell chimed Chopin's Funeral March, and another door, with an ornate satyr's head carved on it, opened on spoken command.

Anton was soon included in Dr. Nixon's Saturday night soirees, where the likes of Harry Houdini, pianist/composer Ignace Paderewski and actress Gertrude Lawrence had once gathered. While aging socialites sang operatic selections, Anton accompanied them on the ornate Wurlitzer. He provided appropriate background music for dramatic recitations, magic acts, or simply to set the proper mood for those he called "Potted Palms."

The palmiest was one Onezoma Dubouchelle, who, recalls Anton, "always made little finger sandwiches for the soirees, out of questionable meats and spreads. They weren't very good but no one wanted to say anything. I would constantly find tiny dried-out sandwiches hidden in the organ bench, or stashed behind the console. It was anyone's guess how long they'd been there.

"Dr. Nixon considered Onezoma (pronounced Oh-NEZ-a-muh) Dubouchelle a grand lady by whom all others should be judged. She shared the upstairs with a pleasant and capable woman named Betty Sedgewick. Each had her own room, ostensibly sharing the single bathroom. But rather than reduce herself to such a plebeian level, Miss Dubouchelle walked a block to a Shell gas station when her needs demanded. That was what Dr. Nixon admired most about Miss Dubouchelle, even more than her craggy beauty. She always reminded me of a blend of Mount Rushmore and Margaret Dumont but the Dr. maintained, in one of his most brilliant *faux pas*, that 'she must have been a real beauty when she was 22 dollars.'"

When Anton came into his life, Dr. Nixon felt he had discovered someone with whom he could really communicate, who was self-educated in the same fields he himself was, and to whom he could confide his deepest secrets. He admired Anton a great deal — his skills as an accomplished musician (Dr. Nixon built an elaborate pipe organ in his home but couldn't play), engaging magician, hypnotist and cynic. He also appreciated the fascination Anton elicited in women. "When you come into the room," Dr. Nixon said of Anton, "the girls give a little start." Dr. Nixon himself had a great romantic respect for beautiful women and felt that, while it was unnecessary to constantly engage in "base sexual calisthenics," there was nothing more pleasurable than "fondling a beautiful woman under the quilts." He liked Carole and spent many evenings in the LaVey home. Dr. Nixon adopted Anton as a magical son, a younger reflection of himself, and shared things with him he would share with no other.

The most captivating invention Dr. Nixon ever created still survives, and continues to impress both scientists and conjurers to this day. "Isis," named after the Egyptian goddess, was presented as a carved automaton who lounged on her couch and played the zither to an incredible repertoire of 3000 tunes. Dr. Nixon spent 15 years on her, "applying 150 scientific principles in her construction." She is filled with a series of complex gears, cams, sprockets, solenoids and electro-magnets — and only Dr. Nixon knew the precise vibrations necessary to activate her. After some time of working on Isis with Dr. Nixon, he confided the secret of her operation to Anton, giving him his own typed instructions with handwritten notes which Anton locked in a vault and has refused to reveal to anyone, in accordance with Dr. Nixon's wishes.

*"I always end up regretting it when I give away secrets — I might be tempted to give bigger ones away if I hadn't seen the effect of giving the little ones away."*

For a time, Dr. Nixon tried to interest Anton in constructing a blonde automaton named Galatea who played the violin. Dr. Nixon also spoke of his plans for a "Castle in the Air" in Calistoga, a Northern California hot springs resort town. He explained it was to be a large house on a knoll, with mirrors set all around the base of the house at 45-degree angles so they reflected the sky. Surrounding the house at a certain distance down the rise would be an iron fence through which visitors could look and see the house apparently floating above the ground. Besides these projects, Dr. Nixon was working on an autobiography entitled "The Castle of Indolence."

*"The only problem with having older friends is you have to see them all die off. It sure would be nice if there really was some place where you could see all your old friends again after you die."*

Following Nixon's death in 1962, at the age of 82, Bill Harrah, of Nevada casino and automobile collection fame, bought Isis, but his museum's curators were never able to make her operate. The museum sold her at auction in 1985. The present owner, John Gaughan, a master craftsman and conjurer in his own right, is, at this writing, restoring Isis and hoping to restore her to her former glory.

*"I am all that was, and is, and is to be, and no mortal hath lifted my veil."* —engraved on Isis' base

Another illustrious member of Anton's original Magic Circle was underground filmmaker Kenneth Anger, who, after establishing himself as a leading force in that genre, has since become known as one of Hollywood's most notorious historians, publishing much of the juicier tidbits about its stars in *Hollywood Babylon* and *Hollywood Babylon II*. Starting out at a very young age as an actor himself (as the changeling prince in *A Midsummer Night's Dream)*, Anger discovered as a teenager that he liked it much better behind the camera, creating his own unique moods and images. Anger had already filmed *Scorpio Rising*, which kicked off the popularity of leather and motorcycles, and was filming *Inauguration of the Pleasure Dome*, based on the "stately pleasure dome" of *Kubla Khan*, by Samuel Taylor Coleridge.

Anton and Anger had much in common. Both were born in the same year. Both built cities when they were children (though Anger built a volcano in the middle of his and destroyed his creation in a spectacular display inspired by the eruption of Vesuvius). Both frequented the same childhood haunts as children, predictably encountering each other. Many years later, during pre-production research for *Pleasure Dome*, Anger traveled to two of Crowley's haunts — Cefalu on Sicily (where he restored much of Crowley's retreat) and Boleskine in Scotland. While there, he also gathered much of the Great Beast's recordings and texts for magical rituals. Anger introduced LaVey to Marjorie Cameron, John Parsons' widow, who was starring in *Pleasure Dome*, and who confided to Anton the details of her husband's explosive demise during one of their Thelemic rituals.

During the time he was developing his Magic Circle, Anton had maintained his job playing at Mori's Point a few nights a week. One Sunday night in 1959, a young woman came in who would play a very important role in Anton's life. Diane, a 17-year-old beauty with long blonde hair and enchanting green eyes, worked as an usherette in nearby Pacifica, and was escorted to dinner by her manager who was obviously smitten with his charming employee. As Anton spoke at the manager's table of magic and ghost-hunting, Diane could not hide her enthusiasm.

It was not the first time Diane had seen Anton. Once, on a fog-shrouded night by the ocean, she was entranced by a wraith-like white sedan she saw cutting soundlessly through the fog. A mysterious-looking man in black was behind the wheel. She didn't know then that it was Anton LaVey prowling the night in his 1937 Cord.

Anton was pleased to see that Diane had talked her escort into bringing her to Mori's Point the next Sunday. Anton took the opportunity to gather a little more information about this voluptuous girl, aptly named after the bewitching Huntress of mythology. Anton was impressed with Diane's beauty — she looked strikingly like Marilyn, in the shape of her face; the white, translucence of her flesh; and in a certain unsureness underlying her movements. She seemed to Anton to be a perfect composite of "Sheena, Queen of the Jungle," and artist John Willey's "Sweet Gwendoline." But he was also impressed with the devotion she felt for her family, working nights in the theater and days doing office work in an insurance company, turning over a large portion of her paycheck to her mother.

Anton gathered that Diane, like himself, had always been something of a black sheep, an outcast, no matter how much she might have wanted to "fit in." Her long, straight hair was not the commonplace sight it was 10 years later in the late '60's. At a time of Jackie Kennedy flips and shellacked beehives, only exotic dancers had long, luxuriant hair. But that was the way Diane liked to wear it, regardless of public opinion. She immediately admired Anton's strong bearing, his mystery, tempered by the sensitivity with which he played. It was obvious there could be no other man for her. She came back to Mori's Point several times until her manager finally realized that he was no match for the man who had won Diane's heart. By that time, Anton and Diane were meeting secretly, and she was slowly becoming more and more an integral part of his life.

Over the next few months, Anton spent as much of his free time as he could with Diane, sometimes resorting to sneaking her out through the secret passages of the house and departing with her hiding in the trunk of his car. His love for Diane grew steadily in response to her unbridled devotion and unquestioning support of all he was doing. Carole and Anton finally divorced late in 1960.

The San Francisco Fox Theater was generally conceded to be the grandest movie palace ever built. It had been decided the space could better be used for an office high-rise and the wreckers were to begin tearing it down. Anton was one of the entertainers present the night the Fox closed its doors forever. Diane, then working as a telephone information operator, pleaded with her supervisor to let her off for the night, explaining that her boyfriend was playing at a very important event. When the supervisor refused, Diane quit.

Celebrities and admirers of the lavish theater crowded the aisles that night, paying final homage to an era of opulence that would never be repeated. As the crowd filed out the doors after the show, Anton LaVey played the last organ chords that would ever echo through the building.

The Fox Plaza in downtown San Francisco, built on the site of the Fox Theater, is thought to have a curse on it — offices housed in the building seem to have one problem after another...

Diane had the pleasure of taking over Carole's role as hostess to the Magic Circle. Eventually, Anton began to formalize the magical lectures, holding them every Friday night at midnight, the witching hour, and opening them to the public, charging $2.50 per person. In no time, the place was packed to capacity. Anton's lectures included not only occult topics, but esoteric knowledge such as: vampires (not only the horror-movie version but some vampires from history and modern days); werewolves (man into animals of various kinds, and methods for achieving transformations); freaks (drawing from Anton's experiences on the backlots of carnivals—fat ladies, midgets, strong men, pinheads, giants, and other human anomalies, along with sword-swallowers, geeks, and carnival fakirs); methods of torture and various devices for pain, including the methods of self-mutilation established by the Church; sex theories and revitalization techniques, including gland transplants from monkeys or goats, and recipes for aphrodisiacs. Others topics included haunted houses, ESP, zombies, and homunculi. Most of the seminars were illustrated in some way and, of course, the lecture on the Black Mass concluded with an authentic ritual that Anton devised, putting together elements from a number of sources.

*The Black Mass was the original psychodrama — purging the participants of the pain induced by certain societal sacred cows through a lavish ritual of ridicule, parody and satire. The subject of the ritual changes according to the needs of the group at that time. The Catholic Church, with the mental traumas it induced through repression and guilt, became a prime candidate for lampooning. In order to free the stifled and trauma-*

*tized from their religion-inspired psychic burdens, Satanic ceremonies employed the inverted cross, black candles instead of white, desecration of the Host, and the backwards recitation of prayers.*

One seminar on "Cannibalism and Human Sacrifices" covered the subject in more than just words. Students were invited to partake of a cooked thigh of a young white woman. The leg had been biopsied and provided by a Berkeley physician who attended Anton's lectures regularly. Diane basted the main course of *puaka balava*, "long pig," in Triple Sec, fruit juices and grenadine. She served it with fried bananas and yams, just as the Fiji Islanders did, adding Tonka bean wine and caterpillars to round out the meal. The meat was described as tasting somewhere between pork and lamb, with a consistency rather fibrous like pork chops, but sweeter, and not quite as tender or salty as lamb. The diners exhibited little squeamishness except when it came to eating the caterpillars. But the LaVey's three-year-old daughter, Zeena, polished them off with enthusiasm.

Anton also developed "Witches' Workshops" as an adjunct to the regular seminars but concentrating more on the skills of applied magic, enchantment, love potions, fortune telling, and such things specifically pertinent to witchcraft.

In 1964, Anton began getting his first wave of heavy publicity. Monique Benoit, society columnist for the *San Francisco Chronicle*, wrote of Anton as a psychic investigator, spending nights investigating haunted houses and cemeteries, and now holding strange rituals in his menacing black house. Herb Caen included him in his columns again, describing Anton attending the opera, resplendent in a formal black cape with scarlet lining, and carrying an antique sword cane.

Zoltan, Anton's big "black cat," seemed the perfect pet for his "black house." Zoltan loved his place in the kitchen, causing problems and startling guests. There was only one time Anton cursed ever keeping an animal like Zoltan in a large city. He disappeared once when he was about five years old. Anton and Carole were frantic. Day dragged into day, and week into week, and still no sign of him. After three or four weeks, Anton heard a familiar sound in back of the building. Investigating, he found Zoltan crouched at the foot of the stairs.

He was a pitiful sight. His jaw was broken, hanging slackly from its original position. His paws were raw and bloody, as if he had traveled a great distance. The veterinarian said his jaw had been broken for some time, possibly with a baseball bat or heavy pipe. He tried to mend it with a steel pin. "I hate to think what he must have gone through during all that time," Anton recalls. "He might have traveled 50 or 100 miles to get back to us after wandering into a truck being loaded or something and being carried off. Perhaps he traveled only at night, keeping to the bushes and trees, frightened — who knows what he'd been forced to eat. We'd given up hope of ever seeing him again." But Zoltan bounced back to health with a lot of love, a broken fang and a trick jaw.

Three years later, when Anton was out one evening, Carole opened the front door at the wrong time and Zoltan darted out into the street. It looked as if he was trying to jump into the window of Anton's car — one of his favorite tricks. But before he could reach the car, he was hit by a passing car and killed. Anton wrapped him in one of his jackets that Zoltan had loved to curl up with to sleep, and buried him in the backyard of his home. He buried Zoltan on the Fourth of July and as he dug into the earth, a calliope could be heard playing faintly in the distance.

Diane knew of Anton's background with big cats and was prepared when one of Anton's associates purchased a ten-week-old Nubian lion for him which Anton named Togare. Along with her duties as hostess, model enchantress, mother, and magician's wife, she helped Anton raise the lion cub. Diane divided her time between Togare and their daughter, Zeena Galatea. Karla, now 12, had chosen to stay with Anton and Diane instead of with mother Carole, now a real estate broker, and was included in many of Anton's outings with his cohorts. The Victorian house was bustling with activity.

Since Anton was the only musician listed in the union directory under "calliope" (also the only one listed under "band organ" and "una-fon"), he was contacted by anyone who needed a calliope for parades, grand openings and fairs. It wasn't long before Anton found out about the calliope he had heard playing distantly on that Fourth of July when he had buried Zoltan. The owner had salvaged a steam boiler from a locomotive and adapted it to create a calliope with excessive pressure. Like the old-timers,

Anton developed a playing technique with one eye on the pressure gauge, playing fuller chords to release the pressure when it got too high.

*"People got the idea that the reason they used to put calliopes at the end of circus parades was to act as a kind of gleaming Pied Piper, merrily leading all the children to the circus grounds. Actually the reason they put the calliope at the end of the parade was so that if it exploded, it wouldn't hurt any of the animals."*

The sponsors of the holiday parades Anton was hired to play were usually Rotarians or Elks, who selected some fresh young beauty pageant winner to act as queen. Dressed in a tasteful bathing suit, the appointed ingenue pasted on a smile and waved stiffly from a shiny open car. Invariably, the calliope would lead the way. Anton, disdainful of the sterility of it all, began putting some of his Satanic principles into action. He had Diane and a few of his sexiest witches dress in flashy, low-cut red, white and blue outfits and ride on the calliope truck with him. With dresses that were too short and too tight, make-up that was too heavy, and bright red lipstick, they had every male onlooker fairly drooling with lust. The parade's queen would wind up hardly noticed. Again, Anton was satisfied to see the Forbidden, or in this case, the clearly unacceptable, triumph.

As publicity swelled, the curious began showing up at the Lost Weekend to ask Anton questions about magic spells, hypnosis and other phenomena. A significant number of his petitioners were typical barroom drunks. Finally, one of Anton's long-time associates, a police inspector with the unlikely name of Jack Webb, raised the inevitable question: "Why don't you make some use of all this magic stuff and the philosophy you've spun around it? You know, you've got the material for the founding of a whole new religion. Do you realize that?"

Perhaps Anton had already realized that the principles he was formulating, standardizing *could* be blended into a new religion. But not a religion of worship and blind faith; he would have to establish something new which would apply his black magic while smashing the ignorance and hypocrisy of by the Christian churches. Anton became convinced he was learning methods to harness the dark forces which cause "a change in situations or events in accordance with one's will which would, using normally accepted methods, be unchangeable."

There were little things at first — when he was running late, parking places fortuitously appearing in front of crowded theaters where none should have been, rare books or other items he had recently been coveting suddenly falling into his hands through strange circumstances, people appearing who Anton had just been thinking abouts — as if they had been summoned. Could there be such an increase in "happy coincidences" or was there more going on than was readily apparent? When Anton applied expanded formulas to the Magic Circle rituals and began achieving precise and desired effects — professional advances, unexpected rewards, monetary gain, sexual or romantic satisfaction, the elimination of certain enemies — it was apparent to everyone involved that Anton had indeed tapped into that mysterious force of Nature.

There was the magic — and there was a workable philosophy to go along with it. A down-to-earth, rational, bedrock philosophy that emphasized the carnal, lustful, natural instincts of man, without imposing guilts for manufactured sins. To break apart the crust of ignorance and irrationality the Christian churches had fostered over the past 2000 years, Anton knew it was necessary to blast their very foundations. His ideas could not be just a "philosophy" — that would be too easy to pass off or overlook. Anton would have to blasphemously form a *religion* and, even more — he would call his new organization a *church,* consecrated not in the name of God but in the name of Satan. There had always been a Satanic underground, centuries old, but there had never been an organized Satanic religion, practicing openly. Anton decided it was high time there was.

While there has never been a Church of Satan before, there have been groups dedicated to similar principles. In the mid-18th century, Sir Francis Dashwood formed a group known as the Hell Fire Club. Several of the most influential men in England, at the height of England's power, gathered together for Satanic feasting, reveling and debauchery, while shaping the destiny of England and the American colonies. Many historians have minimized the group, saying they were little more than fops and dandies, even though the then Prince of Wales, the Prime Minister, and the Archbishop of Canterbury were included in their number. Benjamin Franklin's association with Dashwood and other members of the group helped lay the foundations for the emerging nation of the United States.

LaVey maintains, "If people knew of the role the Hell Fire Club played in Benjamin Franklin's structuring of America, it could suggest changes like: 'One nation, under Satan,' or 'United Satanic America.'"

Other enclaves of Satanism: 1) The Abbey of Thelema as described by Rabelais in *Gargantua and Pantagruel* as a temple of perpetual indulgence. The motto invented by Rabelais for his monks, "Do What Thou Wilt" *(Fait ce que Voudras)*, was reported adopted by Dashwood, used at his abbey at Medmenham, and eventually also taken up by Aleister Crowley for his own Abbey of Thelema. 2) Group of Hollywood actors and writers in 1930's who forthrightly paid homage to Satanic forces and, 3) Fortean Society: Group of skeptics gathered around Charles Fort, master compiler and investigator of strange phenomena, in 1930's and '40's, several members of which later became part of Anton's Magic Circle.

Anton knew the date upon which the first Church of Satan must be established. It would have to be during the traditional night of the most important demonic celebration of the year, when witches and devils roam the earth, orgiastically glorifying the fruition of the Spring equinox: Walpurgisnacht, the night of April 30th - May 1st. Anton shaved his head as a part of the founding ritual, in the tradition of medieval executioners, carnival strongmen, and black magicians before him, to gain personal power and enhance the forces surrounding his newly-established Satanic order. It is the enactment of an allusion at the end of Coleridge's *Kubla Khan*, an incantation rejecting the Holy Trinity and the spiritual life in favor of one devoted to Hell and material pursuits.

Traditional to the Yezidi devil worshippers is a rite of passage that the emerging adept must perform. A razor is washed in the waters of Zamzam, the subterranean well of Islam said to be the point of origin for underground streams flowing under the Seven Towers of Satan. The caverns beneath the Towers are supposedly tributaries leading to the place of the Satanic Masters, known as Shamballah, or Carcosa. The razor is employed to shave the magician's head. Then, shorn of his locks, he leaves the world of the descendants of Adam. To make the ritual complete, Anton declared 1966 Year One, Anno Satanas — the first year of the reign of Satan. The new Age of Fire had been inaugurated, and though the ceremony on Walpurgisnacht, 1966, was a highly personal, private one, Anton would soon feel the tremors it was to produce around the world.

# Chapter Seven

# Court of the Crimson King

It is not yet midnight on this wind-chilled street near Seacliff in San Francisco, but the Satanists are gathering in anticipation of their Friday night revels. They've come to this infamous black Victorian house to renew their dedication to Satan, to ask that He favor them in their desires, and free them for fleshly indulgence.

Gathering in the antechamber, they seem like any group of amiable, successful people you might find chatting at a cocktail party. Most of the men are dressed in dark suits, though some are less conservative, wearing brighter shirts, perhaps leather jackets or pants. The women are more provocative. They wear bright colors, spiked heels, heavy makeup, short skirts or sheer dresses clinging tightly to outline their ample curves. More than one woman has a necklace peeking from between her partially-exposed breasts. Many of the men are wearing the same necklace over their shirts. They stand in groups of two or four speaking of the latest stock trends, astrology, old cars, and telling tales of modern-day vampires.

Finally, a tall, black-robed figure enters and announces the ceremony is about to begin. Cigarettes are extinguished and the two dozen men and women assemble quietly behind the figure to be escorted into the ritual chamber. Not a word is whispered as the congregation moves solemnly into their darkened chapel.

Eyes begin to adjust to the dimness, the only illumination filtering through from the antechamber. The air is a few degrees colder in here, the atmosphere thicker. As soon as the congregants take their seats the door slams shut behind them, leaving them in pitch-black silence. Almost immediately the silence is shattered by the booming chords of an organ. The ear picks up strains of old church hymns, and Wagnerian themes blended with sound effects from old horror movies. The group listens in darkness for a full five minutes or more, the sounds clearing their minds for what is to come.

The music ends in a thundering fanfare. After a beat a gong sounds three times and the lights are brought up just enough to see the celebrants now assembled at the front of the ritual chamber. The central figure is a large man, strong-looking, his steady eyes glittering as he peers at, and through, everyone in the room. His shaven head is fitted with a black cowl coming to a sharp point at his forehead, with horns made of bone on either side. The cowl extends to a floor-length cape, lined with crimson satin lining. His presence is one of quiet but irresistible command. He is the High Priest — Anton Szandor LaVey — the first man ever to found an above-ground organization dedicated to Satan and the delights of the flesh.

Behind him on the wall is a large Sigil of Baphomet, the symbol of Satanism adapted from the design used by the Knights Templar in the 14th Century — an inverted pentagram containing a goat's head, surrounded by five Hebrew letters, one at each point of the pentagram. The letters spell out "Leviathan," one of the crown Princes of Hell. The same symbol is on the necklaces of the assembled Devil worshippers. Below this lies a curvaceous redhead serving as the altar for tonight's services. She has draped herself across the large stone mantle over the fireplace, her flesh gleaming in the dim light. She bends her knee modestly, allowing the hair from her head to fall over the edge of the mantle. She too wears the symbol of Baphomet, almost hidden between her naked breasts. Tonight she is a living altar of flesh, evoking lust and making the blood burn. She becomes the point of concentration for all in the room, the carnal focus of the will of the Satanists.

Two men in black hoods stand ready at either side of the High Priest, with another hooded assistant manning the gong to the right of the altar. A woman with long blonde hair flowing over her velvet robe stands near to the High Priest, holding a sheathed sword, point downward, in front of her. The organist also wears a black hood as he begins to play "The Hymn to Satan," a corruption of Bach's "Jesu Meine Freude." Two naked female acolytes stand reverently near the altar.

The ritual chamber itself is painted black, with a ceiling of blood red. Amber bulbs burn dimly in the sconces on the walls giving the room an indistinct glow. A coffin stands upended in the corner, forming a looming hexagon shape, upon which a large stuffed owl glowers down on the participants seated below. One of the female acolytes moves about the altar now, lighting the black candles in preparation.

It is time for the ritual to begin. All eyes focus on the High Priest. As the organist continues "The Hymn to Satan," LaVey picks up a large brass bell, waves it over the altar to sanctify it, and slowly revolves counterclockwise before his followers, his cape billowing around his feet as he turns. He rings the bell nine times — Satan's number — to clear the air, then returns the bell to its place on the mantle. Turning to his blonde assistant he smoothly unsheathes the sword she has offered him. LaVey points it over the altar of flesh and somberly intones his evocation: "In nomine Dei nostri Satanas Luciferi excelsi!" The organist plays improvised rumblings to accent the High Priest's words. "In the name of Satan, Ruler of the earth, King of the world, I command the forces of Darkness to bestow their Infernal power upon me. Open wide the gates of Hell and come forth from the abyss in answer to your most Unholy names:

"Satan (extending the sword to the South), Lord of the Infernal Regions;

"Lucifer (turning to the East), Bringer of Light and Wisdom;

"Belial (turning to the North), King of the Earth;

"Leviathan (turning to the West), Ruler of the Watery Abyss.

"Come forth and greet your loyal brothers and sisters of the Left-Hand Path. Shemhamforash!"

The congregation shouts in response: "Shemhamforash!"

"Hail Satan!" chants the High Priest.

"Hail Satan!" Their defiant cries ring out. The gong is struck.

One of the hooded assistants moves to the altar and hands LaVey the Chalice of Ecstacy — a silver goblet filled not with wine or even blood but with LaVey's current favorite: bourbon whiskey. He takes the chalice, drinks deeply and passes it among his assistants to enjoy with him, finally returning it to the altar. The two naked acolytes step forward. One holds a candle slightly above their heads. The other opens a large black book in front of the High Priest and holds it for him as he thrusts the sword aloft and reads in a harsh echoing voice:

"Hear me, Dark Ones. Appear among men and be driven back no longer.

"Come forth and creep into the great councils of those without, and stop the way of those who would detain us.

"Grant me the indulgences of which I speak! I have taken thy name as a part of myself! I live as the beasts of the field, rejoicing in the fleshly life! I favor the just and curse the rotten!

"By all the Gods of the Pit, I command that these things of which I speak shall come to pass! Come forth and answer to your names by manifesting my desires! Oh, hear the names!"

LaVey fiercely growls the infernal names — gods and goddesses once adored, revered, now debased and defiled, hated and feared by all but the Satanists. Loki, Balaam, Tchort, Mammon, Shiva, Asmodeus, Shaitan. All considered evil by conventional religions. The congregants echo each name after LaVey. The organ music climbs to a crescendo and again the gong is struck three times. "Hail Satan!," the group shouts after their High Priest.

When the infernal names are concluded LaVey recites a passage in the pre-Biblical magician's language, Enochian. The syllables are hard, guttural yet strangely compelling:

"Ol sonuf vaoresaji, gohu IAD Balata, elanusaha caelazod: sobrazod-ol Roray i ta nazodapesad, Giraa ta maelpereji, das hoel-qo qaa notahoa zodimezod... Zodacare, eca, od zodameranu! odo cicale Qaa; zodoreje, lape zodiredo Noco Mada, hoathahe Saitan!"

LaVey steps toward his fellow Satanists, summoning them forth to speak their deepest desires before their Dark Lord. Each in his turn whispers his untold dreams and needs to LaVey. "Help me do well in my new job ... Make the man in the apartment across the hall fall madly in love with me ... Let my wife return to me in wild passion ... Destroy my competitor so I can get the contract I'm working on..." Human drives and goals, no murky spirituality draped in hypocritical selflessness. The emphasis is on applying whatever power they feel their demons wield to help them gain worldly power for themselves.

After each desire is repeated aloud by the High Priest, shouts of "Hail Satan!" are echoed by the congregants. The air is electrified with adrenal energy as the goals are sent out to the ethers and the ritual draws to a close.

While the organist quietly plays triumphal strains in the background, LaVey opens his cape wide before the nude altar, his hands held up in the Sign of the Horns: two fingers upward to affirm the duality of Nature with the three middle fingers folded down in denial of the Holy Trinity.

"Forget ye not what was and is to be! Flesh without sin, world without end!" He lowers his arms. "All rise and give the Sign of the Horns." The members rise and thrust their left arms forward, returning the sign. After turning to the altar to pass a traditional Sign of the Flame over her, LaVey shouts three "Hail Satans," with his congregation repeating each one. After each, the gong booms forth. The purifying bell is rung nine times once more, as the organist plays "The Hymn of the Satanic Empire." When the music ends and the last ring of the bell fades to silence, LaVey pronounces, "So it is done."

\* \* \*

The Church of Satan was founded on the night of April 30th, 1966. Within a year and a half of its creation, the organization had been the center of three separate media sensations that splashed front page headlines about Satan's Church around the world. The first of these was the marriage of two of Anton's members on February 1st, 1967. John Raymond, a politically radical journalist and Judith Case, New York socialite and daughter of a prominent attorney, asked Anton to perform the wedding ceremony, blessing their union in Satan's name.

It was not the first Satanic wedding ceremony LaVey had performed; that distinction fell to another of Anton's flock, Forrest Satterfield. But due to the "good family" status of Raymond and Miss Case, word got out. On the day of the ceremony, newspapers from California to Europe had "more reporters and photographers than any event since the opening of the Golden Gate Bridge" crowding the Black House to witness this supreme blasphemy. There was such a mob that police had to cordon off the area. Photographer Joe Rosenthal, who took the immortal shot of soldiers raising the American flag on Iwo Jima in World War II, was assigned by the San

Francisco Chronicle. The Los Angeles Times, among other prominent newspapers, devoted four columns at the top of their front page to one of Rosenthal's pictures of the wedding. Most of the accompanying stories lingered on the naked female altar, the array of personalities present, and Togare, the Nubian lion, roaring from somewhere further inside the house. The press was delighted. They dubbed Anton "The Black Pope" and clamored for interviews with him.

Anton rose to the occasion, making the most of the tricks of dramatic presentation, costuming, props, and stage magic he had learned on carnival and circus lots. While many of the early magazine articles were published in men's magazines because of the nude girls, mainstream magazines became interested as Satanism gained popularity. Eventually all the major magazines were doing in-depth cover stories on the rising tide of Satanism led by LaVey.

The rituals for the first year were largely intended as cathartic blasphemies against Christianity. The elements were consistent with the reports of Satanic worship from the famous writings of diabolists, such as the description in Joris-Karl Huysman's *La Bas*. Some of the people attending their first honest-to-Satan Black Mass would say their "Hail Marys," cross themselves quickly and rush out of the ritual chamber to scratch their names off the registration book at the door. In Anton's church all the Satanic fantasies became realities.

It was during this public prankish period that Anton held his Topless Witches' Review at a San Francisco nightspot in North Beach. One of the girls he hired to emerge menacingly from her coffin as a vampire was Susan Atkins. Atkins was not yet involved with Charles Manson and it would be two years until she committed the murders in Sharon Tate's Benedict Canyon home, licking the blood from her fingers after the deed. But in her post-conversion expose, *Child of Satan, Child of God,* Atkins indicts LaVey as the catalyst for her downfall. Anton remembers her as just another Haight Street burnout, perhaps a bit more drug-befuddled than some. "She'd beg off rehearsals, saying she had a fever of 108°. But in the end she made a fine vampire."

"We utilized a formula of nine parts social respectability to one part outrage," says LaVey. "We established a *Church* of Satan — something that would smash all concepts of what a "church" was supposed to be. This was a temple of indulgence instead of the temples of abstinence that had been built up until then. We didn't want it to be an unforgiving, unwelcoming place, but a place where you could go to have fun."

After a while Anton got tired of simply mocking Christianity and decided to work up rituals which would be blasphemously positive and exciting. "I realized there was a whole grey area between psychiatry and religion that had been largely untapped," said LaVey. He saw the potential for group ritual used as a powerful combination of psychodrama and psychic direction. Instead of just throwing off the bio-electrical energy and releasing it to be dissipated in the surrounding ethers, that energy could be structured, shaped, and directed to accomplish a specific goal. He didn't want to do parlor tricks but real applied magic.

The formalized curse, for example, is more than an exorcism of pent-up emotion. It is a true destruction ritual with all reserve tossed aside to generate wild emotion and focus it on the object of contempt or anger. That way the person who caused the pain is made to suffer rather than the one who harbors the feelings — the destruction is turned back on the one who deserves it. LaVey saw his ritual technique as much more powerful than the "psychics" who made claims to all kinds of magical powers. "The amount of energy needed to levitate a teacup," thought LaVey, "would be sufficient force to place an idea in the heads of people halfway across the Earth and motivate them in accordance with your will."

LaVey promised no miracles, and perhaps that is what most inspired people to listen to him. "I do not mean to tell you that magic alone can attain anything for you. If you are a talentless person, you can't be a great musician just by wishing for it or working a spell. If you are an ugly woman, you can't expect to attract a handsome movie actor by magic alone. Magic requires working in harmony with nature. Bearing that in mind, I can assure you that I have stumbled onto something. Magic works. I would do it whether people attended the Church of Satan and did it with me or not."[6]

Anton decided it was time to perform the world's first public Satanic baptism. People would be forced to see that Satanism is not drinking the blood of babies and sacrificing small animals. LaVey declared, "Rather than cleanse the child of original sin, as in the Christian baptism imposing unwarranted guilts, we will glorify her natural instincts and intensify her lust for life." Who better to be baptized in such a public ceremony than LaVey's own three-year-old daughter, Zeena? With her soft blonde hair and engaging smile, she captivated reporters with the image of such an angelic child being dedicated to the Devil.

> *"If real Satanism were allowed the kind of television time that Christianity has now, the kind of drawing out and patience that interviewers give sports figures now, or the kind of coverage that a baseball game gets, Christianity would be completely eliminated in a few short months. If people were allowed to see the complete, unbiased truth, even for 60 minutes, it would be too dangerous. There would be no comparison."*[7]

The date was set for May 23rd and photographers started showing up at 6 a.m., even though the baptism wouldn't begin for another 15 hours. One of the Church members, survivalist Kurt Saxon, designed and made a special amulet for Zeena just for the occasion. It was a colorful Baphomet with an ice cream cone, lollypop, and other things a little girl would like included in the circle. Her mother dressed her in a bright red hooded robe and sat her on the edge of the altar while photographers from New York to Rome snapped away.

Anton recited an impressive invocation, later adapted for inclusion in *The Satanic Rituals:*

"In the name of Satan, Lucifer ... Welcome a new mistress, Zeena, creature of ecstatic magic light.... Welcome to our company; the path of darkness welcomes thee. Be not afraid. Above you Satan heaves his bulk into the startled sky and makes a canopy of great black wings.... Small sorceress, most natural and true magician, your tiny hands have power to pull Heaven down and from it build monuments to your own sweet indulgence. Your power makes you master of the world of frightened, cowering, and guilt-ridden men. And so, in the name of Satan, we set your feet upon the left-hand path.... Zeena we baptize you with earth and air, with brine and burning flame. And so we dedicate your life to love, to passion, to indulgence, and to Satan, and the way of darkness. Hail Zeena! Hail Satan!"

The entire ceremony was designed to delight the child, welcoming her into a world of indulgence with sights and smells that were pleasurable to her. Unlike the Christian method of dunking already frightened children in water to baptize them, Zeena sat cheerfully chewing gum throughout the ritual, basking in the attention she was receiving from admirers and the press.

While many Christian organizations and other "concerned citizens" were outraged at the spectacle, there was little they could do. Today, LaVey probably would have been charged with Satanic child abuse — there were no such legal avenues for religious hysterics in 1967.

In December of that year, Anton was approached by Mrs. Edward Olsen who wanted the High Priest to perform a funeral for her recently deceased husband, a naval officer killed in a traffic accident near San Francisco's Treasure Island station. Both she and Edward Olsen had become members of the Church of Satan, despite his Baptist-oriented upbringing and his earlier membership in Youth for Christ. When he had entered the Navy, seen more of the world and married a sexy brunette, he realized Satanism was a more realistic way of life. "He believed in this church," said Mrs. Olsen, "and it is in this church that he would have wanted his funeral."

Though the Navy officials were a bit nonplussed, they agreed to Pat Olsen's request without much discussion, considering it their duty to comply with Mr. Olsen's last request with dignity. There was a chrome-helmeted honor guard in attendance at the ceremony, standing rigidly at attention alongside the black-robed witches and warlocks wearing their Baphomet medallions. The sailors held an American flag over the coffin while LaVey recited a eulogy emphasizing Edward's commitment to life in choosing to walk the Devil's path. To end the funeral, the Navy guard fired three volleys with their rifles, and a Navy musician played taps after the mourners shouted, "Hail Satan!" and "Hail Edward!"

Even though the Archbishop of San Francisco was upset by the whole affair, immediately sending an outraged letter to President Johnson, most San Franciscans, including the Naval officials, felt Olsen should receive the same consideration as any other Navy man. The response from the White House was actually quite fortuitous for the widow and her young son. Olsen, a machinist-repairman third-class was erroneously referred to by White House aides as "chief petty officer." Mrs. Olsen was able to use those letters to file a claim for a posthumous promotion for her husband and receive higher survivors' benefits. LaVey credits "demonic intervention" for Mrs. Olsen's good fortune. Because of the sharp increase of declared Satanists in the military, Satanism was soon outlined in the Chaplain's Handbook for the Armed Services as a recognized religion, with the description updated each year by the Church of Satan.

The rituals continued at the Black House. Besides the Friday night ceremonies every week, Anton was conducting Witches Workshops and various seminars as well which attracted personalities from up and down the California coast. Madness rituals, fertility rites, destruction rituals, shibboleth rituals, and psychodramas in the form of Black Masses were devised for the public to participate in and be entertained by every Friday night.

*"Where were they, all these people who claimed to be doing the same thing or were thinking the same thing before I came along? All the ones who were going to write* The Satanic Bible *but never had the time to actually sit down and write it. I looked, I couldn't find anyone. Who started the 'Church of* Satan'? *Not Church of Lucifer, or Temple of Abaddon, or Order of Thelema, of Brotherhood of Beelzebub — it wasn't in vogue to call yourself a Satanist until we came along."*

By the time *The Satanic Bible* was released in 1969, membership in the Church of Satan had already grown to well over 10,000 worldwide. It was originally published as a paperback (with a later edition in hardback) and has never been out of print — something of a phenomenon in today's short-lived paperback market.

When *Rosemary's Baby* was about to be released in 1968, publicists took advantage of the High Priest's high visibility by passing out small black buttons which read, "Pray for Anton LaVey." Anton remembers the audience's reaction to the ending of the film, when it clearly showed the Satanists had no intention of hurting the child, as everyone expected, but glorified it as the son of Satan. "People got very angry — stomping their feet and showing general disapproval. Sometimes the reality of Satanism is a lot more terrifying to people than their safe fantasies of what it's supposed to be. For the first time, they've been confronted with a Devil that talks back."

# Chapter Eight

# The Devil and Saint Jayne

On June 29th, 1967, Jayne Mansfield was riding along U.S. 90 near the Rigolets, a waterway between Lake Pontchartrain and the Gulf of Mexico, on her way to New Orleans. It was a little after 2 a.m. and the young man who had volunteered to drive, 24-year-old Ronnie Harrison, was trying to pick up some time. Jayne would need a little sleep before her television appearance at noon. Sam Brody, Jayne's attorney, was also in the front seat while three of her young children, Maria, Zoltan, and Mickey, Jr., nestled sleeping in the back. Jayne had been performing at Gus Stevens Restaurant and Supper Club, Harrison's father's nightclub in Biloxi, Mississippi, and they'd rushed off right after her last show.

Suddenly a fog appeared on the deserted stretch of road. A tank truck crept along in front of them, forming an impenetrable mist from behind as it released clouds of mosquito spray. By the time Harrison was able to see anything, they were going too fast to stop. They plowed into the back of the tank truck, killing Harrison, Jayne, and Brody instantly. The top of the car was forced back like a sardine can lid. The children were rescued from the wreckage, shaken but surprisingly unharmed. Officers on the scene reported that Jayne Mansfield's head was almost completely severed from her body. Investigators set the time of death at 2:25 a.m.

At his home in San Francisco, Anton LaVey was working in his study, clipping photos from the German news magazine, *Bild Zeitung* — pictures taken by photographer Walter Fischer of Anton placing flowers on Marilyn Monroe's grave. When he was ready to paste the articles into one of the Church of Satan's scrapbooks, he noticed a story on the back of the clipping, concerning a trip to Ireland that Jayne had been forced to forego. LaVey was distressed to see that in clipping the article about Marilyn, he had inadvertently cut a photo of Jayne right across her neck.

Fifteen minutes later, a reporter from the New Orleans Associated Press bureau called Anton to inform him of Miss Mansfield's tragic death and to ask him for comments. He had gotten LaVey's name and number from the address book Jayne carried with her. Anton could not speak. The journalist, hearing only silence on the line, pressed LaVey, asking if he knew she had practically been decapitated in the accident. LaVey hung up the phone. He was all too familiar with the web of incidents which had led to Jayne's death — a pattern of events reporters had no way of knowing at the time. LaVey's own ritualistic words demanding retribution, must have echoed in his mind during those moments. Anton had placed a curse, not on his devoted witch, Jayne, but on her attorney, Sam Brody after being harassed, ridiculed, and slandered one too many times. Despite numerous verbal warnings, and several close calls, it seems Jayne could not keep Brody away. Even on the night she died.

* * *

When Jayne Mansfield asked to meet Anton LaVey in the fall of 1966, she was already established as the reigning platinum blonde in America. From her first important stage appearance in *Will Success Spoil Rock Hunter?* in the 1950's (which she later brought to the screen with Tony Randall in 1957), Jayne's ecstatic squeal and trademark pink delighted reporters. It has been said that Jayne Mansfield invented "pink journalism." She certainly kept flashbulbs flashing wherever she went. Jayne had come a long way from her early life of beauty awards and shopping mall openings, eventually making several films in Europe besides her movies in the United States. But Jayne discovered her real forte was public appearances — nightclubs, talk shows, guest shots where she could interact spontaneously with the audience. Her forty-inch bust, entertaining wit, and playfully lustful, uninhibited demeanor, kept her constantly in the public eye.

Accompanied by a small entourage of doting men, she was in San Francisco preparing for the annual Film Festival. Jayne heard about Anton and his Church of Satan and insisted she must meet this Satanic High Priest. The local publicist Jayne was doing promotion with thought it was a good idea — Jayne Mansfield and Anton LaVey would make a titillating news item, maybe interest Herb Caen enough for a column drop. From the moment they met, Jayne was intensely attracted to Anton — an attraction that would quickly grow into an obsession. He was like nothing Jayne had ever known before. For professional reasons, Jayne bowed to the necessity of having obsequious men around to handle the business and promotion end of things. Taking a cue from Mae West, she recognized the visual impact of a beautiful blonde surrounded by her panting admirers. But Jayne was hardly the dominatrix type. Her own sexual predisposition was much more submissive.

During the first few hours they spent together, Jayne confided to Anton her overwhelming sexual passions, her fears concerning a custody battle she was involved in at the time (with former husband Matt Cimber, who charged Jayne with being an unfit mother), and intimately described her frustrating relationship with her attorney, Sam Brody, whose insane jealousy seemed to be getting more dangerous all the time. Upon meeting Jayne in Las Vegas, Brody had offered to represent her in the case against Cimber. But soon Brody, already married, close to 40 years old and almost a head shorter than Jayne, became her most ardent suitor. Even though he was almost exactly the opposite from what Jayne found physically appealing, she agreed to a relationship with Brody because she imagined it would ensure her custody of her four children. Almost immediately Jayne had second thoughts. Brody showed a side of himself that was violently jealous, imposing impossible constraints on Jayne. She was in the process of trying to ease out of the situation, but Brody was becoming only more protective, using her pending custody suit to maneuver her deeper into a relationship.

Anton questioned Jayne's naivete concerning Brody's manipulations but remained sympathetic, offering to do what he could to alleviate her troubles. Jayne had no previous interest in the occult, but she had a sincere thirst for knowledge and was intrigued by the philosophy Anton espoused. She asked him to place a curse on Cimber so that he would lose the custody battle. Anton agreed. Within a few weeks, Jayne was awarded custody of all her children from her three marriages.

Jayne became a full-fledged member of the Church of Satan, along with her road manager, Victor Houston. Brody, immediately jealous of Anton's influence, refused to let Jayne wear her custom-designed pink and black Baphomet medallion, ripping it from around her neck when Jayne refused to take it off. Several times Jayne called Anton from Beverly Hills, crying uncontrollably, and screaming that Brody wouldn't let her wear her amulet, that he was dragging her career down, and causing her nothing but pain. Brody, listening from the adjoining room, would eventually relent. When she wore her Baphomet to the Fall 1966 San Francisco Film Festival, Brody grew enraged over Jayne's public display of allegiance to LaVey and his Church. The glinting black and pink medallion nestled between Jayne's ample breasts, barely covered by her low-cut evening gown, prompted an insinuating comment from a reporter covering the event. That was all Brody needed. He lunged at Jayne, trying to grab the medallion off of her. She dodged his hand, and they fought in front of baffled onlookers.

When Jayne requested a chauffeur to take her to the Black House the following day, Brody invited himself along. He could see Jayne was falling in love with Anton and was determined to prevent them from being alone together. Victor Houston also came along. Anton entertained his guests for awhile and then was called into his den to take care of some business. As soon as Anton was out of earshot, Brody began chiding Jayne for taking Satanism so seriously, strutting around the room, finally wandering into the black chapel, where Church of Satan magical rituals were held. As Brody picked up priceless items from the stone altar and waved them around the room, laughing about LaVey and the Church, Jayne followed him, trying to get him to stop. Finally Houston could take no more and rushed to find Anton.

"That jackass is going through your religious objects, making fun of everything," Houston reported to LaVey, "he's lighting candles and laughing." As soon as Anton heard "lighting candles," he dropped what he was doing and strode quickly to the ritual chamber, afraid of what he would find. As LaVey suspected, Brody had lit a skull candle used for destruction rituals. Anton quickly blew it out and leveled his gaze at Brody: "You shouldn't have done that. You don't know what you've done. That candle is used only for curses. I don't know what's going to happen to you now. I only hope I've put it out in time." Brody only laughed.

About a month later, Jayne had cause to believe the skull candle was haunting her. She had told her four children about Anton's full-grown

Nubian lion that lived with him in his big black house in San Francisco, and they made her promise to take them to see the lion. The children were used to exotic animals. Jayne kept, at one time or another, a monkey, an ocelot, and four chihuahuas, among other pets, in the kennels at her "Pink Palace" on Sunset Boulevard. LaVey says Jayne bought her pets like toys. "She was very much like a child in that respect. When they were new, they got a lot of attention, but the novelty soon wore off." But Jayne had never had a lion and the children were very excited to meet Togare. When Brody heard about the trip, he forbade them to go. Jayne's six-year-old son, (coincidentally named Zoltan, just like LaVey's black leopard) was terribly disappointed. As a consolation, Jayne arranged for Zoltan to accompany her to Jungleland, a private zoo in Thousand Oaks, north of Los Angeles, where animals that work in movies and television were boarded and trained.

While Jayne posed for publicity shots, Zoltan wandered off to talk to a lion chained some feet away under a tree. Jayne had been assured by zoo officials that the lion was tame, so she was pleased that Zoltan could meet a real lion after all. Jayne glanced over and saw Zoltan laughing and talking to his new friend, then the next moment she looked over to see her son down on the ground, his head bleeding profusely, the lion grabbing Zoltan in his powerful jaws. Jayne screamed for someone to help her little boy.

A lion needs only a few seconds to kill, and if that had been his intention, this lion would have had the time to kill Zoltan. He had probably intended only to play with his new admirer, not realizing the fragility of his frame. Zoo officials pried the lion's jaws from around Zoltan's small body and drove him to Conejo Valley Hospital in Thousand Oaks. Immediately, he was wheeled into surgery where doctors worked on his fractured skull, ruptured spleen and bone fragments at the base of his brain.

Though the doctors were doing all they could to save the boy, Zoltan's chances were growing slimmer as the evening wore on. Jayne was frantic. How could this have happened to her son? She had been assured by Jungleland officials the lion was friendly and tame. The answer kept coming out the same: all of this was due to the effect of the skull candle. It had grown to be a full-fledged curse and there seemed no way for Jayne to escape it. She telephoned LaVey in a panic, quickly explaining what had happened and pleading with Anton to work his magic to stop the curse, to help her son. "I give you my word," vowed LaVey, "that I will do everything within my power."

LaVey felt the impulse to act immediately on the boy's behalf, and he followed his instincts, even though a rainstorm raged throughout the Bay Area, along with ferocious winds. He wasted no time. Draping himself in a black ritual cape, Anton jumped into his black "carryall" coroner's van he used to carry his own lion, Togare, and headed across the Golden Gate Bridge toward Mount Tamalpais, the highest peak in the San Francisco Bay Area.

As he drove through the pounding rain, LaVey reviewed the intricate threads of coincidence leading to this moment. Anton's concentration blinded him until he reached the highest point in the road, then he continued to the top of the mountain on foot. On the 25-minute drive from the city, Anton had composed his invocation. Now as he held his cape out like great leathery wings against the raging wind, the rain beat hard on his face, and, summoning all the power within himself, LaVey called upon his Brother Satan to spare Zoltan's life.

In remarkable time, Zoltan recovered from his wounds. But complications set in: lion feces had worked its way into one of Zoltan's gashes and finally seeped into his spinal fluid, developing into spinal meningitis. The boy once more hovered near death. Jayne called Anton to help once again. Anton gathered a few dozen members of his congregation together and conducted a Church of Satan ritual, applying their combined power to invoke Satan's blessing upon Jayne's son. The doctors were surprised by Zoltan's speedy recovery. Jayne vowed her eternal gratitude to Anton for saving her son, then directed Brody to initiate proceedings on a $1.6 million lawsuit against Jungleland.

Jayne's enthusiasm for her newly-discovered philosophy grew stronger, as did her feelings for LaVey. She told Anton that Satanism was "Kahlil Gibran with balls," and that it was the only way of thinking she had ever found meaningful. As with others, Satanism had been a discovery rather than a conversion — an experience of "I've felt this way all my life but never knew there were others like me." Jayne loved talking about Satanism, and its rational approach to life. It gave her an opportunity to show off her knowledgeable side. She wasn't stupid enough to believe that, faced with her overpowering physique, people would take her mind seriously. But *she* took it seriously. She realized how far her full, sensual mouth and protruding breasts had gotten her, and used those attributes to her advantage, but at the same time she liked to tell people she had an I.Q. of 163. "Jayne was intelligent," says LaVey, "but she never had any reinforcement for her intellect. When she was around me, she would often try to be 'intellectual' — recite Browning and use a drawn-out 'ah' sound. She liked to say 'om-u-let' when she meant amulet. She thought it sounded classier. She made it sound like some obscene breakfast dish. Unfortunately, intellectualism clashed with the image she presented. People would laugh. There was this sexy buxom blonde in front of them, lowering her squeaky voice, trying to recite Byron and Baudelaire.

"Jayne really had an appreciation for music, though. She had just cut a record of herself reading the classics with a musical background and wanted to re-cut it with me playing the background instead. Jayne would have me believe I was the world's greatest musician — she must have liked the kind of stuff I play. Gershwin, Cole Porter, Irving Berlin ... our tastes were similar in music. She always gave me an exaggerated buildup to people — told them I was a concert violinist, a child prodigy, that I could pick up any instrument and play it in concert style. She was the same way with my paintings, always talking them up to people. She wanted to commission me to do paintings for her home when she moved to San Francisco. I suspect she vicariously liked to think of herself as an artist. She did little drawings of the Baphomet on the back of envelopes to me — things like that.

"Jayne had taken violin lessons as a child and really wanted to accompany me. I had a violin around the place so I brought it out for her one night. She was surprisingly articulate after all those years, just very rusty. She remembered how to tune the strings, knew how to hold it, which was pretty good considering she hadn't played since she was a little girl. She wanted to learn violin again. She wanted to do everything that was a departure from what she was doing."

After experiencing the effects of the skull candle firsthand, and seeing what had happened when Anton applied his magic to help Zoltan, Jayne had seen what Satanism could do and was more impressed than ever. Anton, in turn, was delighted with Jayne and her natural abilities as a consummate witch. He gave Jayne personalized rituals to perform: compassion rituals, lust rituals, and the "Shibboleth Ritual," useful for purging oneself of stifling anger and frustration by taking on the characteristics of the person causing the anger.

In Jayne Mansfield, Anton happily discovered a woman who shared, encouraged, and complemented, his kind of playfully enthusiastic sex. Jayne was already adept at performing her own little Satanic rituals, using many of the Lesser Magic techniques of "accidental" exposure LaVey would later include in *The Satanic Witch*. She had ingenious methods for strategically weakening the seams in her tight capri pants or on the miniskirts she seemed to be busting out of so that, when the time was right, all she needed to do was stretch a little for the seam to rip open. She did the same thing with buttons so they would pop off with a twist of her buxom body. Then it was just a matter of carefully maneuvering the cloth to show a bit of bare flesh, or bare breast, or pubic hair peeking out, all apparently without her knowledge. "Jayne was not a flirt. She was an exhibitionist," says LaVey. "She would jump at the chance to expose her breasts or spread her legs a bit too far to give a show to any man she felt would be appreciative."

She liked to shock men just to see the reaction. For instance, in the presence of men, Jayne would wet herself enough to make a spot show through on the back of her skirt, giving the impression she was so intensely excited she couldn't control herself. Jayne unabashedly encouraged men to leer at her, to desire her. She reveled in the lust she evoked in men. Perhaps she would forget to wear her panties under the most revealing miniskirts. Then when getting out of a car, she would innocently remark, "Don't look at me now," which would, of course, ensure the attention of every male within earshot, straining to glimpse the white flesh between Jayne's legs.

More than once when Anton went to pick Jayne up at her hotel, he found the door to her suite standing open, while bellhops, delivery men, and male lodgers hovered near the open door, scurrying along their way when Anton came down the hall. When Anton went inside, Jayne greeted him in a terribly disheveled state, her clothes all askew. He didn't know what the hell Jayne had been doing with herself but all the men passing by had certainly seemed interested.

Anton recalls one particularly embarrassing incident when he stopped at a busy gas station to use the men's room. When he came out, he found Jayne perched on a pipe railing, sipping a can of 7-Up, her legs spread enough to see everything under her miniskirt. Work had come to a complete halt as the patrons and attendants ogled Jayne. Smiling brightly at Anton, she confided in a loud voice, "I'm not wearing any underpants." Anton escorted Jayne back to the car and hurried away from the gawking attendants, who left their station unattended and followed Jayne and Anton for some blocks before getting lost in traffic.

"Jayne had a native understanding of the application of prurience," says LaVey. In *The Devil's Avenger,* he described Jayne as "... a lewd, lascivious virago who was happiest when rolling on the floor with masochistic, orgiastic energy." He adds, "Jayne liked to be humiliated, liked to be degraded. There was nothing forbidden in bed, and she reveled in her lusts. I don't know how she was with other men, but she made it crystal clear to me what she wanted, how she wanted it, and when. Then she would chide and maneuver until she got it. She longed for a stern master who could dominate her — a father figure.

"Most people have to manufacture turmoil in their lives, or have it manufactured for them, to satisfy their masochistic yearnings. But Jayne was a self-realized masochist — she didn't need emotional turmoil. She wanted to get it out in physical, sexual ways instead. That's why Brody's endless hounding was so distressing; Jayne needed physical torment, not emotional.

"I say she was a 'self-realized' masochist because she goaded me with the spoken understanding between us of exactly what she wanted me to do ... throw her to the ground, pull her by the hair, that sort of thing. It was chiding, but it was playful — we both knew what she was really asking for. That's a lot different from those who want you to smash them but won't admit it — they'll manipulate you every way they can to make you destroy them, without ever admitting to themselves what they want and why they might need it. That's the height of hypocrisy. Brody was that kind. They always get what they deserve — but maybe not what they want.

"Jayne hated emotional upset and manipulations but, because everyone adored her, she needed ritualized degradation. In the public arena, she wanted people to like her, wanted to keep everyone happy, harmonious and to bring people together — she didn't want chaos and disharmony. But in her private life, Jayne wanted debasement, degradation. For her own ego gratification, she knew she needed public admiration, men fawning after her. The more fawning Jayne received, the more she needed an antidote. But that takes incredible perspective to be able to remove yourself enough to recognize your own needs so clearly. Most people don't have the courage to take such a realistic look at themselves. That's why she enjoyed being with me, I suppose. I wasn't afraid to give her what she needed."

Diane, Anton's wife, did her best to accept Jayne's adoration of her husband just as she accepted other facets of LaVey's role. "Diane understood as best as any human could. I'm the High Priest of the Church of Satan, not some Sunday school minister. Diane was often the one who answered the phone when Jayne called. As my wife, she was discreet and tactful — realizing the potential good for the Church. I don't think Jayne liked Diane, though. Whenever they were together, Jayne would sit with her back to Diane. Diane didn't seem to mind — she was more amused than intimidated. The fact that Jayne was a movie star didn't seem to faze Diane. She knew she was 'it.' She had to deal with a lot of people. Jayne's kind of enthusiasm was one of the hazards of being married to a public figure.

"Jayne would've moved right in if she'd had half the chance. She already had a lot of stuff here. She had her makeup all over the bathroom, her clothes strewn all over the place, half in and out of suitcases, shoes left under beds.... When she took things off she just let them fall, crumpled in heaps. Diane wasn't about to pick up after her. They stayed where they were, Jayne didn't care. She was a lot like Marilyn that way.

To honor Jayne's natural abilities as a Satanist, LaVey made her a Priestess of the Church of Satan, and presented her with a certificate declaring her position which she proudly displayed on her wall, despite Sam Brody's protests. Undaunted by Brody's continuous jeering, Jayne began a serious study of witchcraft and black magic. She made regular calls to LaVey to tell him of her progress, share some new discovery, avow her love for him, and ask for a happiness spell.

*"The difference between Marilyn's and Jayne's approach to intellectual pursuits is that Marilyn carried big heavy books around and hung out with brainy people to absorb their intellect, while Jayne really had a thirst for knowledge. Jayne was very proud of the fact that if she liked something enough she would commit it to memory. At the time,* The Satanic Bible *was still in monograph form, and Jayne had pored over those pages until she knew most of it by heart."*

Part of LaVey's relationship with both these women was the sharing of books. "Marilyn gave me a copy of Stendhal's *On Love,* and I still have a copy of Walter Benton's *This is My Beloved,* which we bought together on Sunset Boulevard. Marilyn turned me on to it — wanted me to read it and write something in it for her. I got as far as writing her name in it, but I ended up with the book. It meant a lot to me during a particularly dark period in my life after I left L.A. Jayne kept insisting I read *The Story of O* and *I, Jan Kramer.* She gave me a dog-eared copy of each. It seems a distinctly feminine trait to want to share books with people they care deeply about.

In her reading one night, Jayne ran across the term "incubus." The word is used to describe a male demon that comes to women in their sleep, making passionate love to them. Magicians have been accused of sending such demons in their own images to enthrall innocent women. Brody, ever watchful, forbade her from traveling to San Francisco to see LaVey. When Jayne read about the incubus, she grew excited at the thought of LaVey sending his image through the night to make love to her.

Jayne immediately phoned LaVey to tell him about what she had read, and to ask him if it was true. Anton confirmed the legends but tried to skirt around her obvious requests. When she called from the Acapulco Film Festival in December, 1966, she was more insistent, asking Anton to describe in lurid detail the incubus he would send: "Will I be able to feel him? How big will his cock be? Will he make me as hot as I am right now?"

At the height of Jayne's breathy description of exactly what she wanted the incubus to do to her, the Mexican operator who had been monitoring the call cut the connection in an attempt to protect the morals of international telephone conversations. Jayne was not distracted from her purpose, replacing the call immediately through another operator. "How should I lie on the bed to wait for him — should I be on my back with my legs spread far apart? How hard will he be? Will he be gentle with me or rough, fast or slow? Is he getting harder now?" She concluded by reminding LaVey, needlessly, "Now make sure the incubus looks like you."

Since Jayne was so persistent, LaVey was obliged to promise to send an incubus to her that night, more as a way of getting off the phone than as a true magical exercise. But, to please her, he did send some positive energy her way. The next day, Jayne called to thank Anton for sending the incubus. She then went on to describe in every detail what she felt all over her body as the incubus made love to her.

*LaVey speculates on the similar attractions certain women feel to the ideas of satyrs, snakes, demons, the Romantic beast in the classical sense — sleek, enchanting, rather than a slavering, coarse creature. Could these women be direct descendants of what have come to be known to us as sylphs, nymphs, and other female creatures of the glade? Perhaps they develop an archetypal compulsion that needs to be satisfied, compelled to LaVey because of certain satyr-like qualities. It wouldn't matter whether he was the High Priest or not — the attraction would be the same. Marilyn Monroe: fascinated by Dark Side, she had dreams of the Devil when she was young, attracted to Anton long before he formed the Church of Satan. Jayne and Diane had similar compulsive attractions. "You have to wonder how atavistic these reactions are."*

Sam Brody continued to try to interfere with Jayne's relationship with LaVey and the Church. Jayne had to resort to ridiculous tactics to try to shake him. It seemed Jayne could not travel anywhere for any reason without Brody tagging along. Once, desperate to see LaVey, Jayne bought a plane ticket to Seattle, knowing that Brody would buy a ticket for the same flight and wait until the last minute to board the plane. She let him follow along. When they stopped over at the small Portland airport, Jayne left the plane to stretch her legs. Brody remained on board, not wanting Jayne to spot him. When the announcer called the passengers back to the Seattle flight, Jayne watched the plane taxi away from the gate and down the runway, then she went to the ticket counter to buy a ticket to San Francisco.

When Brody was busy in court, Jayne made as many trips to the Bay Area as she could. When she arrived, she would demand Anton's immediate attention. If he happened to be lecturing or talking on the telephone, she would insist he come outside and meet her in the waiting limousine. LaVey would be expected to escort her to her favorite restaurants in San Francisco, Ernie's, Trader Vic's, The Blue Fox.... "Jayne could be a demanding woman," LaVey remembers. "It was almost like being her personal 'sorcerer-on-call' at times.

"Jayne would call from the airport when she got in. If I didn't pick her up, if I was busy and couldn't make it, she'd call Mrs. Halsey [Jayne's close friend, Lucia, wife of Admiral "Bull" Halsey] to send her Bentley from the city, or she'd call a local TV or radio station — they always wanted publicity on her. They'd waste no time sending a driver to pick her up and she'd have them drive directly to my place. They'd be waiting in their Chevy around the corner and I'd get called out of a seminar I was conducting with maybe 40 or 60 people crammed into the room for one of my lectures. I'd leave the room for a moment, hurry her in downstairs to wait for me then rush back to the waiting crowd. I'd hurry as fast I could to get through the lecture too. If I didn't, Jayne might start playing pinball machines downstairs, blasting music on the jukebox or start pounding on the ceiling to get my attention. I'm not saying I would have done it for anyone else — but anyone else wasn't Jayne Mansfield."

Though Jayne never attended a public Church of Satan ritual, Anton arranged private ceremonies for her. "Jayne didn't want to get involved with groups of people for rituals, seminars, parties — the whole idea, for her, was to get away from crowds. That's why she didn't quietly slip into the back of the room during my seminars. She wanted to get me all to herself." "She didn't want any other woman in the room," recalls Karla LaVey, "not even a 14-year-old girl." "But there were always people around," continues LaVey, "there had to be. Diane, Victor Houston, Jayne's entourage.... So she would use the pretext of performing a ritual, or going out to dinner, or wanting to show me something. But even in the ritual chamber, I was afraid of who might be watching us, or if someone had to come in if they needed me for something. Jayne didn't care. She was a real exhibitionist. Sometimes it seemed the more public it was the better she liked it. She loved sex where people would see us, might walk in on us, or where people would be shocked by us."

*Once, when LaVey was a guest of Jayne's at a society party held at Mrs. Halsey's penthouse on Russian Hill, Jayne maneuvered him into the master bedroom where many of the guests had put their coats. There were windows from floor-to-ceiling across one wall. The view was beautiful. Jayne wanted Anton to lay beside her on the chaise lounge in front of the window. Of course, as Jayne rubbed and cajoled, one thing seemed to be leading to another. She had a way of goading Anton, saying, 'Don't you want to shake them up a little, it'll do them good. What kind of devil are you? Don't you want to have a little fun?'*

Jayne grew to demand always more of Anton's attention and time. She was tired of being driven around by publicity agents and flattering admirers. She wanted to see more intriguing places. "Where do you go at night, Ahn-tohn? I don't want to just hear about these places — I want to go where you go." Jayne decided she wanted to accompany Anton on his forays into the night, investigating haunted places, mysterious disappearances, graveyards, and strange illuminations — trying to pick up psychic impressions of places the way he did. Anton opened the gates to his black world for her. He showed her places of murder and mystery, explaining his theories of diabolical angles and unseen influences. They drove to an abandoned mansion in the hills above Belmont, California, where calamity struck several generations who lived there. Anton took Jayne to "Nut Hill" in Berkeley where Isadora Duncan and her sister were said to have lived in a Grecian temple. They explored an abandoned brickworks near San Quentin Prison — the site of a number of unsolved murders. Jayne was overjoyed that Anton would share these places with her.

"It's an interesting phenomenon that when I was with Jayne at airports, restaurants, hotels, there were always people crowding around with cameras flashing. But when we went out late at night and stopped in some greasy spoon for breakfast, people would look or stare but they probably wouldn't know who we were. It was out of context. It afforded great opportunities for anonymity."

When Brody saw Jayne's unswerving devotion to Anton, he became desperate. He threatened to blackmail her, claiming he would release photos of Jayne's sexual liaisons. She was incensed, telling Anton that on this one occasion Brody had drugged her until she was senseless, planted a dope dealer in her bed and a photographer in her bedroom to snap the incriminating photos which Brody threatened to use against her. "Brody was like many guys who become obsessed with sex symbols," says LaVey. "They secretly relish the fact the woman is having sex with other partners, but they want it to be on their terms, in a controllable scenario — it's not uncommon for such a man to arrange lovers for the woman. Eventually their emotions overcome them, compulsion leads to rage and then the situation gets completely out of hand."

When Jayne did nothing to respond to Brody's threats, he decided to concentrate on making trouble for LaVey. One night when he accompanied Jayne to San Francisco, Brody scoured North Beach's Broadway strip for some black "superfly" types to invite to a fictitious party at Anton's house, as Brody apparently felt this would be the best method of intimidating LaVey. Brody promised there would be plenty of food, drink and drugs flowing, and as a special bonus, they could meet America's sex goddess, Jayne Mansfield. There were plenty of takers. Brody showed up at Anton's doorstep with two carloads of street people he picked up from the seediest parts of town. Brody pushed by the man watching the door and showed his "guests" into the front parlor, where they plopped into the chairs and waited for the party to begin. Brody slipped quickly back out the front door and watched from his car across the street.

Anton was summoned into the front parlor where he tried to explain there was to be no party and that the young men might as well go home. They were determined to meet Jayne Mansfield. Jayne and Diane had retreated to the kitchen in the back of the house where Jayne fretted in near hysterics. After repeated requests to leave, Anton realized tact and courtesy were getting him nowhere. He resorted to threats but still the toughs would not leave. As a last resort, Diane hurriedly called the police. In a matter of minutes, several radio cars screeched to a stop in front of the Black House. Because of the climate of the times, they came in with riot gear ready. The uninvited guests had grown so obnoxious that Anton was preparing to bring Togare out of the back to see if a full-grown lion might persuade them to leave.

Anton knew many members of the SFPD on a first-name basis having worked with them in many guises since the mid-1950's. As the activities at the Black House gained international media attention, the cops regularly assigned to the area had become familiar with LaVey's place, adopting a protective attitude toward LaVey and his organization. Even the sight of the authorities did not seem to dissuade the intruders. They were determined to be entertained by Jayne Mansfield. The threat of jail was the only thing that moved them. Reluctantly they filed back down the hallway and got into their cars. One of their automobiles predictably would not start and had to be pushed by hand for over a mile outside of the area, with a police car trailing slowly behind. The officers then returned for a more relaxed visit with Jayne themselves. Brody was long gone by the time the affair was over.

When Jayne was prevented from visiting LaVey in person, she would call him sometimes three or four times a day from Beverly Hills, or wherever she was in the world, to have intimate conversations, assuring him of her undying love. "Jayne would call at all hours of the day and night, asking for me. If I was with a student, she fully expected me to drop what I was doing and come to the phone. If I was asleep, she'd want someone to wake me up. If the phone was busy, she'd have the operator break in on the line, saying that it was a life and death emergency." "I love you," Jayne vowed, "and it's not just the magic; it's a personal feeling." The ever-present Brody would listen for a time from the next room, then barge in, grab the receiver from Jayne, and slam the telephone down. LaVey was reaching a breaking point with Brody.

On a cool night in January, 1967, Jayne locked herself in her bathroom and, crouching next to her famous heart-shaped bathtub, made a desperate telephone call to LaVey. "Please help me, Anton, help me!" Jayne screamed. LaVey could hear Brody shouting wildly in the background, pounding on the door. "I can't stand it anymore! Please help me get away from him, Anton!" Jayne pleaded. Finally Brody broke the door open, grabbed the phone and shouted at LaVey: "She's never to talk to you again! You hear that? I don't ever want to catch you talking to her again. You're a charlatan, and I can make plenty of trouble for you. I'll expose you..."

LaVey exploded. "Now, just a minute. I don't have to listen to this. I won't let anybody call me a quack. It's too bad you're taking this attitude. I've tried to be pleasant to you even at times when you deserved to be put down. But now you've gone too far. My power exceeds anything you can imagine, and now you're going to feel it. You will be dead in a year. Sam Brody, I pronounce that you will be dead within one year!"

Later that same night, LaVey conducted a private destruction ritual against Brody, ceremonially writing his name on a piece of parchment and burning it in the flame of destruction. As Brody's name was consumed, LaVey invoked the powers of the infernal ones, commanding that Brody, likewise, be destroyed within the specified time. There was no mercy in LaVey's heart, as he could see no redeeming qualities in this "weasel," as he called Sam Brody. He had attacked LaVey's reputation, purposefully caused him endless grief and must suffer the consequences of his indiscretions. LaVey had been more than patient and had only been treated to more of Brody's threats and churlishness. No simple undirected curse would do this time. LaVey would only be satisfied when Brody was dead.

Once the curse was invoked against Brody, LaVey called Jayne to warn her. She told Brody to apologize to LaVey. Three days after the incident, Brody called Anton to say he was sorry. LaVey told Jayne that unfortunately the wheels had already been set in motion against Brody and even if he wanted to, there would be no way for LaVey to stop the curse.

"Jayne, I must tell you bluntly," LaVey stated, "you are traveling under a dark cloud as long as you are around Brody. Nothing will go right for you. Get away from him before it's too late." When Jayne returned to San Francisco, she brought Brody along to patch things up. Even though Brody seemed contrite, he had to show off by driving up to 80 miles an hour within the city limits, and his seething jealousy caused him to try to control Jayne's every move.

In February, 1967, Jayne was headed for a tour entertaining the troops in Vietnam. She wanted to see Anton before she left, but since she couldn't get away from Brody long enough, she left a big flocked greeting card for LaVey when she changed planes at the San Francisco International Airport. Nearly three feet long, with a wide-eyed little red devil holding a pitchfork on the cover, the message printed inside read: 'Thanks from way down deep." Jayne had added in her sweeping handwriting, all the "i"'s dotted with characteristic hearts, "To my Satanic Friend — High in the Eyes of orthodox religion — My probing for truth may be satisfied by my High Priest." And on the outside of the large envelope, she had written "Destination — Elysium!"

Jayne called from all over the world to put other celebrities on the phone that she had been telling all about Anton LaVey, wanting LaVey to explain the merits of Satanism. "She was zealous, to say the least," laughs LaVey. The Lord Mayor of Belfast, original "glamour girl" Brenda Frazier, the chief of some Indian tribe, some assemblyman or senator — too numerous for LaVey to remember.

"They'd call from their table in a restaurant after they'd finished dinner. Before they got on the line, she'd give them a big build-up: 'This fellow is very big here, Ahntohn, very influential. He can do you a lot of good. I've told him all about you ... here he is now.' I'd find myself giving a spontaneous lecture about Satanism and what I was doing. When she called from Mexico, Europe, Japan, or Vietnam, some could hardly speak English, so I'd have to speak Pidjin English to be understood.

On a European tour, Jayne was faced with further disappointments. Her nightclub dates in England came off very well and Jayne was scheduled to go to Ireland next. But when the 82-year-old Bishop of Tralee, Father Denis Moynihan, read in a news story that Jayne was a practicing Satanist, he ordered his congregation to boycott Jayne's appearances. Following his orders, the Irish government cancelled her tour. Jayne, for her part, was not swayed from her commitment to Satanism. To Jayne, it was the only philosophy that accepted her as she was. She was all the more enthusiastic about her High Priest. Of course, this made Sam Brody fume.

Early the month Jayne Mansfield died, photographer Walter Fischer asked Anton to pose with Jayne for some German publications. Fischer, though based in Hollywood, provided pictures primarily for European distribution. His photo of Anton placing flowers on Marilyn Monroe's grave ran in a prominent spot in the June 2nd edition of the *Berlin Bild Zeitung*. Anton was pleased with the response the Church was getting in Germany as a result of Fischer's work so he readily agreed to pose for the photos. Jayne loved the idea of being photographed with Anton, and invited LaVey to stay with her at the Pink Palace.

Fischer snapped pictures of Jayne and Anton by the heart-shaped pool, playing with her pet ocelot and two chihuahuas, Momsicle and Popsicle (later killed with Jayne in her fatal crash), working out in Hargitay's gym, and climbing on rocks with Jayne's children and their pet dogs. (These photos disappeared after Jayne's death, filched from news files around the world.) After the photo sessions were over, LaVey entertained the children with his stories of vampires, ghosts and magic. Jayne Marie, Jayne's oldest daughter, indicated an immediate rapport with LaVey, charming him in her own right while he dazzled them with his expertise at the piano. She directed her attentions toward Anton, completely ignoring Brody. He grew red-faced with jealousy and humiliation as the evening wore on. When Brody discovered Jayne Marie had asked Anton to stay longer, Brody slapped the girl across the face.

The following night, LaVey, Jayne, Brody and Fischer had dinner together at LaScala restaurant in Beverly Hills. After dinner, Brody insisted Anton ride back with Walter Fischer, leaving Brody alone with Jayne. Brody, driving back to the Pink Palace in a flashy new Maserati, smashed into a pole. He ended up with a cracked rib, and Jayne was luckily unharmed.

LaVey soon returned to San Francisco. Not long after he did, Jayne Marie walked into the West Los Angeles police station, covered with bruises, and filed a battery charge against Brody and her mother. She insisted that it wasn't safe for her to return home and placed herself in the protective custody of the court.

Less than a week later, Brody, driving alone, had another auto accident — this one more serious. He ended up with his Mercedes-Benz nearly totaled and a broken leg. He was in a cast the following night when Jayne appeared at Gus Stevens Restaurant and Supper Club in Biloxi.

*"The last time I spoke to Jayne was the day before she died. She called and said she was doing great at Gus Stevens', really packing them in, they wanted her to stay on there, and that the next night would be her last show — then they'd be on their way to New Orleans and she'd call me from there. Of course, she said she wished she was with me and didn't have to go to New Orleans.*

*"Jayne liked to call me every day to get a 'happy spell' from me, putting my blessing on her for the following day. It was important to her. For some reason, she hadn't called me the day of her last performance. I was surprised I hadn't heard from her, though not particularly concerned — I assumed she must have been traveling or something. That was the only time I didn't speak to Jayne every day, when she was en route somewhere. When the phone rang that night with the call from the AP reporter in New Orleans, I thought it must be Jayne calling."*

It was because Brody couldn't drive that Ronnie Harrison volunteered to make the trip to New Orleans the night of June 29th, the night of Jayne's fatal accident. LaVey's inexorable curse had been fulfilled — tragically costing him a dear and most loyal friend and lover.

*"I have little doubt that the reason they were killed was because of Brody goading the driver to go faster. I would stake anything on it. That kid was probably being badgered to go faster right up until the moment they plowed into the back of that truck. Jayne never complained that I wasn't going fast enough when it was just the two of us in the car. The mute evidence speaks for itself — Jayne didn't smash up cars. Only Brody. Jayne might be alive today if Brody hadn't been in the car that night."*

On the Friday night following her death, LaVey conducted a private Satanic memorial service for Jayne Mansfield at the Church of Satan (her public memorial was held on the East Coast). Immediately before the ritual began, as LaVey stood before his congregation beginning to talk about Jayne, they were startled when the dim lights in the black-walled chamber began flaring brightly. An electronics engineer that was acting as an assistant priest in the ritual, was even more surprised, explaining later that any such abnormal bursts of electricity should have overloaded the delicate filaments. But the bulbs didn't burn out. They flashed five times in a brief two-minute period. Diane swore that one of the bulbs glowed in a heart-shape.

To My Satanic Friend —

High in the Eyes of

orthodox religion —

May probing for truth

may he satisfied by

my High Priest —

Jayne

LaVey continued with the ritual, blaspheming Sam Brody's soul and paying tribute to Jayne Mansfield's passions, enthusiasm for her life on Earth, and dedication to the ideals of Satan. Summoning the Princes of Hell to draw near, he asked that Jayne's hedonism and pure, selfish pursuits cause her to be blessed by living on in the hearts and memories of those who adored her during her lifetime. The congregation responded with shouts of "Hail Satan!" and "Hail Jayne!" LaVey concluded the ceremony, as in most Satanic rituals, with the solemn, and now tragically apt phrase: "And so it is done."

# Chapter Nine

# Devil's Advocate

*"In that moment the many masks of Anton LaVey seem to
melt before my eyes. Mad scientist, carnival barker, intellectual
broker: All of these melt, then form again, one sinking into the
quicksand of the next. And when he turns to face me, it is the
most terrifying experience in my life, yet I'm unable to tremble.
For I am gazing only at sleight-of-hand, at a face without a
definable shape, a face both as charming and as monstrous as
any I could possibly imagine. The face of the anti-Christ."*
— Dick Russell, "Anton LaVey: The Satanist Who Wants to
Rule the World," *Argosy*, 1975

In the midst of Woodstock, Vietnam protesters, tattered blue jeans
and LSD gurus "turning on" the world, it became LaVey's role to speak up
for Satanic issues. Perhaps modern Satanism never would have reared its
barbed head had it not been for LaVey's frustration with the barefoot, slo-
gan-spewing "love children." "I considered the 60's and 70's a barren, aesthetically destructive era. America, especially San Francisco, was a mire of
ignorance, stupidity and egalitarianism. I created my own world — the
Church of Satan. That's the only way I could survive. It turned out to be a
real cudgel on the head of mainstream society at that time. Without us there
would have been no counterculture. All the Ken Keseys and Timothy Learys
did was attach great importance to the worthless."

It may have been precisely the era for LaVey to find an appreciative
audience. "In magic," Anton says, "if the timing is right, you can say one
word and it will create the act you will want." So it was with LaVey's first
book, *The Satanic Bible*. "I never set out to be a writer. I wrote *The Satanic*

*Bible* out of disgust. I'd looked for years for a no-bullshit, how-to book on black magic, without the protection of the pentagram and evoking the names of Jesus. I couldn't find anything like what I had in mind. So I wrote one.' Much of the book had already been circulated on brightly colored stock within the Church of Satan as introductory essays in Satanism. Certain members with connections in publishing felt LaVey had potential for a wider readership and the editors they spoke to were just as enthused. "It was a fluke," Anton agrees. "The editor I worked with at Avon Books was extremely supportive — hardly changed a thing from my original except for grammatical errors, didn't touch the content. It probably couldn't be published today. But that's a moot point because there wouldn't be this over-compensating religious climate if *The Satanic Bible* hadn't been published in the first place." The book has gained a certain amount of respectability during its 21 years in print —it's been required reading in certain college sociology classes, with excerpts of The Satanic Bible included in college texts since the early 70's.

A musician first and foremost, LaVey writes with an ear for rhythm, finality, and cadence, choosing some phrases more for sound than strict meaning. He credits writers like Ben Hecht, H. L. Mencken, Horatio Alger and Nathanael West as major influences, as well as the notorious governor of Louisiana, Huey Long, "the closest thing to an honest politician that's ever been elected." LaVey's style is tight and direct; informative, with enough earthy humor thrown in to keep from sounding pompous. People close to LaVey have quipped he should put out a handbook of Satanic "parables" — jokes he uses to illustrate aspects of his cynic's philosophy. Those who have been around him for any length of time develop a shorthand of significant punchlines, often after the joke itself has been forgotten. "Anyone without a sense of humor," says LaVey, "is too pretentious to be a good magician."

After writing *The Satanic Bible,* LaVey continued his Satanic triptych with *The Compleat Witch, or What to Do When Virtue Fails,* which was heavily edited by Dodd, Mead before its publication in 1970 (since reprinted as The Satanic Witch). Finally, in 1972, *The Satanic Rituals* was published by Avon as a companion to LaVey's first book, a comprehensive collection of history's best authentic black magic rituals.

After establishing the Church of Satan, then codifying his brand of Sin in his three books, LaVey did his share of traveling around the country for talk shows, radio shows and interviews with local papers. Articles constantly appeared in newspapers around the world as editors sent their reporters to find out why everyone was buzzing about this San Francisco sorcerer. LaVey got major coverage in U.S. magazines like *Cosmopolitan, Time, Newsweek, Seventeen* and was on the August 24th, 1971 cover of *Look*. After meriting several documentaries and wax figures of himself exhibited in a dozen museums in various parts of the world cast at Madame Tussaud's wax works in London, cutting a rather unique album of the first recorded Black Mass, writing a long-running "Letters to the Devil" column in *The National Insider*, and performing an elaborate on-camera ritual on Johnny Carson's 7th Anniversary show to summon success for the upcoming year, LaVey moved from being a local San Francisco character to being an international celebrity.

Reactions to what the Exarch of Hell had to say ranged from decidedly hostile to immediately supportive. Among the first articles written about the new High Priest of Satan was Shana Alexander's "The Feminine Eye" column in February, 1967, then running in *Life* magazine. Titled "The Ping is the Thing," the article opens by describing a ping that is often heard when idly listening to the morning news broadcast: "This ping seems to signal that something funny, or weird, or maybe even profound may have just occurred, although one is never sure." Alexander goes on to give a wonderfully engaging account of LaVey and his activities in those early days, describing, as she says, "the jarring clash between the exotic and the utterly banal."[8]

Besides *Rosemary's Baby,* the movie which LaVey has said "did for the Church of Satan what *The Birth of a Nation* did for the Ku Klux Klan, complete with recruiting posters in the lobby," there were a few other films made about or including LaVey. *The Brother Buzz Show,* an educational documentary-type series for kids, showcasing unusual animals and people, devoted an episode to LaVey and his lion, Togare, before LaVey even started the Church of Satan. This delightful profile is "narrated" by Togare (Pat McCormack), who describes LaVey (not yet shorn of his hair) as a hypnotist and psychic investigator, and then goes on to take us through a typical day in the life of a man and his lion. There's some wonderful footage of the inside of the Black House, as well as of Diane, Karla and a toddling Zeena.

Because of its innocent enthusiasm aimed at evoking wonderment in children, the episode proves to be one of the best portraits of LaVey to date.

*Satanis,* an extensive feature-length documentary on the Church of Satan was released in theaters across the country early in 1970, often playing on a double bill with another movie in which Anton appeared, Kenneth Anger's *Invocation of My Demon Brother.* The ads for *Satanis,* showcasing LaVey's scowling countenance, promised bloody, sexually-explicit rituals. In true William Castle fashion, cautions were phrased in the most serious manner: *"Satanis* is the most pertinent, and perhaps the most shocking film of our time. But it's definitely not a movie for everyone. If you choose not to see it, we will understand." Sadly, several other foreign documentaries (by Germany's Florian Fuertwangler and France's Victor Vicas), that were made of LaVey's church never got American distribution. Different versions of Luigi Scatini's *Angeli Bianca, Angeli Nera,* were released around the world, the American version titled *Witchcraft '70.* The segment on LaVey and the Church of Satan was one of the few included in every version. Ray Laurent's *Satanis* was available for a time on videotape and has long been the only footage of the Church available for TV producers to use when describing the evils of Satanism to concerned studio audiences.

Late 1970 found Anton LaVey promoting his newly-released *The Compleat Witch* on *Donahue* and other shows across the country, appearing, on many occasions, with Arthur Lyons, author of *The Second Coming: Satanism in America.* Lyons, who has since written a series of hard-boiled detective novels, covers LaVey extensively in *The Second Coming:*

> "Anton Szandor LaVey, despite his accusers, is a sincere and dedicated man, demanding sincerity and dedication from his members. He is mobilizing for a purpose: to control, to gain power through the already existing social channels. 'I visualize a day,' he told me calmly as we talked one afternoon at his home, 'when tridents and pentagrams are thrust into the sky from church roofs instead of crosses. I have a legacy to fulfill, and it will be fulfilled.' Perhaps it will, so long as the group does not lose sight of its present aims and methods."[9]

*The Second Coming* had been the established text on Satanism until

Lyons wrote another book in 1988 titled *Satan Wants You* which updated his first book, providing fresh material on Anton LaVey and dispelling much of the hysterical claims of animal sacrifices and "ritual abuse" of children which have been blamed on Satanists over the years.

*Newsweek* magazine has done a few articles covering LaVey's exploits. One from August 16th, 1971, entitled "Evil, Anyone?," was already raising questions about suspected "Satanic crimes" that have plagued LaVey from his organization's beginnings. Anton's answer has been consistent over the years: "Satanism, he insists, is 'developing two circles, an elitist group which I always intended my church to be, and the faddists who are becoming Satanists because it's the thing to do.'" Discovering murder isn't on Satanism's list of required sacraments, diligent reporters have to find something else to entice thrill-seeking readers. "Indeed, far from preaching sexual or political anarchy, LaVey describes his goal as the creation of a police state in which the weak are weeded out and the 'achievement-oriented leadership' is permitted to pursue the mysteries of black magic."[10]

Because of LaVey's nude female altars (more than a few fetishists wrote letters of inquiry addressed to "the redheaded nude altar"), there were plenty of men's magazines willing to cover the Church of Satan, having a juicy, ready-made excuse for nudie shots. Though most of the stories accompanying the pictures were limited to recounting ancient myths of Devil's orgies and naked, nubile acolytes tied to sacrificial altars, several were written by Burton Wolfe, who eventually wrote a much-needed biography of LaVey in 1974. Wolfe's vision of LaVey is clear and concise, packing a wealth of information into his book, *The Devil's Avenger.* An established writer with three previous books to his credit, Wolfe explained his interest in LaVey this way:

> "One of the reasons I became involved with LaVey and eventually wrote about him was that he did make sense. I first heard him speak at a Sexual Freedom League meeting in 1967 and was immediately impressed by his knowledge and practicality. All of the other occultists I had met, heard about, or read of turned out to be frauds, quacks, and madmen. But not LaVey. He may be the first occultist ... ever to work out a rational and even a partly scientific basis for his beliefs and rites."[11]

Burton Wolfe joined Anton's church for a brief period in 1968 when, as he writes, "LaVey was still in his prankish stage. The rituals and parties in his black house were full of fun and humor, and I thoroughly enjoyed capers such as playing the role of the director of the insane asylum in the Madness of Logic rite."[12] Wolfe continued to fan interest in LaVey with articles up into the early '80's and, though he had to drop out the Church of Satan because he felt it was evolving into a "harsh, vindictive, crypto-fascist style organization,"[13] Wolfe wrote a comprehensive introduction to *The Satanic Bible* which has served as the only biographical reference on LaVey since *The Devil's Avenger* went out of print.

*"Someone paid me a great compliment long ago," LaVey recalls, "when he said, about me, 'He's no fun any more.' That's when I knew I was getting somewhere. This was when the Church was two or three years old and I realized people were beginning to regard us as more than just fun and games."*

Being a public Devil could open doors in the right places. LaVey developed an intimate friendship with David Pleydell-Bouverie, the Vickers munitions heir and "godson" of Sir Basil Zaharoff. Bouverie had become a legendary *bon vivant* in his own right with his estate serving as a gathering point for the wealthy and notorious few. Through him, LaVey met Lady Sylvia Ashleigh, Clark Gable's widow, whom Anton describes as a well-bred, pleasant, pigeon-breasted woman, much like Elwood P. Dowd's mother in *Harvey*. LaVey also met Abigail Folger's mother. Abigail was the first baby born under hypnosis and, since Zeena had also been born under the same circumstances, Diane and Mrs. Folger had enough in common to strike up a ready friendship. Alan Watts went skeet-shooting with LaVey once and Anton found him to be rather absent-minded, but "a nice enough guy. There was a haziness about him, like Leary, whom I met on a *Donahue* show when he was still broadcasting from Cleveland. Leary's daughter was with him and she seemed almost articulate. In Dr. Nixon's words, he was 'a simple soul.'"

By contrast, Bouverie's enclave also established LaVey's meeting Joseph Cotten and his wife Pat Medina, who once assisted LaVey in shoving a balky Togare back into his carryall when the big lion decided he was reluctant to leave the estate. Speaking of Cotten: "He is first and foremost a circus man, a real trouper who has an uncanny kind of perception of the world and human nature. It's no accident — and not acting ability alone — that he's played the roles he has."

As might be expected, LaVey finds he can communicate with the highest strata of people best, no matter how supportive a "lower-wattage" person might be. "Support alone is not enough," LaVey confesses, "understanding is primary. And you can't get that without a modicum of intelligence. I don't appreciate being supported for all the wrong reasons, with no regard for underlying motivations — that's less than helpful. I don't need warm bodies just to fill the pews, fill out membership figures or make charitable donations. In most cases it's a drain of vital energy from me, not them.

"I would like to think that presidents and world leaders of any kind would have some special appreciation for someone who really understands their roles — the pressures, the constituents they have to satisfy.... That requires Satanic perception or acumen. Even though a leader always appreciates his supporters, who may be very much with him and sympathetic, they may not have that added level of empathy or rapport. When it comes right down to it, on a scale of one to ten, I have an intuitive feeling I'd find a greater rapport, share a deeper understanding with the Pope than I would for someone like John Kennedy, for example. I don't perceive that John Kennedy had much I might relate to. When it's right, it often goes without saying we share the same likes and dislikes in music, movies, books, fascinating places — we can practically talk in shorthand. I couldn't see that with Kennedy. I could sympathize with the pressures of his position, but not for the man himself. It's a frequency."

In the early to mid-70's, LaVey spent some time back in Los Angeles, living in Jayne Mansfield's Pink Palace at 10100 Sunset Boulevard, which had been acquired by another Church of Satan member after Jayne's death. Anton's associations in the movie business from years before now expanded to include still more actresses, actors, writers, directors and producers. Movie stars found it easy to align themselves with LaVey and his philosophy — they always like to experiment a bit more than average people. LaVey found a very welcome, unabashedly admiring atmosphere, with people accepting him for what he was rather than challenging his "dramatics" or "theatrics." Hollywood glitteratti could sympathize with LaVey being accused of posturing when in reality he was just being true to his archetypal self. And LaVey, in turn found himself energized by familiar sights and friends in Hollywood.

Two of LaVey's Hollywood friends, director Milo Frank and his wife, actress Sally Forrest, owned the infamous Jean Harlow/Paul Bern suicide house that Jay Sebring happened to be living in at the time of the Manson murders. They approached LaVey with a tempting deal to trade residence in the house for filming opportunities in Anton's now famous Victorian in San Francisco. At the time, the LaVeys had already come under scrutiny so soon after the murders and felt it wouldn't be prudent to create any more connections for reporters to exploit than they already had. LaVey has since felt a modicum of regret he didn't avail himself of the opportunity. Supposedly the house has a curse on it, with secret panels and a history to rival LaVey's notorious Victorian. Other homes in Hollywood were also available to him, and still are. LaVey maintained his residence in San Francisco, motoring up and down the coast sometimes two and three times a week. Karla and Zeena stayed in San Francisco most of the time, usually attended by one or more of LaVey's members. Karla, then in her early twenties, was following in her father's footsteps — giving lectures in Satanism and taking a degree in Criminology.

Being the Devil's representative on Earth not only opened celebrities' doors to LaVey but many of their hidden hearts and minds as well. Secrets became known to him; secrets someone could only tell the Devil himself without risking rejection or disapproval. It has always been part of the mythos that, as the keeper of the gates of Hell, a fit and proper devil must bear the burden of men's wickedness, hidden from other mortal men. LaVey doesn't balk at this aspect of his role. Yet, true to his unwritten underworld code, he is reticent to disclose that which he, feels, is better left hidden. "I wouldn't stick my neck out and say what I know; I'm already unpopular. I wanted to expose myths at one time but the real terrifying part was people's reactions to enlightenment. The myths weren't nearly as frightening as what happened when I tried to expose them."

In 1973, a year after *The Satanic Rituals* was released, publishers decided the public had heard enough Satanic thought. When LaVey's agent presented his next book, *The Devil's Notebook,* at the annual international book fair in Frankfurt, enthusiastic bids were placed for the manuscript. But when editors brought it back to New York to take a closer look, LaVey was quietly put off. Portions of the unpublished work surfaced over the years in the Satanic newsletter, *The Cloven Hoof,* but it was considered by major houses to be too inflammatory for the general public. One publisher, after reading a chapter on Lycanthropic transformation, exclaimed, "Why, if this was published, the streets would be running red!"

Membership in the Church of Satan expanded steadily. LaVey tried to include visits with his constituents around the globe wherever he traveled, blessing them with papal visits to their grottos, where he was greeted with an excess of pomp and black capes. "It became rather embarrassing after a while. I'd step off the plane and there they'd be, all huddled together to meet me in their black velvet robes and capes with huge Baphomets around their necks. Many of our grass-roots people didn't know much about subtlety then, or decorum. I was trying to present a cultured, mannered image and their idea of protest or shock was to wear their 'lodge regalia' into the nearest Denny's."

At the same time, Anton was beginning to experience the negative aspects of being the center of high-profile publicity. LaVey was besieged from both sides: from those who didn't like what he had to say and from "fans" who created problems by just wanting to hang around. After pictures and descriptions of Rueben, LaVey's malformed skeleton, appeared in *Paris-Match,* the doctor who had treated the man with Paget's Disease before he died called the U.C.S.F. Medical Center and demanded they retrieve the skeleton. Though the hospital officials were hesitant to do it, the doctor raised such a fuss they were forced to take Rueben away from LaVey. "That was a real shame. That skeleton got more attention and appreciation with the Church of Satan than he ever could have otherwise. We rescued him! He probably would have been destroyed among the wreckage. Even in a museum, he would just be one more skeleton among hundreds. With us, he was special."

LaVey had a similarly unhappy experience with Togare, his Nubian lion. Anton kept Togare with him as his constant companion for three years, much to the delight of the Bay Area media and schools, where Togare often visited to promote goodwill toward wild animals. Neighborhood parents brought their children by LaVey's odd home to pet the lion. But once the Church of Satan was founded, a small band of LaVey's neighbors petitioned the city to get rid of Togare. Their complaints: he was potentially dangerous to the community, he littered LaVey's backyard with large, smelly bones. They pressed police to arrest LaVey on charges of allowing his lion to make "loud or unusual noises."

Finally, the LaVeys were forced to donate the 500-pound Togare to the San Francisco Zoo in 1967. The separation was wrenching for both man and lion, and LaVey leveled a curse on those responsible. Within a year, several of the neighbors who had been the most vocal about Togare had either moved away, died, or disappeared. Togare sired many cubs both in San Francisco and on actress Tippi Hedren's ranch in Acton, California, where Togare eventually lived out the last of his years. In her book, *The Cats of Shambala,* Hedren described Togare as a "good but fierce papa." Togare died in 1981, on Walpurgisnacht.

In the beginning of the church's activities, LaVey freely printed his address and phone number on posters, fake folded money (to be left lying on the street as a promotional gimmick), and allowed reporters to print his address as they wished. "I don't like to think I was naive during that period of my life. I just wanted the Church of Satan to be honest, open and above-board. I also had a dream of being able to work out of my own home, as most of my friends did who were writers or performers. I envisioned the pleasure of rolling out of bed and having your work right there waiting for you without having to get in your car and drive to an office or another location. I didn't think that was unreasonable. But I didn't understand then how treacherous people could be." Zeena and Karla, who have grown up delighting in their father and his organization, recall that their only fear from being raised a Satanist came from outside, from people who were threatened by what their father was trying to do, or who just wanted to give him a bad time. Zeena remembers coming home from school with a nut waiting on her front doorstep with a butcher's knife. She had been instructed by her parents, in such an emergency, to keep walking past and pretend she didn't live there. Since then, LaVey, like most celebrities, has established living quarters around the world to which he can retreat so that he is no longer trapped by his own popularity.

LaVey grew embittered over the harassment and threats to his family and security. He grew even more wary of his own brewing hostility, recognizing the danger of killing someone with the .45 he carried as a constant companion. As Wolfe relates, "LaVey, heeding G.B. Shaw's dictum that the Superman must tread among the mass of humanity as carefully as though dealing with wild beasts, bore no hopes for kindnesses, or understanding, or sensibilities. Living like the lion trainer among his lions, he had his own peculiar faith: a faith in the ability of black magic to change circumstances in the immediate environment, rendering escape unnecessary."[14]

After a few years, LaVey began cutting back on the administrative demands on his time, concentrating his energies on his own projects more than on public relations and personally ministering to his ever-increasing flock. Following LaVey's plan, it was time to "stop performing Satanism and start practicing it." The Church of Satan was having its impact on the outside world and LaVey wanted to encourage new directions among the members rather than siphoning off the best energy for compulsory performance of rituals. The period of actual above-ground activity coming directly from LaVey's Victorian was relatively brief, but long enough to have an irreparable effect on established religion. "After that original blast," LaVey remembers, "there was no need for the ongoing public spectacle and outrage of an inverted Catholic Mass anymore. Christianity was becoming weaker every day. That was just beating a dead horse. There were plenty of other sacred cows to attack, and that's what keeps Satanism vital and thriving."

All weekly public ceremonies in the Black House stopped in 1972. Responsibility for Satanic activities was shifted to the dozens of Satanic grottos established around the world, with Central Grotto (as LaVey's original Black House was designated) serving only to screen, approve and direct potential active members in the Church of Satan.

By 1975, a reorganization had taken place and those few who were counterproductive to LaVey's Satanic ideals, who were more interested in what Anton calls "Phase One Satanism" (i.e., group rituals, blaspheming Christianity in a rigidly-structured, limited way) were phased out. The grotto system was loosely maintained but no longer strictly managed through Central Grotto. LaVey wanted his Church of Satan to evolve into a truly cabalistic underground rather than degenerating into a long-running public pageant or a Satan pen pal club.

Putting the brakes on the "lodge hall" activities, LaVey emphasized that a person's status within the Church of Satan should reflect his status outside the organization. Highest ranking people in the world outside should hold a commensurate position within the group, since that, LaVey reasons, was the truest measure of how able they were to apply Satanic theories of Lesser and Greater Magic for their own benefit. Anton also shifted the organizational focus to those who could benefit the church in a substantial and material way through who and what they were, not just through spending large chunks of time with nonproductive "psychic vampires" no matter how dedicated.

"There always has to be a fair exchange," LaVey says. "I realized many people were joining our ranks simply because it was a guarantee of friends, or because they wanted the glory of passing tests to earn degrees, much like the lodge hall 'Grand Poobahs' who take off their robes and vestments and become the local plumber again outside their lodge. They were getting more 'spook-appeal' out of being members of the Church of Satan than we were getting esteem from having them among our membership. As an organization grows, group activities only cause contention, drain vital energy that could be better applied elsewhere and eventually become counterproductive. Teaching people that they're all right and society is all wrong, that the only ones who really understand them and that they can relate to are within the group, is damaging in the long run. It only reinforces their own inability to deal with the larger world.

"That's one reason why I dissolved the Grotto system. I wanted to create a forum, a loosely-structured cabal for the productive aliens, not misfits who need to depend on a group. After the re-organization, I was free to be more selective. I would much rather attract and lend support to those individuals who *use* their alienation — just as most leaders are usually different or distinctive in some way. Groups encourage dependence on beliefs and delusions to reinforce their omnipotence rather than applying magic on an individual basis, as *The Satanic Bible* outlines. Instead of fostering self-sufficiency and honest skepticism, I saw my group lapsing into blind belief and unhealthy anthropomorphism. That's not what I intended and I had to make moves to get the Church of Satan back on track." Consequently, LaVey devised a diabolical way to "clean house," which eventually eliminated much of the dross and administrivia that LaVey felt was obscuring the organization's true destiny.

At the same time LaVey was re-focusing priorities within the world he had created, he became more selective about granting interviews, since his doors were no longer open to anyone off the street who wished to drop by for his lectures. Because of this rather abrupt cessation of activity, rumors spread of the end of the Church of Satan and of LaVey's death.

Of course, there were those who wanted to continue the group activities. Rather than seeing LaVey's changes as moving the Church of Satan beyond the realm of a "cult" where all activity is strictly dictated by a central figure, some members felt betrayed by LaVey for discontinuing their avenue for meeting others of like-mind. There were also those who simply felt "sour grapes" toward LaVey from 1966 on, who felt they could do the same thing only better. Groups sprouted up around the world once Anton hit the newspapers, many of them claiming a more illustrious Satanic pedigree than LaVey's original group, and many started by disgruntled ex-members of the Church of Satan: Church of Satanic Brotherhood, Ordo Templi Satanas, Order of the Black Ram, Temple of Set, Shrine of the Little Mother, Church of S.A.T.A.N., Thee Church of Satan, Order of Baal, The Satanic Church, Thee Orthodox Satanic Church, and The Church of Satanic Liberation, to name just a few that have presented themselves to LaVey. Most of these other groups took on a Laurel and Hardy-like "Sons of the Desert" quality and never seemed able to stick together for more than a few years, with infighting and jealousies being constant problems. Some have written disparaging remarks over the years which LaVey passes off as "absurdly self-righteous," and some have reportedly thrown their share of demonic curses in LaVey's direction.

Yet, as Arlene Fitzgerald points out in *Everything You Always Wanted to Know About Sorcery ... But Were Afraid to Ask,* "death spells not-with-standing, Anton LaVey's Satanic Church has gained a certain acceptance and even respectability in American society, thanks to his superb sense of timing."

"'Somehow the counterculture was ready for a Satanic Priest and

Anton was ready to proclaim himself Prince of Darkness...' San Francisco journalist Merla Zellerbach wrote recently of this modern-day version of Satan incarnate in her *Chronicle* column. As Mrs. Zellerbach goes on to observe, "Every success story has its imitators.... But as yet, no Black Mass enthusiast has succeeded in posing any serious threat to LaVey in his prominent role as 'the advocate's Devil.'"

Despite changes in the structure of his organization, publicity for LaVey hadn't flagged since the mid-50's. In 1975, Dick Russell wrote "Anton LaVey: The Satanist Who Wants to Rule the World," a chillingly perceptive article for *Argosy* magazine, following Anton from Hollywood, to Durango for the filming of *The Devil's Rain*, then finally ending the interview with LaVey in Mexico City. Already, LaVey was being described as "all but inaccessible to the public. Moving between three California homes and retreats in the eastern U.S. and Europe, he has become an almost mythical recluse." Russell weaves purely personal reactions to LaVey among his abundant facts, blending his article into an almost fictional interpretation of how profoundly he was effected by their meetings. The result is a bewitching portrait of a frighteningly prepossessing man — haunted, supernaturally perceptive, possibly unstable.

> "Uncontrollably, I begin to laugh. Soon Terrazina is laughing, and LaVey is laughing, and it seems the whole restaurant — the whole world — must be laughing.

> "There are tears in my eyes when I glance up at him. He is bringing a glass of wine to his lips, grinning like a large whiskered cat. The grin brings me back to reality. In my mind I try to construct my next question."

> ... "Do you believe that you will leave your mark on history?" The question leaps from me so quickly that it takes LaVey by surprise.

> "He contemplates a moment, then replies: 'I'd be maudlin to say I didn't. I honestly feel that a hundred years from now, when most of these Watergate figures are long forgotten, people will know who Anton LaVey was. Selfish as it may appear on the sur-

face, I also sincerely believe I'm doing something that will elevate man's self-awareness. Even if it's a tiny, tiny little step.'"[15]

Fred Harden's 1979 *Hustler* article on LaVey acted as a bridge between LaVey's splashy publicity of the '60's and early '70's and what LaVey terms the "second wave" of Satanism which began, suitably enough, in 1984. Harden's detailed article apprised *Hustler's* readers of some intimate details of LaVey's relationships with Marilyn Monroe and Jayne Mansfield, and discussed LaVey's continuing influence in the film industry.

> "For all his strangeness, LaVey remains a strict law-and-order man, working with police in the investigation of crimes, especially murder, where there emerge signs of witchcraft or demonomania. He does not smoke. He drinks, but not to excess. And he continues to appreciate women, especially well-developed blondes.

> "Far from the scandalous and prankish antics of the '60's, LaVey now stirs his cauldron of Satanic witchdoctory with a truly evil objective in mind — to make the world a more fit place for devils. 'We Satanists pride ourselves on being ladies and gentlemen — sinful ones, perhaps — but nonetheless, ladies and gentlemen.'"[16]

# Chapter Ten

# Life at the Edge of the World

LaVey truly lives in the Devil's realm — in that misty borderland between sanity and madness, acceptability and outrage, between science and the supernatural — yet remains always (as one associate puts it) "beyond the pale." LaVey maintains it's only in this Borderland of all times and no times, with spatial and chronological reference points suspended, that magic is initiated, and the magician's will can be projected outward to superimpose his desires on the Is To Be.

"Everyone's looking for independence now. Identities are at a premium, a precious commodity. The common man is sold individuality with every beer ad or shoe commercial. Only by isolating yourself as completely as you can from the mainstream, can you accomplish real magic," says LaVey. "There's great power in doing something that, at that moment in time, there is probably no one else in the world doing. If you listen to a piece of music that everyone was humming once, but which has been neglected over the years, you're doing something unique, gaining energy from that 'lost' song. That's the power of *exclusivity*. When you do something that few others even think of doing, you shine forth like a beacon. If there are forces which can carry out your bidding, you would attract their attention, and sympathy, through your uniqueness."

LaVey himself lives an inverted life. True to his vampiric nature, he slips off to bed near dawn, doing his best work in the hours shortly before sunrise. He's isolated himself from media events and tabloid personalities, depending on a satellite system of associates around the world to give him a filtered sketch of pertinent information. In the last few years, LaVey has initiated a campaign against the mind numbing effects of television, reasoning that, if exclusivity is a potent magical tool, nothing can be accomplished by staring into a tube that measures its audiences in millions. He's labeled TV "The Great Stratifier," likening it to "God" in its omnipresence and universal standardization.

"In previous centuries," LaVey writes, "the Church was the great controller, dictating morality, stifling free expression and posing as conservator of all great art and music. Instead we have TV, doing just as good a job at dictating fashions, thoughts, attitudes, objectives as did the Church, using many of the same techniques but doing it so palatably that no one notices. Instead of 'sins' to keep people in line, we have fears of being judged unacceptable by our peers (by not wearing the right shoes, not drinking the right kind of beer, or wearing the wrong kind of deodorant). Coupled with that fear is imposed insecurity concerning our own identities. All answers and solutions to these fears come through television, and *only* through television. Only through exposure to TV can the new sins of alienation and ostracism be absolved."

Satanists, by LaVey's definition, are those rare individuals who (among other things) natively avoid contact with masses of people, whether in thought, dress, taste in music, entertainment, or automobiles. When reviewing an applicant's file for possible further involvement in the Church of Satan, LaVey looks closely at the person's unconscious alignment with media issues and personalities. He makes a distinction between born iconoclasts and media-saturated rebels who only dress or act out "shocking" behavior because they want to be accepted by another peer group. LaVey uses factors like disdain for television, and favorite movies, books and jokes as a gauge for determining the depth of one's Satanic alignments.

"A major determining factor by which a superior human can be isolated from his average counterparts is his very isolation — the degree to which he naturally removes himself from mass-media input and stimuli. You cannot be an elitist, a Magician, and be plugged into the system."

One issue of the *Cloven Hoof* contained a tightly-written bombshell of disdain titled "Misanthropia." In language comparable to that used in *The Satanic Bible,* though matured, LaVey begins by saying, "A long time ago I tried to be a full-time dear fellow sweet guy. I should have known better." From there he goes on: "There are countless books I wish to read, musical compositions I would like to play and listen to, objects I would like to create, paintings and drawings I would like to render. Undesirable men and women rob me of those opportunities."[17]

LaVey has little charity when it comes to aiding the less fortunate of the world. "People don't realize they take their lives in their hands when they talk to me about 'helping' the starving and downtrodden and homeless—my fellow man!" says LaVey. "I consider that a most ignoble endeavor. The only way I would like to 'help' the great majority of people is the same way Carl Panzram 'reformed' people who tried to reform him. It would be most merciful to help them by relieving them of the life they seem to hate so much. People should be happy I'm not a humanitarian — or I'd probably be the most diabolical mass murderer the world has ever known."

Perhaps it is just this callousness toward human beings that allows LaVey to align himself more closely with animals, and to value inanimate objects much more highly than humans. On the last page of Arthur Lyons' book, *Satan Wants You*, LaVey describes the real threat of Satanism: "Like an old Duesenberg sitting at the curb is more alive than the people crowding around it, drawing energy from its beautiful chrome pipes, the object will become more valuable than the people watching it. When things become precious and people expendable, that is the horror of the true Satanic society. That is when the nightmare begins."[18]

LaVey cherishes and preserves orphaned items — books, sheet music, clothes, movies, memorabilia. Much of his extensive collection is contained in a "storeroom" far below one of his homes, a place best left to the imagination, monstrous not in size but in content. His purpose is not only indulgence but also saving obscure bits of history that might otherwise be lost forever: "Here's to the conservators! They provide the world with a memory." Among LaVey's treasured icons of bygone eras are lost or banned songs, like a collection of "Gloomy Sunday" recordings he inherited from an early member of the Church. Because of LaVey's perverse reverence for inanimate objects, he seems more influenced by the written word and movies than by real people. Just as he has always adopted ideas others shy away from, LaVey admits to being fascinated with houses dangerously close to elevated freeways, beyond the pavement's end, precariously perched on stilts; houses literally on the fringes, that others wouldn't feel comfortable residing in. Antique or unusual cars, sleazy paperbacks, pulp magazines ...

LaVey is a collector of "bizarrary" that others overlook, cast aside or shun as disturbing or disgusting. People are envious only when his orphaned items (or ideas for that matter) become monetarily valuable, then the unscrupulous but ever-present few will try to abscond with what he's preserved, even if it takes court action.

Perhaps it's directly because of LaVey's adoration of unique items that things taken from him or lost often return after many years. He seems to be a vortex for rare books, which he regards as physical entities that preserve and communicate our past. All books are treated with extreme care, to the point that even many long-time friends are discouraged from touching them. A sign posted in a section of his extensive library declares, "Anyone caught removing books from these shelves will have their hands amputated." "Something always happens when people mistreat these books," LaVey warns, gesturing to the shelves filled behind him. "Almost as if they're living entities. If someone hurts them, I find out the person later met with some tragedy." LaVey's keyboards seem to have the same effect on people. LaVey is a private man. He has few people he involves closely in his life. If someone intrudes in LaVey's private domain uninvited, or sullies the atmosphere when he is granted inclusion, the intruder can blame no one but himself for the harm that befalls him.

Yet in his perverse way, Anton LaVey preserves our memories for us, treasures them and keeps them alive and fresh. Everyone tells us the past is impossible, even worthless, to experience again. LaVey, in contrast, encourages his followers to live in a world of their own choosing, their own making. Going back in time to experience worlds you missed, or returning to a time that once gave you vitality, isn't an option in LaVeyan thought, it's a necessity. "It's not a crime to wish for other worlds. You'll get taxed for it but they can't throw you in jail for creating your own private world ... yet. Dramatics are fun, an indulgence. 'You can't go backward,' 'You can't live in the past,' they tell you. Why not? 'You've got to put all that behind you and move on to other things,' they say. Bullshit! These are all expressions of modern disposability. It's a mediocritizing technique — trying to get rid of what I call 'past orthodoxies.' It's our past that makes us unique, therefore it's our past that economic interests want to rob from us, so they can sell us a new, improved future. Society now depends on a disposable world — out with the old, in with the new, including relationships. But how we weep and wish we could hold onto those cherished moments forever, to those long-whispered dreams, those tortured nights — how we want to grasp them and stop them from sifting through our fingers. I say, 'Don't let it happen. Keep things the way you want them and let the rest of the world be duped.'"

But LaVey's advocacy of chosen total environments goes beyond simple entertainment. Evoking certain periods with appropriate music, clothing styles, manners, and patterns of speech that have been abandoned can give a would-be magician unparalleled power. LaVey has a theory that it even can increase longevity if a person is allowed to remain in exactly the era that is most pleasurable to him. Perhaps time can be suspended. LaVey himself hasn't seemed to age over the last 20 years. In fact, his ideas remain what they were when he was ten years old — he has just found avenues to flesh them out more completely. And he stays in the world that makes him happy.

Total environments can be an expression of unique knowledge, secrets that you might be privy to, which makes the environment all the more magical. Satan has always been a keeper of secrets, and LaVey has described secrecy as a process of empowerment in itself. "A secret organization is secret not to preserve a given body of information per se, but to gain power from having and transmitting secrets to its members. The process of learning, and more importantly keeping, hidden information, gives you power. If you just tell someone a secret they won't learn a thing. A stage magician can show how a trick is done but he can't teach all the years of skill and practice it has taken to learn how to do that particular trick in a few short minutes."

Holding secrets about other people, sometimes what they can't even tell themselves, is like being the keeper to the Gates of Hell. LaVey sympathizes with the fortune-teller "Apollonius" in a novel by Charles Finney, *The Circus of Dr. Lao.* When a lonely older woman comes into his tent hungry to hear that she'd soon meet a handsome man, or begin an adventure, Apollonius is compelled to tell her:

> "Tomorrow will be like today, and day after tomorrow will be like the day before yesterday. I see your remaining days each as quiet, tedious collections of hours. You will not travel any-

where. You will think no new thoughts. You will experience no new passions... When you die you will be buried and forgotten, and that is all... And for all the good or evil, creation or destruction, that your living might have accomplished, you might just as well never have lived at all."[19]

"I can't tell people what I really think. Like Apollonius, I have a loaded gun. What I see in people is truthful, but it's concerted cruelty to hold a big mirror up to people. I don't have it in me to use it in a cavalier manner. I can't tell people what would devastate them. It might be better, less stressful for me if I could, but I hold back. It's different when it comes from me. I and I alone can allow them to feel content, even satisfied with the very imperfections that others would stigmatize — likewise I and I alone can make people feel devastated if I point out the same imperfections others might point out. If you have that ability, you don't put your perceptions forth often. You know what one word could do. It's a tool you don't use unless you intend to destroy — like a curse. I don't even like to think such thoughts about certain people. It's dangerous coming from me. Cursing people with themselves is the worst curse of all."

As LaVey says, he often admires in people that which others would consider stigmatizing. One of the strengths of Satanic philosophy is to take that in yourself which would be considered by most to be a liability, and invert it. Make it work for you rather than against you. Perhaps this is where the image of Satanic inversion holds true. An accomplished Satanist takes what is considered "evil" by mainstream Judeo-Christian society, turns it upside down in unexpected ways and gives it back in spades. By applying LaVey's rule of "nine parts social respectability to one part outrage," Satan, church, religion, Bible, must all be re-defined in the post-1966 era. LaVey advises, "To be really outrageous, make your alienation work for you. Use their own fears against them. Take the givens and throw it back at your accusers so they get more than they bargained for.

"The difference between me and someone like Manson is he's playing poker and they're playing poker, but I'm playing blackjack. Maybe that's not what he wants to play but that's how it's worked out. I'm playing a totally different game than they are, with the hand they dealt me. Using what they give me, implementing them in a way they don't expect and don't like

— visuals, music, archetypes, — they deal eustress and I give them real distress. It's all in the application.

"Endowing stereotypes, endorsing what people say Satanists do according to Christian definitions — sacrificing animals, killing people, stealing, destroying property, criminal behavior — is endowing and empowering the system. You're playing the game right. That's actually an acceptable option in the Judeo-Christian framework — to be a criminal. You're no threat behind bars. You can be safely locked up so they can poke sticks at you. They get eustress and you get distress. That's not Satanic."

Instead, LaVey instructs his witches and warlocks to develop unique competence and skill in one thing; develop something you're very good at so you can transcend the consciousness of it. Learn to play the oboe, or build a model city from scratch, or learn to draw a horse that looks like a horse. When you learn a skill and claim it as uniquely your own realm, with endless practice you'll be able to do it so well you won't even have to think about it. That's magical meditation, trances, out-of-body experiences, the magician standing in the middle of the Circle and pronouncing the words he alone knows, the use of magician's tools — all the metaphors are there. "This is applicable to music or magic," says LaVey. "When it becomes a form of expression, that's when the auto-pilot takes over and the medium becomes incidental — I lose consciousness of the method or tools.

"Once you familiarize yourself with your tools, you should forget about them. It will only throw you off-balance. In all these 'rolling shit into little balls' types who spend hours of time and reams of paper saying nothing, literary masturbators, they concentrate on the vehicle more than what they want to produce. That impedes the end result and defeats the purpose. You must lose consciousness of the medium or mechanics to do the impossible. Like Nijinsky who explained how he gave the impression of hovering in mid-air — 'I just pause when I get up there.' In a child-like way, real magicians innocently do the simplest thing. The objective is all they think about. I just want to make music the way I hear it. The ends justify the means, and the means become inconsequential."

LaVey uses various forms of artistic expression to evoke his creative demons. Though he has written a few rousing songs and done some soundtracks, his passion so far has been in dynamically interpreting music already written but long-neglected. Only recently has LaVey agreed to release some of his musical compositions and interpretations to a wider audience. LaVey has also managed over the years to turn out some rather startling paintings and photographs. At a time when only Charles Addams and the artists for *Weird Tales* were doing their darkly wicked work, LaVey painted and exhibited some delightfully eerie paintings. His artwork is bleak, with figures haunting and haunted. Almost primitive in their stark concentration of timeless, suspended focus, a few have had to be removed from their exhibition spots because they were "too disturbing." The same quality can be found in his photography — lonely, dismal scenes that would only appeal to grisly, perverse appetites.

LaVey explains the power of alienation, finding interest in things most dismiss as old or insignificant: "Something that once had importance might be forgotten by most people but because millions of people once knew it, a force is present that can be harnessed. There might be so much significance attached to a song, for example, or a fact, that it can't die but only lies dormant, like a vampire in his coffin, waiting to be called forth from the grave once again. There is more magic in the fact that the first mass worldwide photo of the Church of Satan was taken by Joe Rosenthal — the same man who took the most famous news photo in history — the flag-raising at Iwo Jima. There's real occult significance to that — much more than in memorizing grimoires and witches' alphabets. People ask me about what music to use in rituals — what is the best occult music. I've instructed people to go to the most uncrowded section of the music store and it's a guarantee what you'll find there will be occult music. That's the power of long-lost trivia. I get irritated by people who turn up their noses and whine 'Why would anyone want to know that?' Because once upon a time, everyone in America knew it.

"Suppose there's a repository of neglected energy, that's been generated and forgotten. Maybe it's like a pressure cooker all this time, just waiting for someone to trigger its release. 'Here I am,' it beckons, 'I have all this energy stored up just waiting for you — all you have to do is unlock the door. Because of man's cupidity, he's relegated me to this state of somnambulism — dreaming the ancient dreams — even though I was once so important to him.' Think about that. A song that was once on millions of lips now is only on your lips. Now what does that contain? Those vibrations of that particular tune, what do they evoke, call up? What do they unlock? The old gods lie dormant, waiting."

As a metaphor for using alienation to it's greatest advantage, LaVey uses the image of the vampire. He started investigations into vampires in 40's and 50's, and included the subject in his weekly lectures. Florescu and McNally *(In Search of Dracula)* and Leonard Wolf *(The Annotated Dracula, A Dream of Dracula)* contacted LaVey when they first started their projects since he was the only one doing research on vampires at the time. In 1988, LaVey was called the "Chief Ideologue of Modern Vampirism" by German *Tempo* magazine.[20] After the Church of Satan got underway, he was invited to host "Dracula Tours" to Transylvania, but he demurred. They wanted him to go as the "Devil man." He used "VAMPYR" license plates in 1969 (an associate has "NOS4A2"), and, of course, coined the term "psychic vampire" in *The Satanic Bible,* a phrase that has since found its way into common parlance.

When he was doing his "Letters to the Devil" column in a national tabloid in the late 60's, LaVey had more than one occasion to explain the traditions surrounding the vampire, and the deeper meanings behind them. The drinking of blood has its roots in devouring the love object. Blood or "essential salts" were nice ways to say sexual secretions (semen or vaginal juices) in the 17th and 18th centuries. Our thirst for metaphorical blood also represents the forbidden, the secret, hidden self, and it shocks *because* it is forbidden. A secret fascination for vampires becomes more intense with increased technological society. Bloodletters and butchers weren't always looked on with revulsion, just as professionals. Everyone saw blood more — we slaughtered our own livestock, fought wars with swords, saw charnel houses. Anything that's that far removed from our everyday experience now becomes more shocking, more compelling. We're protected, insulated. We never see blood in our clean, stone and steel, chrome and glass environment. But as we grew further away from the constant confrontation with blood, vampire lore was refined. What we now know as specific vampire characteristics are a relatively recent phenomenon — mostly from Bram Stoker and then Hollywood.

LaVey has explained, in his articles, the reasons why vampires don't look (or reflect) in mirrors; why native soil, the homeland, is so important (he points to a modern counterpart in R.V.'s, where people want to take their homes with them); what might cause the aversion to garlic and sunlight; and the beneficial effects of the shape of coffins (the closeness and soundlessness is conducive to "traveling out" on the night). Subsequent research has been done in those directions which has affirmed much of what LaVey has written. The possibility that people who were once labeled "vampires" actually suffered from a rare blood disease has been given no small amount of credence.

"People would like to think of vampires as parasitic — they aren't. True vampires (as opposed to psychic vampires) always have something to offer — *immortality*. Therefore a modern true vampire must have a place in society or must have done something that has conferred immortality on him so that he in turn can pass it on to the victim. Immortality is a metaphor for power. But a true vampiric relationship is never a one-way street. Passion, vitality is conferred on the vampire's host as well.

"A vampire doesn't look for an unwilling victim; he can gain significantly more energy from willing victims. Vampires need fresh blood but of a particular kind. It's a good interchange when it gives the victim a thrill while the vampire gets the energy from one who's already 1) enthusiastic, and 2) fetishistically stimulating to the vampire. The victim, in her turn, enjoys the Svengali hold, the unquenchable compulsion, the summoning over long distances, the obsessional dependence on the vampire.

"A vampire would only pick a deserving, unwilling victim to exercise his sadistic tendencies. Then he'd choose someone often looking for fun-fear and taunting him for it. The deserving victim would want to gain energy from the vampire by making him hurt her or punish her. You can't draw energy from worthless people — releasing hostility against them can turn a negative into a positive by providing the vampire with a sense of well-being and calm. When the point comes when it's beyond fun for the taunter, into distress, then it becomes fun for the vampire. Otherwise it's enervating. Vampires actually get drained by most human interaction.

"Now that the Gates are pretty much open, saying you're a vampire or interested in vampires is one way to get people looking in your direction. But, as is always the case, the people who work at anything the most are the least what they're supposed to be. It's like Satanists who want to get together for lots of group activities. They just want to draw energy from others (true psychic vampires!). The people who talk about it, aren't really doing it. Sometimes the people who are true vampires, who are involved in vampiric interchanges for mutual benefit, don't even realize it themselves."

In the late 50's and early 60's, LaVey developed several files on a real modern vampire — a young man named Robert Hammersly — about whom he has only vaguely alluded. He speaks so eloquently on the subject, one wonders if all his speculation comes merely from his objective research or if LaVey sees any vampiric tendencies in himself. Not surprisingly there are a few notable comparisons. LaVey is diagnosed photophobic, has a strong allergic reaction to garlic, and has always maintained peak productivity in a nocturnal sleep pattern. He was sleeping in a coffin long before anyone else thought of it, discovering it had much the same benefits as a sensory deprivation tank. People who work closely to LaVey can attest that he likes the air unbearably cold, finds pleasure in quiet, dark surroundings, and, as any self-respecting vampire would, shuns mainstream culture to create a world of his own. Though LaVey doesn't drink blood, he does need rare, red meat — no other protein will do. When asked, LaVey freely admits to the similarities. "Yes, in drawing life from energetic people; in shunning the light and reacting to certain foods, like garlic, which contain mitogenic radiation ... there are certain common elements of a vampiric personality. In the image of the earthbox, as representative of the homeland from which I sprang. My home is very important — I cherish the familiar sights, sounds, smells — which is, again, the opposite of a disposable society.

"The vampire is a soul doomed to walk through eternity searching for a lost love, a lost past, a place to light peacefully from those who would hunt him down and kill him for his romantic attempts to recapture the past, and live in the splendor of an era long-decayed."

"I am all that is vile, reprehensible and evil in the world," snorts LaVey. As he wrote in "Misanthropia," "I will never die, because my death enriches the unfit. I could never be that charitable."

# Chapter Eleven

# Music As Necromancy

Like a mad scientist impatiently blending chemicals in his laboratory to get just the right philtre, LaVey stands before his keyboards adjusting the controls to achieve a precise combination of tones. The attack, sustain, and decay envelopes are carefully altered in the ways he knows will summon the most effective sounds for his purposes. What begins as something of a hissing noise slowly changes tone, running up and down the scale as he depresses the keys. Another twist of a knob and a slider pushed up sharpens the overtones to a more metallic ring. After a half hour or so of trial and adjusting, the hissing sound has become a disturbingly accurate reproduction of a burlesque-style sizzle cymbal. LaVey smiles, giving his new sound a test run with a raunchy version of "Night Train."

After spending years playing wheezy calliopes, trying to keep the steam pressure steady so they wouldn't blow up in his face, or old theater organs that had only one or two pre-sets functioning, with a quarter of the notes either not working or cyphering (a note that continues to play after the player's finger leaves the key), LaVey is dismayed by how far we've come technologically while falling behind musically. "The old Hammonds were great fun to play, though. They're built like pinball machines — you could just play the hell out of them. You didn't have to worry about complex registrations — just play the music. But you just couldn't get any of the range of sounds you can get on the simplest synthesizers today."

Most people lack the patience and skill it takes to adequately reproduce the complex sounds he uses. "I spent hours creating a kazoo on a synthesizer costing thousands of dollars — a Prophet 5 — when I could have had the real thing for 25¢." Time and again he has been told certain things are "impossible" or "unnatural" to the programming possibilities of the synthesizer. Unheeding of these widely accepted limitations, LaVey develops authentic approximations of real instruments. *"I can play the Flight of the Bumblebee with my feet, I can play the Minute Waltz in 45 seconds, and I can play Faust slow."*

"I probably had the best keyboard training possible by playing on circus lots and along the carnival midway," says LaVey. "What the keyboards lacked in realism you had to make up for in technique. You can't play a trumpet sound, for example, like you'd play a sweeping strings sound. A live trumpet player would run out of breath! The tuba is an easy instrument to blow into, but by the time the notes emerge, they're in big fat belches. When you play an accordian, you're moving the bellows in and out all the time, so when you play it on a synthesizer, just using the swell peddle to make it louder and softer makes the illusion more believeable."

LaVey hardly plays the top 40, nor does he play "elevator music." His single qualification for good music is strict: it has to be evocative. *"I refuse to be a 'musician's musician.'"* The lyrical, romantic tunes of the 30's and 40's predominate, though he also uses effective music from the 20's or 60's, as long as it fits his criterion. Music has been a consistent element in LaVey's life and he has always played songs largely neglected, the real "occult" music.

*"If I didn't have these keyboards I don't know what I'd do. It's the one thing that acts as a kind of anchor. Whenever someone starts minimizing me, and I hear it so much that I start believing it myself, I can sit at these keyboards and I can do things that no one else can do — remember songs that no one else remembers, play songs in a way that they aren't played any more."*

LaVey admired the almost exagerrated technique of organist Paul Carson on his "Bridge to Dreamland" radio program in the 30's and 40's. Carson also did the music for other shows, like "One Man's Family" and "I Love A Mystery." Professional musicians used to joke about how LaVey would milk emotion from a song. "I like 'No Bullshit' music," says LaVey. "Straight renditions, not jazzed up or be-bopped; but *augmented, supercharged,* to bring out the real strengths of the piece. It's all in the arrangement and orchestration. People don't play that way anymore except in Las Vegas supperclubs, Italian picnics, Jewish weddings — Klezmorim — and junior high bands ."

Consider that when you are listening to a piece of music largely forgotten by the rest of the world, the chance that someone else is listening to that same music at the same time you are is not very high. If it is evocative music, it is all the better because, if there *is* indeed some unnameable power we can tap into, your heightened experience of that music at that instant in time will shine forth like a beacon. LaVey feels this uniqueness is essential for a successful ritualization. "Tiny Tim was a wonderful medium for those old songs, sung straight — he learned them by listening to scratchy old records. He was too far *ahead* of his time."

Considering Anton LaVey's more diabolical concentrations, one might suspect that he would inevitably blend these two obsessions in experimentation. In fact, he's been doing just that for a very long time — and credits music as the catalyst for some of his most successful magical workings.

His explorations on the physical effects of music led him to Tesla's work with his "black box." It was a small device that produced "black sound," vibrations at such a low frequency as to be hardly audible to the human ear but which have a disastrous effect on any structure that the sound is focused on, causing it to vibrate against itself and eventually break apart. It's the sound of earthquakes and a lion's roar, a dull throb which is felt more than heard. To test his black box, Tesla attached it to a building under construction not far from his workshop. Upon his return, he found the building had suffered severe structural damage.

LaVey experiments with "white" and "pink" noise, as well as "black sound." He incorporates Pythagorean theories and the advantages of Just Intonation for bringing out textures in sounds by pitching each tone separately. Blending this knowledge with the emotional reactions he has observed in people, he develops methods of creating effects with music that go far beyond simply playing the tunes. "Music is a complete evocation — like a smell. It can bring an entire memory and feeling back to you in a rush. Much more complete than even a photograph. You allow yourself a certain visual distance with photos — not music. It envelopes you — there's no way to escape it. It's a great test of sensitivity — the degree of reaction to music. I use it all the time. I call it my 'Music Test.'

"People today don't want to hear the truth. They're really afraid of tranquility and silence — they're afraid they might begin to understand their own motivations too well. They keep a steady stream of noise going to protect themselves, to build a wall against the truth. Like African natives, beating on their drums, rattling their gourds, shaking their bells to scare off evil spirits. As long as there's enough noise, there's nothing to fear — or hear. But they will listen. Times are changing."

There are, according to LaVey, certain irresistable "Ur song" reactions universal to all beings on a very primitive level. This response crosses over into animals, even plants. "Chord progressions of one kind will make us laugh, while another will make us blue. Hitler used this kind of universality to his advantage with his impelling marches of the Third Reich. The music of Herbert Windt and others during WWII in Germany will have to eventually be recognized as great music.

"Unusual applications for commonplace things — thousands of people have synthesizers but how many use them the way I do? Right now it's practically illegal to use keyboards for my purposes; it might as well be written on the books. Evoking emotions and energy with songs like 'I Remember You' might as well be against the law. How often do you hear that kind of music on the radio?" Since LaVey has learned most of the songs he plays by ear, and he is not limited to a small repertoire of songs, he doesn't rely on sequencers. He likes the freedom to tap into whatever tune he might feel compelled to play at the moment. When he records his music, he usually does it in one take, allowing his intuition to guide him, to use the spontaneity of a live performance.

*"I probably won't play a song the same way tomorrow as I play it today. Only a pitchman says the same thing the same way twice, without varying a word. If music is a language, why don't people use it with the same subtlety, nuance, and facility as they do the spoken language? Probably because they don't verbalize with the same vocabulary and tone they once did. It has been said that a people's character is reflected in their music. Our culture is a perfect example. If people here walk around using one-syllable words with no color, no variety, no shading, how can we expect our musical language to be any different?"*

LaVey is disdainful of the keyboard music composed and performed today. "It's like the emperor's new clothes — sure they can sit and make wild noises on their syntheisizers and call it music — who questions? But ask them to pull up a chair and play 'Gal in Calico' or 'Temptation,' or even a straight dramatic version of 'The Star-Spangled Banner' and they can't do it. They're too pretentious. They can't just play songs."

Rock music isn't any better in LaVey's estimation. He sees modern rock as part of the current desensitizing and de-emotionalizing trend of the country. LaVey does have a kind word for Sid Vicious' version of "My Way." "It was so far out that it really sounded inspired. It fit. The song is enjoyable to listen to again." As for the links between rock music and Satanism in the form of "Black Metal" — if the music Anton LaVey plays and loves is any indication, there is no association between the two. As outlined in *The Satanic Bible,* Satanic principles emphasize an increase in physical awareness, not the deadening of the senses that loud music causes. About the myth of Satanic influence in rock music, LaVey says, "They needed an adversary. What would they do without us?

"Actually Satanic symbology is the only thing that has kept rock music alive for the past few years. Since MTV, bands rely entirely on visuals. What else can they sell? They certainly can't rely on any musical merit. Kids buy records as badges of affiliation now. They say themselves that they don't listen to the words, they just like what the visuals communicate — and Satanic imagery is the most dramatic. Plus they get the feeling of rebellion which most kids seem to need. The music industry had nothing else to sell so they reached for the most powerful icons they could think of — Satanism. David Lee Roth even included a little in-joke in the title of one of his 1987 hits, using the last words from *The Satanic Bible,* 'Yankee Rose.' But all these bands, with the single exception of King Diamond, who has the courage to openly support Satanism and makes no secret of his dedication, stridently deny charges that they are advocating actual Devil worship — it's all in fun. It's the old story of using the Devil's name to make your millions but not wanting to play the Devil's game."

Young people now have been exposed to Satanic symbols all their lives. They call themselves Satanists because it's cool, it's rebellious, and all their friends are doing it. They give the sign of the horns as a high sign, a greeting, like the peace sign in the 60's. LaVey wrote in *The Satanic Bible,* "The sign of the horns shall appear to many, now, rather than the few" but he had no idea how prophetic those words would become. But for every young person you see holding up the sign of the horns at rock concerts, ignorant of the Satanic thought behind it, there are others who hold communion with the true Satanic principles in private, between classes at Harvard or before a big meeting at the office.

Satanic music is not heavy metal rock and roll. The real Satanic influence is seen in the revival of the lyrical, evocative music LaVey has been playing all his life. "The music industry has gone as far as it can in one direction — all that does is create a climate for a backlash, in this case a return to lyrical music. When people get a taste of evocative music, they drink it up like a thirsty man gulps water. It is so satisfying compared with the noise that has been foisted on us for the past 30 years.

"The revival has already started. All it needs is a name. You can't market anything without a catchy label. Someone smart will come along and give it a name so record stores can set up new sections of records. The music I advocate is not big band, not jazz, not soul, not swing. These are straight renditions of popular songs that probably had a short burst of attention on the radio when they were first released, but then were forgotten because maybe they didn't quite become million-sellers or they weren't featured in the right movie, even though they might have been used as background music. They're already being recorded by singers like Linda Ronstadt and Pia Zadora — and the number of re-released songs by Rudy Vallee, Buddy Clark, Al Jolson, and Nat King Cole are growing larger all the time. It's inevitable."

Of course, when everyone is playing this "new" music, one aspect of the magic will be gone: exclusivity. With this music playing everywhere, the power of its uniqueness will be less. "That's all right," replies LaVey. "The emotional strength of the music itself will never be diluted, as long as it's played straight. Everyone will make the great discovery and try to sell it back to me in a new package. It's always a trade-off. But the world will be a much more pleasant place to live."

**Top Right:** Playing hooky; probably before an evening stint at the poolhall.

**Top Left:** Young Anton LaVey seen with scarf later "stolen" by Marilyn Monroe.

**Bottom Left:** LaVey liked to dress in zoot-style clothes, and was derisively labeled a hood or pachuco.

**Bottom Right:** LaVey in carny pitchman's jacket. Note loud handpainted tie.

By 1948, when LaVey was playing in the pits of Los Angeles burlesque houses (like the Mayan Theater where he met Marilyn), he had already established that blending of Satanic and *film noir* imagery that would become his trademark.

**Top Left:** LaVey's circus I.D. photo.

**Top Right:** The scar Anton received in a knife fight is clearly visible on his cheek.

**Bottom:** LaVey was encouraged in his interest in firearms during the time he spent in newly-developed Las Vegas with his uncle's "business associates," Bugsy Siegel and Meyer Lansky.

**TOP:** LaVey in his early 20's at the Mighty Wurlitzer theatre organ
**BOTTOM:** Scene of one of Anton's earliest erotic imprints, the Sally Rand Live Nude Ranch at the 1939 World's Fair on Treasure Island.

LaVey and friend.

In the Clyde Beatty circus, Anton worked his way up from cage boy to lion trainer. By the time he was 17, LaVey was handling eight Nubian lions and four Bengal tigers in the big cage at once. During his circus and carnival days, he made friends with many unusual characters like Lou Jacobs and his midget sidekick, Jimmy Armstrong.

Here, Anton plays for one of his Friday night gatherings, a year before shaving his head and establishing the Church of Satan on Walpurgisnacht, 1966.

LaVey and live-in friend.

**TOP**: LaVey with *Weird Tales* literary cronies (from left) George Haas, Robert Barbour Johnson and Clark Ashton Smith.

**BOTTOM:** The late Dr. Cecil Nixon, with his carved automaton, Isis, who played a repertoire of 3000 tunes on voice command. Only Dr. Nixon knew the precise adjustments necessary to activate her, and passed on his secrets to Anton.

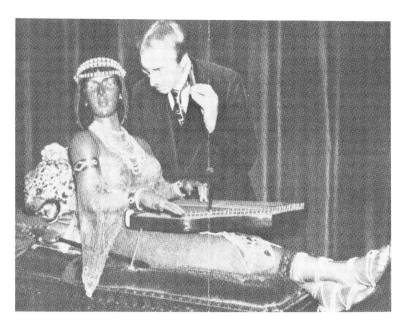

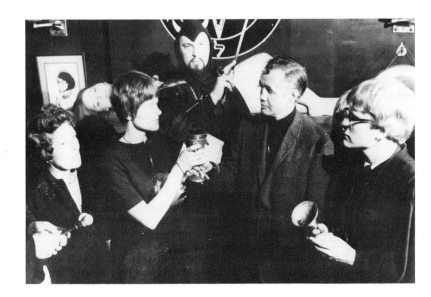

**TOP:** The first internationally publicized Satanic wedding. LaVey joins socialite Judith Case and radical journalist John Raymond in unholy matrimony. Photo by Joe Rosenthal, who shot the flagraising on Iwo Jima.

**BOTTOM:** The first public Satanic funeral, conducted for Edward D. Olsen. Kenneth Anger is the black-robed warlock seen at center of photo.

**TOP:** Murderess Susan Atkins emerges from a coffin in her pre-Manson vampiric role in LaVey's Topless Witches' Review.

**BOTTOM:** The Devil's chief spokesman.

LaVey is seen with his personal magical symbol, an inverted pentagram thrust through by a lightning bolt.

LaVey stands on the front steps of his Black House with Togare, Anton's Nubian lion, a constant companion in the early days of the Church of Satan.

The Black Pope encourages a nubile acolyte to earthly indulgence. Many such photographs were published in men's magazines during the early years of the Church of Satan.

Anton and devoted disciple, Jayne Mansfield. Inset: LaVey, Jayne and family. Photos by Walter Fischer.

**TOP:** LaVey's photograph of his androids in agony.
**BOTTOM:** A known LaVey haunt, near Calais.

**TOP:** Anton with one of his early paintings, circa 1955.

**BOTTOM:** A representative photograph from LaVey's brief career as a police photographer for the San Francisco Police Department.

**TOP:** LaVey steps out of one of his cars, assisted by his longtime driver and major-domo, Tony.

**BOTTOM:** Anton's ghostly 1937 coffin-nosed Cord.

**TOP:** This famous deathbed sketch of John Barrymore was drawn by John Dekker on a piece of brown wrapping paper. Dekker and Barrymore were part of a cabal of Hollywood writers, actors and bon vivants, which also included W. C. Fields, Ben Hecht and Gene Fowler, who wrote odes in homage to Satanic forces and took on the names of various devils.

**BOTTOM:** Though his true name was Boehm, Ellis Island officials characteristically renamed Anton's grandfather by his last place of residence, LeVey (France). He kept his new surname, changing the first "e" to "a."

**TOP:** LaVey on the 20th Century Fox lot with compatriot and writer Will Fowler (son of Gene Fowler), who is seen here practicing his phrenology.

**BOTTOM:** Anton with *Famous Monster*-man and sci-fi potentate, Forrest J. (Forry) Ackerman, left, and Hollywood historian, filmmaker and Magic Circle member, Kenneth Anger.

**TOP:** LaVey receiving mythic visions from *Dr. Phibes* creator, Bob Fuest.

**BOTTOM:** The High Priest seated between ufologist, computer scientist and iconoclast, Jacques Vallee (left), and French publisher *(Morning of the Magicians)*, spelunker, and Gnome King, Aime Michel.

**TOP:** Anton's first wife, Carole.

**BOTTOM:** Diane, LaVey's companion of 24 years.

**TOP LEFT:** Zeena Galatea LaVey. (Photo: Nick Bougas.)

**TOP RIGHT:** Karla Maritza LaVey on the cover of Brazil's most popular magazine.

**BOTTOM:** Stanton Zaharoff LaVey, Anton's grandson, born in 1978. (Photo: Gisela Getty.)

In this recent portrait, Anton Szandor LaVey counters the forces of the Invisible War. (Photo: Nick Bougas.)

# Chapter Twelve

# Hell on Reels

*"...no occultist has had as direct an impact upon formulaic cinematic presentations of satanism as has Anton Szandor LaVey. Ritual and esoteric symbolism are central elements in LaVey's church and the films in which he has had a hand contain detailed portrayals of satanic rites and are filled with traditional occult symbols. The emphasis upon ritual in the Church of Satan is 'intended to focus the emotional powers within each individual.' Similarly, the ornate ritualism that is central to LaVey's films may reasonably be seen as a mechanism to involve and focus the emotional experience of the cinema audience."*
— Sociologist Clinton R. Sanders, quoted by Burton Wolfe in his introduction to *The Satanic Bible*.

LaVey credits the confiscated *Schauerfilmen* he saw in Europe in 1945 for launching him on the trail of an actual Black Order of Satanists, existing not in some medieval witchhunter's mind but in Germany between the two world wars. The rituals LaVey eventually developed in the Church of Satan utilized the startling angles, conflicting sound frequencies and disturbing reflective planes introduced in those cinematic rites. Movie historians have also traced the roots of *film noir* to the same sources, so it's not surprising that the American *noir* genre of films is LaVey's element.

Roughly spanning from 1940 to the early 50's, *film noir* is best epitomized by films like the original *Scarface, M, Scarlet Street, The Harder They Fall, The Asphalt Jungle* and others, with sincere hoodlum anti-heroes prowling rain-slicked streets toward ever more treacherous circumstances. Charles Higham and Joel Greenberg conjured the foreboding intrigue of *film noir* in their 1968 book, *Hollywood in the Forties*:

"A dark street in the early morning hours, splashed with a sudden downpour. Lamps form haloes in the murk. In a walk-up room, filled with the intermittent flashing of a neon sign from across the street, a man is waiting to murder or be murdered...the specific ambience of *film noir*, a world of darkness and violence, with a central figure whose motives are usually greed, lust and ambition, whose world is filled with fear, reached its fullest realization in the Forties...."[21]

"To me," LaVey states, "*film noir* is epitomized in a film like *The Gangster.* It's almost like a surreal stage set; the angles are so disquieting and the whole feeling is so oppressive and claustrophobic." In the 1981 *Book of Movie Lists,* LaVey numbers Barry Sullivan's lead role among ten highly Satanic screen portrayals, and describes *The Gangster* this way:

"This is a small and neglected film. It's almost a lost one. It opens and ends with a satanic statement, and you know that the man, played by Barry Sullivan, is doomed. This is not a Legs Diamond or an Al Capone story; it's a psychological tale about a gangster who is perhaps too cultured and too sensitive and too kind to be a ruthless gangster. He has risen from the slums into the only role he could, into his destiny. Much like Lucifer, the fallen angel, he finds himself a victim of his circumstance. At the end, just before he's shot down in the rain, which is typical *film noir,* he's castigated by this young girl whose father wants to hide him. She refuses him refuge, and just before he plunges into the rain to his death, he delivers a bitter diatribe.... It's a purely satanic soliloquy, of a victim in a role he should never have been thrust into."[22]

Among the other Satanic portrayals on his list, LaVey selects Edward G. Robinson's roles in *The Sea Wolf* and *Key Largo* as reflective of the essential satanic attitude, as LaVey interprets it. "Wolf Larsen [in *The Sea Wolf*] ... only degrades those who have already degraded themselves; he brutalizes only those who know only brutalization; he preys upon those who deserve to be preyed upon. Robinson, in this, is a purely Satanic figure."[23] LaVey adds: "Robinson had always wanted to play Wolf Larsen, from the time he first read Jack London's book. He was delighted to be chosen for the role;

but he lost a number of liberal friends once he did. My reaction to the film has paralleled my growing disdain for the human race over the years. When I first saw it, I thought, 'The character of Larsen is too brutal.' The next time a saw the film a few years later, I could understand the brutality a bit more — it didn't seem so extreme. Finally by the next viewing, I'd developed a real empathy for Wolf Larsen!"

Regarding Johnny Rocco, the character Robinson plays in *Key Largo,* LaVey describes him as, "a very self-centered, refusing-to-go-under hoodlum and totally hedonistic ... sadistic, brutal, and at the same time very satanic, and at the end pathetic." LaVey is so taken by Robinson's characterization in *Key Largo* that he is wont to borrow a couple lines from that film while making conversation. "All through the film, the only interesting characters are the villains! Bogart and Bacall are used merely as one-dimensional, cardboard good guys, playing 'straight men' for the gangsters' satanic one-liners. Barrymore's part is written as a crotchety but honorable old coot confined to a wheelchair. Mean 'ol Rocco shows no respect for the man's handicap. When Barrymore harangues Robinson and threatens, 'If I could only get out of this wheelchair...,' rising menacingly, Rocco laughs and replies, 'If you could get out of that chair, old man, you wouldn't be talking that way!'

"Robinson actually did a number of Satanic films — *Hell on Frisco Bay, Little Caesar, The Night Has a Thousand Eyes* — most of his roles had satanic overtones. In his personal life, he was an avid art collector and had one of the finest private collections in the world until he lost it in a divorce suit. Chernobog — the devil in Walt Disney's *Fantasia,* the one who looms up from the mountaintop during the 'Night on Bald Mountain' sequence was actually inspired by Edward G. Robinson's features, not Lugosi's as is usually believed. He exuded the diabolical perhaps better than any other actor — with the possible expansion of that statement to include Erich Von Stroheim. He was an actor, and director, who cast himself in some of the finest satanic roles yet filmed — *The Great Flammarion, The Great Gabbo,* and *Sunset Boulevard,* among others. His arrogance and swagger didn't win him any friends but he also allowed his satanic sadness and doomed romanticism to come through."

Another actor LaVey mentions as particularly attuned is Walter Huston: "... his most Satanic role was in *The Treasure of the Sierra Madre,* where he was the only one who came out unscathed. He was the old geezer who knew the score, who was nobody's fool when it came down to survival ... Walter Huston certainly had finely honed Satanic sensibilities, exhibited not only in his acting but also in this wonderful recording he once did of a sad little tune called 'September Song,' a love theme about a man growing older and developing a romance with a young girl. It was written for him to sing onstage in *Knickerbocker Holiday*. Everyone was very enthused about having Huston in the play. When composer Kurt Weill wired Huston requesting what range he sang best in and what quality of voice he had, Huston wired back, 'No range. No voice.' The song was written and Huston recites it more than sings it — which is the best way it could be done. He sounds like a misty romantic saddened that he has so little time left with this girl he loves so deeply.

"Walter Huston's son, director John Huston, certainly showed Satanic vision in a lot of his films. One that stands out in my mind, that was obviously a kind of diatribe for him, is *Wise Blood*. It's based on the Flannery O'Connor story about this boy's adventures when he returns from the service to his Southern home and eventually starts, what he calls, 'The Church of Jesus Christ Without Christ.' Just relating the story doesn't do the film justice — the terribly detailed characters are what make the film excruciating. They're painfully realistic! So stupid and intense and tragic. There's no one in the whole film you'd want to identify with. Harry Dean Stanton does a fabulous job as a fake blind preacher, with a real lout of a daughter who's borderline retarded — but so are most of the other characters. The worst part is that some people watch it and don't get the joke — they think everybody's supposed to be like that! It's a finely-wrought film, and certainly satanic in that Huston was able to portray all these sad, stupid people exactly as they really are! — a real misanthropic exercise. It's so realistic it borders on the surrealistic."

To reassure us all that certain established "scary" actors are indeed what he would deem Satanic, LaVey points to Vincent Price who, he feels, is a Satanist both on and off the screen. In his roles in *The Abominable Dr. Phibes* and *Dr. Phibes Rises Again* (1971 and '72), Price played the title role of Dr. *Anton* Phibes — more than a mere coincidence, the movie's Anton plays dramatic organ and hatches a diabolical plan to avenge his beloved wife's death at the hands of incompetent doctors. In *Movie Lists,* Anton compliments Vincent Price's portrayal in which "he pulled out all the stops and created a camped-up essence of Satanic characterization." Anton goes on to mention another of Price's films he admires: *The Masque of the Red Death*. "That's an evocative film with some wonderfully Satanic dialogue that Vincent Price delivers as only he can. Off screen, Price is a debonair devil with some truly dark, obsessional aspects in his life."

Peter O'Toole in *The Ruling Class* is another of LaVey's favorite devilish portrayals: "This is an oddball film that they tried to sell as a comedy, but it's really a tragedy with comedic overtones. O'Toole's transition in the film starts with him being quite naive, a total innocent, and takes him to the brutalizing total cynic at the end, when diabolically, he takes on the role of the devil incarnate. He starts the film thinking he's Jesus Christ, but he's very anti-Christ because he's blasphemous despite himself. And, of course, everyone thinks him insane. Then as he transcends, or descends, from the Christ-identification to thinking he's Jack the Ripper, he finds that people more readily accept him, and rejoice that he's now cured of his insanity. He's normal now that he's a real rotten son-of-a-bitch who dresses in black, advocates torture, and kills people. At the end there's that blasphemous scene where he's leading the decaying corpses singing 'Onward Christian Soldiers'." LaVey adds: "*The Ruling Class* is one of the all-time great Satanic films. And it also happens to have one of the best authentic cake-walk scenes I've seen on celluloid, which Peter O'Toole leads to the tune of 'Dry Bones.' The only other film that has as much of that perplexing blend of comedy, musical and tragedy has been *Pennies From Heaven,* with Steve Martin. This was a real box office bomb because people went who were Steve Martin fans, expecting to see him being a funny guy. He's not — he's rather sad and sincere. It's set in the 30's and he really fits into the era surprisingly well. As in *The Ruling Class,* the music selected for *Pennies From Heaven* is terrific. They used period recordings, including the title song recorded by Arthur Tracy, who happens to be one of my favorites. The sets and characters were 100% authentic. It was filmed in almost a sepia wash to enhance the mood of the period. Again it's a wonderfully sad, disturbing film."

LaVey can, and will, talk for hours about films — their relative merits, anecdotes about various actors and actresses, comparing directors and cinematographers — and has built up probably one of the finest collections of obscure films in the country. LaVey reasons if a movie is easily obtainable from the corner video shop there's no point in keeping a copy — but he has literally hundreds of cassettes chock full of rare or "extinct" films, on tape and celluloid, that are not to be found in any other film vaults.

As might be expected, LaVey's main interests have always been in the dark, the disturbing and the forgotten films. He is responsible for reviving a number of films that would have forever languished on dusty shelves in distributors' warehouses. *Freaks,* one such film Anton resurrected, "had to go underground for many years, even though it was produced at MGM as a sort of competitive film for Universal's *Frankenstein.* [Tod] Browning used real freaks and malformed people, which disgusted not only much of MGM but audiences as well. It's purely Satanic in that audience sympathies lie with the freaks themselves, and the villains are the straight people, who are the cruel exploiters of human misery. You cheer at the end when the freaks rise up and turn their [tormenter] into one of them." *Terror of Tiny Town,* another of LaVey's discoveries, also utilized unusual actors and actresses with an all-midget cast. Not only is it an archetypical western storyline but it also contains some good tunes including one Anton particularly admires — "Mr. Jack and Mrs. Jill."

When LaVey first started pushing the more unique movies — what many would now call "schlock," or "low budget/no budget" classics — there was no underground appreciation of the genre as there is now. "I remember when, at my insistence, Herschell Gordon Lewis was approached about re-releasing some of his films like *2000 Maniacs* and *Color Me Blood Red,* he couldn't imagine anyone being interested in those films. He thought we were putting him on." In an entry reviewing *2000 Maniacs* for the *1978-79 Audio Brandon Film Catalogue,* LaVey described Lewis' film as "A horror version of *Brigadoon...* (a) tale of a Southern town which was savagely destroyed by Union troops and rises from its swampy site every hundred years.... Because, rather than in spite, of its low budget and unknown performers, amateurism transcends into chilling super-realism." In describing Lewis for the catalogue, LaVey described his attitudes regarding the whole genre of "schlock" — "The discerning viewer will find Lewis' films to be much more than superficial gore, rather an eerie reflection of the repressed sado-masochism in us all that even the smallest voice inside seldom admits to. From *Bonnie and Clyde* to *The Exorcist*, from *The Wild Bunch* to *Jaws*, fragments of Lewis' kaleidoscope radiate."

"There's a whole genre of films that are just little evocative low-budget gems that I certainly wouldn't call schlock but that are also being revived as a consequence of more attention in those directions. Director Curtis Harrington's first movie, *Night Tide,* filmed around the Santa Monica pier and Venice, California, in the late 50's, is a psychologically intricate story about a young sailor (Dennis Hopper) who falls in love with a mermaid. *Carnival of Souls* is another richly evocative film that has been completely lost until recently. Producer/director Herk Harvey did industrial films and this was his brilliant excursion into a world of nightmares. It's just wonderful to see these precious works of art being finally given the attention they merit."

With the founding of the Church of Satan in 1966 came a new excuse to film "unspeakable rites" and "wild sabbath orgies dedicated to Satan." There has been a ripeness for evil characters since LaVey had been thrust in the public eye just as he, himself, actualized certain previous fictional characters in lifestyle and looks, like "Ming the Merciless" from the Flash Gordon movie series and Count Zaroff in *The Most Dangerous Game.* Out of all of the dross, LaVey points to a handful of movies that contain better than average Satanic visuals, or that portray Satanists in a manner closer to the truth. *"The Black Cat* and *The Seventh Victim* are certainly two pre-Church of Satan movies I would consider worthwhile examples of the way true Satanists behave. Val Lewton's *The Leopard Man,* from a story by the champion proponent of darkness, Cornell Woolrich, certainly has some supremely satanic moments in it. *Bell, Book and Candle* at least portrayed witches as something other than ugly old crones. I like the idea of the children being inhabited by the dying Satanists in *The Brotherhood of Satan,* a film I was unfortunately called in on too late to change the extravagant altar they'd already spent too much money on to rip it apart for authenticity's sake. But most of the post-1966 fare I would categorize, with John Fritscher (author of *Popular Witchcraft)* as what he terms 'Pop-Ugh' ("...the deliberate commercialization of the Pop that people like spontaneously.") The same goes for the endless occult T.V. movies and magic-oriented T.V. series spin-offs Fritscher lists — *Bewitched, Nanny and the Professor, I Dream of Jeannie, My Favorite Martian, The Ghost and Mrs. Muir, The Munsters, The Addams*

*Family, The Flying Nun, Topper, One Step Beyond, Outer Limits* — any of them that you see listed in the *T.V. Guide* and your immediate reaction is 'Ugh! Not another one!'

"Yet I know a whole generation of Satanists grew up watching those things, so I shouldn't complain. That's why *Dark Shadows* and *The Twilight Zone* are two television series I choose not to include in my 'completely worthless' list. I recognize that *Dark Shadows*, with its positive characterizations of vampires and werewolves, served as an incredibly influential ECI experience for hundreds of thousands of then-school age kids who are growing up to align themselves 100% with my philosophy! It's probably the single most universal thread among Satanists of that age group — an identification with the characters on that show. *The Twilight Zone* and *Night Gallery* may not have thrilled me because I'd been lucky enough to be around when *Weird Tales* was being published — I saw most of those stories in their original form. But people who were 10, 13, 15 years old when those shows were first broadcast were just as fascinated and compelled to them as a personal expression of their own secret obsessions as *I* was when I was young. I'd be crazy to overlook the influence such series have had on the present and future of Satanism."

When LaVey describes the best recent films communicating Satanic attitudes, chances are they won't have "devil" or "Satan" in the title, and they probably won't even contain scenes of actual rituals, in the accepted definition of the word. "The original *Texas Chainsaw Massacre,* in which all the victims are deserving ones, is more along the lines of truly Satanic. Another authentically diabolical film in which I actually got some credit was *The Car.* The automobile in that film was modeled after one of mine, right down to the rumbling exhaust system and meatcleaver fenders. That's a very gratifying film to watch because, again, comparing the relative worthiness of the victims with the sinister, dramatic quality of this mysterious car, the audience is rooting for the car. *Death Wish* was a catalyst for a lot of Satanic feelings — where the hunted becomes the hunter. But every competent sorcerer knows that's the only way to survive magically. There was a movie about a young man, *Evilspeak,* who uses a computer at military school and a *Necronomicon*-like grimoire to summon demons to do his bidding. He's basically a bright, well-mannered kid. But after jealous schoolmates kill his puppy, which is the only creature in the world who understands him, he unleashes his demons in their direction to get revenge."

Hollywood will no doubt be disappointed to learn that the High Priest of the Church of Satan never saw *The Exorcist* all the way through. "Nor do I want to. I did see *The Omen* all the way through, though. They negotiated with me to be able to film a scene in the original Church of Satan ritual chamber by the stone fireplace, where the main character, Damien, would be formally baptized into the Devil's flock. They wanted to fly the boy in from England; they even said they could just bring in a cardboard cut-out of him standing there if I didn't want the place messed up. I said no dice. The place got enough curiosity seekers — all the occupants needed was a new rash of tourists 'looking for Damien.'"

Is there, then, a concise definition of the "Satanic film?" "That can be many things," according to LaVey, "from a delightful Bobby Breen film to an excruciating Wheeler and Woolsey movie to an obscure schlock film like *Mother's Day* or *Tourist Trap.* Is it blasphemous in itself — saying something no one else has had the guts to say? Are the 'good guys' really deserving assholes who get their comeuppance while the 'bad guys' — Satanists or otherwise — are actually more innately moral than those accepted by society to be All Right? Is the film practically illegal to watch now because of 'objectionable' content — not just pornographic but offensive to the status quo? Is it nearly impossible to find now? These are a few of the elements that can make a film Satanic. The great Satanic films are yet to be made. As with so many avenues concerning *true* diabolism now — the streets are paved with gold."

It seems, though, that LaVey is constantly disappointed by modern films. "I've tried to watch them, Lord knows I've tried. But each time I watch a new film it depresses me, no matter how Satanic the theme is supposed to be. I always have to have an antidote right afterwards — a good Marx Brothers movie or something to rinse out the palate. Modern horror films are nothing more than video splatter versions of amusement park dark rides, complete with spider webs falling over your face. The purpose isn't to communicate anything or even to entertain; it's to challenge your audience's nerves and stomach — see how long they can take it."

"Every day a great actor or actress or director or screenwriter dies," comments LaVey, "forever. There is *no one* to replace them. Hollywood has become a very barren place creatively. What a terribly tragic, sad thing to be of an earlier era, trapped in the wrong time and having to watch all these people die before me. All these vestiges, links with the past, who have seen, touched, experienced — who will eventually pass completely from the Earth. Leaving only the cold, dead, unfeeling, fake world."

> *"My sins? My sins are that I wasn't tough enough. I wasn't low or dirty enough, I should have trusted no one; never loved a girl. I should have smashed first. That's the way the world is."*
> — Shubunka (Barry Sullivan) in *The Gangster*

# Chapter Thirteen

# Angles of Madness

*"From prisms wrought within the twilit grotto I speak through angles mirrored with thoughts senescent and supreme. O learn the Law, my brothers of the night — the Great Law and the Lesser Law. The Great Law brings the balance and doth persist without mercy. The Lesser Law abideth as the key, and the shining Trapezoid is the door!"*

— Anton Szandor LaVey, *"Die elektrischen Vorspiele," The Satanic Rituals* [24]

Before the Church of Satan began, LaVey's group of savants which he called the "Magic Circle" experimented with rituals exploring the realms of angles as passageways to the fourth dimension. Those first members wore a trapezoid surrounded by a bat-winged demon that could be removed to reveal the inverted pentagram/666 design beneath. (In 1966, after the formation of the Church of Satan, this symbol was replaced by the now-familiar Baphomet.) The Magic Circle emerged as the governing body of the Church of Satan, known as the "Order of the Trapezoid" (see the Sixth Enochian Key, *The Satanic Bible).* The Order of the Trapezoid continues as the inner circle within the Church of Satan today (red trapezoidal membership cards were issued early on but proved too unwieldy for wallets and were redesigned sans trapezoid). In describing the requirements for a Satanic altar, LaVey specifies a trapezoidal shape, three to four feet high and five to six feet long. At least two Satanic rituals pay homage to angles ("The Law of the Trapezoid — *Die elektrischen Vorspiele,"* and "The Ceremony of the Nine Angles") while many others include passing references to haunted geometry as well.

In *The Satanic Bible,* LaVey reveals that John Dee scryed the Enochian Keys in the early 1600's using a many-faceted crystal trapezohedron, and not a crystal ball as it is generally believed. It was through this angled crystal that Dee perceived the 19 Keys (or "Calls"), which LaVey claims have been deliberately mistranslated through the years due to "metaphysical constipation." The first "blasphemous" English translation of the Calls, as well as the original Enochian, are laid out in the final section of *The Satanic Bible.* "Now the crystal clears, and the 'angels' are seen as 'angles' and the windows to the fourth dimension are thrown open — and to the frightened, the Gates of Hell."[25]

For those of us who may not immediately apprehend profound magical significance in a common geometrical form, LaVey has published several articles for our enlightenment. To begin at the beginning: a trapezoid can be described as a triangle with its top chopped off. Pull a dollar bill out of your pocket and look at the back side. The stone edifice with the eye in the triangle hovering over it is a trapezoid.

The shape conveys special magic wherever it is seen. Although the Egyptians may have entombed themselves in pyramids, the Aztecs and Mayans made sacrifices to their Gods atop the grand stone trapezoidal temples. Every Charles Addams-style haunted house is topped with a mansard roof — a perfect trapezoid. While fairytale castles are usually envisioned as crowned with conical spires, wicked queens have always lived in stark, angled, well-fortified monoliths. Other buildings echoing the trapezoidal shape include the black John Hancock Building in Chicago (which now stands over LaVey's birthplace), and the brooding Ennis House in Los Angeles, designed by Frank Lloyd Wright to resemble a looming Mayan temple. Old-style coffins were trapezoidal (two placed bottom to bottom), as is the Golden Gate Bridge, viewed from the side. Childhood research revealed to LaVey that the trapezoidal form was used continuously in the architecture of war.

A 14-year-old LaVey expanded his theories on visual patterns when he discovered *The Command to Look* by William Mortensen. Ostensibly a guide to picture-taking, the small book forever changed the way LaVey perceived the world around him. In it, Mortensen explains composition and what makes a compelling photo or scene. He puts forth certain visual laws which LaVey immediately applied to areas beyond photography. What Mortensen termed "dominant mass" coincided precisely with what LaVey was formulating about the hulking visual (and therefore magical) power of the trapezoid. Beyond that LaVey learned other aspects of the command to look — the necessity of archetypal themes, such as Sex, Sentiment or Wonder; and Mortensen's "Is, not does" principle, which explains that true visual power is attained by timeless composition of elements than simply shooting away at movement.. LaVey was so intrigued by the possibilities that he began applying Mortensen's ideas in his own drawings and paintings. One painting, for example, titled "The Sentinel," shows a murky trapezoidal building far in the background, a sorcerer silhouetted in its doorway. The open tower of the house emits an unearthly blast of light into the night as a drone-like winged demon fills most of the foreground, sent out to do the sorcerer's bidding.

Putting Mortensen's theories to practice well-prepared LaVey for the position he was to assume with the San Francisco Police Department. Not only was he trained in effective photography, but by the time LaVey started handling "800" calls, he had already formulated possible explanations for compelling spots, "haunted" houses, cursed areas and mystery spots. Perhaps the nation's first "ghostbuster," LaVey was excited to test his theories on actual haunted spots.

From his carnival days, LaVey knew how contrived visual puzzles like mystery spots were constructed to use angles and false perspectives to fool the eye and throw off people's equilibrium. Perhaps blighted houses, LaVey speculated, are caused by sloppy builders or architects who did not realize the effect of weird angles to the occupants of the building. After investigating and photographing murder and suicide sites, LaVey surmised that certain abnormal configurations can lead people already predisposed to madness to perform aberrant acts. "Angles and space-planes that provoke anxiety — that is, those not harmonious with the visual orientation—will engender aberrant behavior, translate: change. Exceptions occur where a sort of reverse polarity exists in a creature — extreme mental imbalance or perversity, or perhaps even extreme rationality and awareness."[26]

LaVey expanded the ideas to apply to businesses as well, where something is "off" just enough to turn people away. "Sometimes you walk into a room and there's something at an odd angle, disturbing somehow, in an offensive position that needs to be changed. That one thing turns everything off-kilter so badly you have to do something drastic about it. It's the story of blighted buildings. They just need a drastic change. I've seen buildings, often on corners, where businesses will move in maybe twice a year. They'll try everything. Nothing seems to succeed there. People would say the building is cursed. It is. Usually the angles are all wrong, thrusting outward when they should come inward to bring people in... A lot of times they can't do anything about it. They'd have to raze the building and start all over again."

By 1962, LaVey had formulated "The Law of the Trapezoid," and he explained it in a 1976 issue of *The Cloven Hoof*. "I had ample evidence that spatial concepts were not only able to affect those who were involved in visual confrontations, but far more insidiously, other parties with whom a viewer came into contact. As in any other form of contagion, family, friends, and co-workers are affected by the signals of anxiety projected by another. The most tranquil and stoical person can be drawn into a chaotic situation if his surroundings are sufficiently disturbing. Often I discovered that subtle aberrations had a more profound effect than readily-recognizable and overt spatial distortions."[27] It is often the case, one particular room of a blighted house might be identified as the "mad" room. Only one wall might be "off" vertically, but that would be enough to create an unconscious disturbance in its occupants. Whole buildings identified as "haunted" might prove to be infested with obtuse, untrue angles, useless nooks, or an erratic, asymmetrical exterior — perhaps one that had a crouching appearance or looked like it might have a face. Specific objects can trigger intense disturbances in a household as well if they are of an odd shape. Furniture, picture frames, murals, appliances, "jinxed" automobiles can be the catalyst for dreadful acts. As far back as the late 50's, LaVey was asked by an associate to design a proposed housing development. One can only guess what kind of horrors LaVey conjured up for the people who have lived in the houses he designed.

The same thing can happen naturally, LaVey found, with a peculiar rock formation, oddly-sloped hillside or inadvertently aberrant landscape. A particular setting, where angles are askew and one's equilibrium is thrown off, can be heightened by unusual natural phenomenon to a point where legends of hauntings become inevitable. Swamp gases, for instance, might produce "ignis Fatui," "need fires" or "vampire flames" — little blue flames formed by rotting wood in swamps. They are said to show where a vampire is sleeping, a suicide is buried, or where treasure is hidden, depending on which old wives' tale you believe. Such natural formations can cause beliefs that a particular place is magical, haunted or evil. Fairy rings, cairns (standing stones as seen in parts of Great Britain); unusually deep, dark woods; clearings in woods; edges of cliffs; mountaintops; coves; caves ... all these are expected settings for horror stories.

At LaVey's lectures on "Time Warps and Peculiar Areas," he discussed his personal research into areas like Devil's Slide, a coastside vortex just south of San Francisco where a number of unusual fatalities have occurred. LaVey has in his possession a manuscript of an unpublishable book by a crony, fully documenting the inexplicably gory history of the area. LaVey himself admits he has fallen under the winding road's spell on at least one occasion when he and Diane were traveling down the coast. It was all he could do to bring his car to a stop along the narrow shoulder. On Walpurgisnacht a year before the Church formed, a couple of LaVey's witches disregarded his warnings and their car went over the cliff. They landed on a ledge a few hundred feet down and barely survived.

Another natural vortex LaVey has discussed is the White's Hill area in Marin County north of San Francisco, which he describes as second to Devil's Slide. In a three or four mile stretch around the hill — particularly on one "Death Curve" — there have been a number of unexplained car accidents. Surviving motorists have described a feeling of being pulled off the road by some unseen force. LaVey explains this is caused by an improperly graded roadbed. Habitual travelers on the road also claim it takes an unusually long time to get where you're going. It's a commonly accepted rule that you lose about an hour no matter how fast you try to drive.

Certain places attract people and creatures that are out of the ordinary, to say the least. LaVey claims that he has seen some odd creatures in the White's Hill area himself. Riding through once with Robert Barbour Johnson (the *Weird Tales* mystery writer), they saw a four-foot tall vulture eating meat on the side of the road. When they got even with it, it took to the air like a small plane, its wingspan was so large. Another time LaVey saw a thing scuttling across the road. He described it as being about the size of a large tarantula, but spiny, with beady black eyes, moving sideways like a crab — possibly a land crab. And there was the huge undulating caterpillar-like creature, about four feet long, which suddenly appeared from the bushes next to the road, ambled a few feet, then disappeared back into the foliage. What is remarkable, figures LaVey, is not the mysterious identity of these "creatures" but that they have a way of distractingly appearing at the critical onset of the "death curve."

The Land's End section of San Francisco, which LaVey had occasion to visit quite often when he was doing crime photography, consists of dangerously unstable, "molten" land. A young boy was walking with his girlfriend when the hillside came down and swallowed him alive. The girl contended that it happened so fast she barely had time to jump out of the way herself. The earth was quivering while rescuers searched for the body. LaVey has seen sections of the endless man-size tunnels which wind through the underbrush. The organic labyrinths are favorite spots for illicit and illegal activities, including the dumping of bodies. That seems most appropriate since the whole area was originally a cemetery. Human flesh is good fertilizer and seems to create real life in the very ground. Even today, the land keeps churning and slipping though the cause is nothing scientists seem able to analyze. Actually, says LaVey, all soil is a lot more active than we realize. As with many processes in nature, we don't notice the activity. But farmers use it to their advantage by leaving certain fields fallow for a season to allow the land time to rejuvenate itself. There are only two remaining tombstones to mark where the cemeteries once were, one built in an arch. Someone hung himself in the arch of the tombstone several years ago.

With a disciplined blend of ruthless skepticism and magical intrigue, LaVey debunks most claims in order to winnow out anomalous phenomena that might actually exist. The few truly unexplainable phenomena (beyond the effects of the ritual chamber) he has experienced have involved these weird vortexes. His theories to explain the few apparent dematerializations he's seen involve the tendency for all molecular structures to rotate in a singular direction. When items disappear, are gone for a few days, or months, then reappear in an exactly 180° opposite position, is it possible they're passing temporarily into another dimension then rotating back out again?

The Dunwich Horror of H.P. Lovecraft's story comes through the angles of a trapezohedron. "The Lurker on the Threshold", "The Haunter in the Dark" — the entire Cthulhu mythos and much of Lovecraft's poetry makes references to the slavering beasts that find passage into our world through angles. Many of Robert E. Howard's poems and horror stories, *The House on the Borderland* by William Hope Hodgeson, the supposedly apocryphal *Emerald Tablet of Thoth* (from which LaVey derived the text for *Die elektrischen Vorspiele)*, and, one of the most terrifying stories ever written, Frank Belknap Long's *Hounds of Tindalos,* all refer to the flux that angles induce.

Anton LaVey admits to encountering a Lovecraftian entity once on a foray he took deep into the caverns beneath Sutro Baths. The Baths were the largest indoor swimming pools in the world — designed by San Francisco's eccentric mayor, Adolph Sutro, to emulate the Roman baths with several different pools filled with various health-inducing substances. Catchbasins drew from the sea to pipe therapeutic waters into the seven large pools. "Climbing through a dislodged section of wainscoting of an abandoned dressing room, I explored far beyond the building's foundations, so far back I doubt if anyone had been there for decades. My flashlight revealed an expanse of muddy ground reaching beyond the beam of light into pitch darkness. It was as though I had entered a lightless amphitheater. I heard some guttural moaning noises ahead of me and smelled a terrible smell. Peering into the murk, I could barely make out a misshapen shadow moving in the darkness ahead of me. Then, the rustling or flapping of what sounded like huge wings. I had this overwhelming feeling I'd better get the hell out of there. I didn't stick around to see what it was."

If there are elementals we might call demons, existing independently on other dimensions, could they be attracted to such shapes as the trapezoid? Could trapezoids act as a catalyst to evoke or facilitate restless spirits or demons on other planes, creating a window in Einstein's space/time continuum? Might these demons, once summoned, feel most comfortable hidden away in some desolate area — barely accessible coves or bottomless caverns? Could it be that Lovecraft, Long and their ilk wrote fictionally of monsters only because such concepts would otherwise be considered unbelievable?

*"Know ye, all who dwell in the light of professed righteous-ness, that others who know the keys and the angles have opened the gate, and for turning back there is not time. Thou hast been given the key, but thy minds are small and grasp not the word. Therefore, list to the sounds, o ye out there, the great bell sounds of the baying of the Hounds. They are gaunt and unquenched, and through the great blazing Trapezoid they come, their eyes aglow with the fires of Hell!"*

— The Satanic Rituals.

# Chapter Fourteen

# The Witches' Sabbath

> "*You can't erase millions of years of human response, simply by knowing why you do the things you do.... Religions and ideologies will come and go, and the Games will begin and end, but man's basic nature will remain the same. Yet only through understanding himself will he be able to embrace and cherish the demon within him. Then he can revel in his nature and feeling glad, move on to the Final Solution.*"
> — final paragraph of *The Satanic Witch*.

Somewhere in ancient accounts of diablery, there's a phrase about a witch emerging from her hut with hair flowing free and feet bare. Nothing could be further from LaVey's contemporary brand of witchcraft. LaVey avers that women are undeniably different from men, and that a woman's power lies in exploitating her unique attributes. *The Satanic Witch* is LaVey's guide to enchantment, with advice for women on how to unashamedly use artifice, wile and guile to get whatever they desire.

LaVey has always preferred the image of a witch as an enchantress, one who fascinates, rather than the Feminist/Wiccan revision of witch as healer and midwife derived from the Anglo-Saxon *wica* ("wise one"). Feminist stridency aside, most dictionaries still define a witch either as a crone or an unusually attractive young woman. For many years, even after he founded the Church of Satan, LaVey tutored weekly "Witches' Workshops." *The Satanic Witch* compiles most of the field-tested techniques he presented in his classes.

But *The Satanic Witch* isn't just for women. The bibliography of the *Satanic Witch,* along with the original dedication page from *The Satanic Bible,* are considered crib sheets for LaVey's arcane authorities, and the curious have been known to scour the country for the rare books listed there. Also of interest to the non-witch is LaVey's "Synthesizer Clock" reproduced in *Satanic Witch's* endpapers, a typing system based on human physiognomy. The first quarter of *The Satanic Witch* explains how to identify types and learn their likes, dislikes and motivations — vital information gleaned from LaVey's own experience working circuses, carnivals and burlesque houses. It's a carny's view of human foibles, "trade secrets" usually reserved for those initiated into the mysteries of the backlot.

LaVey's Synthesizer Clock takes as its foundation the body-typing systems of Sheldon, Kretschmer and others, and blends them with the traditional magical elements of Fire, Air, Water and Earth. "I provide broad generalities. The idea behind typing is learning to see a billboard-sized canvas so you can recognize the same aspects in a postage stamp. If you train yourself to see the most exaggerated examples then you can recognize certain retrieval cues for personality types when you see them to a lesser degree in other people. If you hone your skills of observation, everything can tell you about a person. That's what is called "cold-reading" in the carnival. For instance, if you see black tennis shoes on a young girl it indicates that she would be inclined to wear entirely black outfits and therefore probably has an interest in the Dark Side, witchcraft, Satanism. Tattoos on a woman's hand can indicate previous biker or gang involvement, hence a rebellious nature. Pay attention to tiny clues. That's what I train my witches to do."

LaVey creates a continuum formed around a clock so each individual can be described as a "nine o'clock" type or a "four o'clock" type, etc.. Starting at the top, a pure twelve o'clock type is described as the masculine archetype — wide shoulders, narrow hips, short legs, firm flesh, domineering, aggressive, always onstage, impulsive and authoritarian. A pure Fire type — flamboyant in the truest sense of the word. A pure Air type, at three o'clock, has a narrow, stick-like build with translucent·skin and sinewy strength. He's intellectual, a thinker rather than a doer, technically-mind, a hair-splitter and a social critic. Blue suits him best. The six o'clock Water type is the pure Feminine element. Just the opposite from the twelve o'clock, she has narrow shoulders and wide hips, a nipped-in waist creating well-defined curves, long legs, marshmallowy flesh, tending toward more fluidic movements. She has a steady, dependable nature, generous, dedicated, carrying out what she says she will. Like the ocean, she can have turbulent moods and be emotionally erratic. Her color is sea blue-green. At nine o'clock is the pure Earth type, with a thick, sausage build and rubbery flesh. She's a social type, agreeable, practical, resourceful, a doer rather than a thinker — just the opposite from the intellectual three o'clock. The masculine or feminine pronouns are used here only as a convenience — males or females can participate to a lesser or greater degree in any of these basic types. A dominatrix-type female can have strong masculine characteristics and be a large, twelve o'clock woman; a man with a lot of feminine characteristics, can naturally fall into the six or seven o'clock range.

As LaVey is quick to point out, "Typing people isn't allowed in our society today. We're all supposed to be equal; we're not supposed to judge others by their appearance. But I say appearance, aesthetics, is everything. In the 30's and 40's great progress was made in character reading. But with the advent of the Great Integration, we're supposed to look beyond a person's physical attributes into a deeper commonality we all share. That's bullshit. Knowing what characteristics go with what appearance is vital to magic. Once you learn to type people, you can see into their souls — and no matter what, they'll remain true to their basic predispositions. It never fails."

After identifying yourself on LaVey's Synthesizer Clock, prosepctive witches are advised to look across the circle to find the type of man they have a tendency to attract. The long-standing phrase, "opposites attract," is incorporated here with the added explanation of why they attract. If a man is a skinny-as-a-rail three o'clock, depending on his intellect and verbal skills to engage people, chances are he will be with an outgoing, personable, heavier woman who enjoys cooking, parties and holidays. We are compelled to our opposites — they fascinate us with their differentness. By our involvement, we access a secret self to show to the world. Our partner provides another dimension, and we are drawn to them whether we like it or not. Likewise, if you see a relationship budding where the parties involved are too much alike, too close on the clock, lay bets they won't be together long and people will be surprised by your foresight. Many types do like to have relationships — for sexual reasons, companionability — with people near them on the clock. But the point is, they aren't *compelled* to each other so they have to work that much harder to stay together.

LaVey defines a unique concept he calls ECI (Erotic Crystallization Inertia). These are women's trappings that, based on a man's initial sexual experience or the time in which he was born, become fetishistic turn-ons. The ECI of men who experienced young adulthood during World War Two would be stockings, tailored dresses and skirts, heavy makeup — because that is what sexually available women wore in 1942. For men growing up in the 60's, their ECI might be something quite different — blue jeans; long, straight hair; politically aware and active women would probably hold special fascination for them.

LaVey provides in his book a short list of fetish-finding comments which you can weave into your conversation with your quarry and gauge the reaction. How you won't "take any guff from a man," discussion about that "hair-pulling match you had with another woman," shame at being chastised by your boss or accidentally exposing yourself. Making mention of some article of underclothing you might be wearing is an obvious fetish-detector. One or more of these types of comments is guaranteed to get a response. "Every man is a fetishist," writes LaVey. "You simply have to *discover* his fetish."

Men's magazines understand fetishes and cater to target audiences. LaVey once gave an interview to the men's magazine, *Hustler* (December, 1979), focusing on his sexual exploits. The article fixated on Marilyn Monroe's farting. Though LaVey never brought up the subject, he was pressed into admitting that yes, like all other humans, Marilyn must have farted. *"Hustler* practically embellished it into a *cause celebre."* After the article appeared, and just as LaVey had feared, about a half-dozen flatulent lonelyhearts sought him out. Needless to say, LaVey was unimpressed. But this apocryphal tale about Marilyn has entered the literature. Subsequently, other first-person "memoirs" and biographies have referred to her windiness.

Successful witches should never forget the Law of the Forbidden. LaVey explains, "The reason there has always been a fascination for witchcraft and sorcery is because it has consistently been considered taboo. Your first duty as a witch is to your appearance. Men are all voyeurs, and most of what they are attracted to is based on what they see. What they see in you, as a witch, must be fascinating, and *nothing* is so fascinating as that which is not meant to be seen.... When it comes to bewitching them all men are nasty little boys at heart ... People have completely negated the value of prurience these days. There's no opportunity like there used to be with women wearing pants and sexually provocative pictures being limited to full-frontal exposure." LaVey cautions women against projecting their own standards for another woman on their sexual attractiveness to men. "What a woman hates most about herself — her feminine odor, her cellulite, her movements, her blemishes — those are just the things I find most appealing on a beautiful woman because those are the things that make her vulnerable, the things that make her a real woman."

Contrary to what white witches may say about working their magic "skyclad," the Satanic witch understands the power of clothing. How can men feel like dirty little boys unless they're seeing something that is absolutely not *supposed* to be seen, that is supposed to be covered by clothing? The true witch dresses in usually more clothes than most women, but that's just to be able to expose more. LaVey cites the provocative example of a topless dancer listlessly shaking her equipment in front of a group of equally unenthusiastic men. A woman spectator steps into the picture clothed rather conservatively with classic three-inch pumps, a close-fitting but unremarkable dress. She is with a man and wears a modest wedding band. When she sits down at the bar, her dress accidentally catches on the back of the stool and she ends up revealing much more than she is aware. The men present are able to strain their eyes past the married woman's traditional beige-toned seamed stockings to view the pale flesh of her thigh. They can even trace a slightly soiled white garter strap up the back of her leg and glimpse a bit of off-white panties. Her undergarments are not the black or red "stage undies" displayed by the girl on stage, but something much nastier — the Forbidden. All the men's eyes direct furtive glances up the lady's dress, no matter what is going on onstage!

*The Satanic Witch,* LaVey suggests the kind of clothes to glamorize a woman's position on the clock. "On women it looks great to expose the neck and back or legs, it's very attractive because it connotes vulnerability and literally baring yourself to ravishment. Vulnerability doesn't work on men. T-shirts with no collar to protect your neck and shorts covering only the minimum part of you makes a man uncomfortable — he feels like a sitting duck. That's what I call 'toddler clothes.' Too exposed." Along with exposure, garter belts, high heels, and straight cut dresses or skirts, LaVey recommends full-cut underwear rather than bikinis (more to show), bright colors in makeup, no excessive jewelry, and no heavy perfumes or deodorants to mask your natural seductive smells.

LaVey released *The Satanic Witch* at the height of feminist fervor. It was meant as an antidote to what LaVey has called the most aesthetically barren period in history. Reactions, as is usually the case with LaVey's works, were sharply polarized. Helen Gurley Brown ran a condensation in *Cosmopolitan*. New York's top deejay, Barry Farber, exclaimed, "My God, man, do you realize what you have here? This is twenty-five years ahead of its time — a breakthrough in understanding human motivation." "Conversely," says LaVey, "the reaction from feminists when my book first came out was incredible — public book burnings, pickets at stores. During the promotional tour, when I made the mistake of announcing on the air I'd be at such and such a bookstore signing copies, they'd show up en masse, with their boots and maxiskirts."

Given his attitudes about the true power of women, it's not surprising that LaVey has little good to say about the effects of feminism. "Feminism negates and inverts the natural male/female interchange. There's a magnetic interaction between men and women that can be exploited for magical results, like a perpetual motion machine. It's been described as yin/yang, active/passive.... In Satanic ceremonies, it's the interplay between the dominant Priest and the receptive female altar. But feminists in their supposed quest for equality have tossed out the baby with the bathwater. It's a real shame too because women are naturally dominant in relationships unless there's an extreme masculine type with an extreme feminine type. The feminist have eliminated avenues for power over men that women have had for centuries. But that system was bad for consumerism. Women are the best consumers and they can't spend favors. In these post-feminist 'liberated' years, men pay *and* women pay — everybody pays — with plastic money according to how God (i.e., TV) tells them to spend it. There's no room for a barter system because women are above accepting favors from men. They have their own money now, that they get by plugging firmly into the economic system. Even prostitutes are trained to get the money and spend it as they should.

"Most men are so threatened and fed up with dealing with women with chips on their shoulders that they place *greater* demands upon women in an attempt to assert power. They're so used to women threatening their masculinity that they take every opportunity to throw their weight around, even with a naturally passive woman. That's what the real crime of feminism is — it's created a situation where receptive, 'bottom of the clock' women have to suffer from what the 'top of the clock' women have thrust upon them. They've been robbed of the thrill of subtle exhibitionism, of prurience. Those women were perfectly happy, and most successful, in the pre-feminist world. Now they have to go out and compete with 'top of the clock' women for office jobs, industry jobs, and suffer because of men's resentment."

When challenged, LaVey admits his views sound more than a bit chauvinistic. "I'm a confirmed misogynist," Anton declares, "but only because I'm such a pushover for feminine women. A misogynist's disdain is based on jealousy. Seeing the power that aggressively passive wield through their feminine wiles, he wishes he had a bit of it himself, secretly admires it, and seeks to capture it before it captures him. But overtly mannish or dominant women create no dualistic yearnings — as I've written, they're useless critters who are too proud for burden and not attractive enough for exploitation. We misogynists need wanton, sleazy, yielding, soft women to augment our masculinity. I consider a well-adjusted, heterosexual misogynist a bulwark against the most devastating form of defeminization."

Another harmful side effect of feminism, as LaVey sees it, is an inversion of sexual roles. "There has been a complete inversion," says LaVey. "Just look around. There's a difference between masculine and feminine metabolisms — women have a tendency to be colder all the time. They have slower metabolisms. I'm always very hot and I asked myself why. Why is it everywhere I go is too hot for me? Then I finally realized what had happened. Maybe it's because I'm a man living in a woman's world. If men become women and women need warmth and kinesis — men are now just as chilly as women once were. Men have taken over women's metabolisms too. They make better women than women these days — it's never hot enough for them. When you're dealing with a nation of women, no one's going to run hot because there are no pure men. You'll be sweltering if you are because everything is geared for lower metabolisms. Lysenko, Lamarck and others have traced changes environment can produce over one or two generations. Such changes don't have to take 50,000 years of evolution."

"Men now go into the marketplace," remarks LaVey, "the way women used to. 'A woman's work is never done' is men's burden now as well. Elvis the Pelvis changed the way men move. Now men do the bumps and grinds and the women pump iron. It used to be all a woman's strength was in her legs and pelvis, and man's strength was in his arms and upper body. Women carried their weight low, men high. Look around now.

"Men don't get 'het-up' the way they used to. The creative, male sex urge is sublimated, lackadaisical now. Women conventionally express sexuality in retention, preservation. Sex is imparted to them. That's what new men need — imparting of sex, heat, potency from women. It's the new plaint of women: 'Where are the real men?' We have a whole nation of barren, cold women huddled together with their male counterparts to keep warm. But women don't generate by nature. They conduct. They receive. Nothing's changed in them — the feminine characteristics are still there, exploited more effectively than ever."

LaVey does have hope though. He sees that Satanic ideas are having an effect on the way men and women interact that will create a forum for a return to the complementary interchange between purely masculine and purely feminine characteristics once again. *The Satanic Witch* was a strong blow for re-establishing sex differentiation during our most androgynous period in history. Now, after almost 20 years of secret leakage into the mainstream, prurience is becoming fun again. "Fantasy (along with androids) is becoming increasingly important in the changing sexual scene (AIDS). People are more circumspect about their sexual liaisons — returning to the only safe outlets, prurience and voyeurism. Women are relearning the arts of flirting and subtle exhibitionism. We must have a return to glamor and prurience whether feminists yell about women 'exploiting their bodies' or not.

"Women can relearn to exercise their differences to gain more power. But they must be highly evolved women. Most women will continue being sheep and buying what they're programmed, emotionally, and economically. Advanced, Satanically-oriented women can choose their own lifestyle rather than having it thrust upon them. They can participate in all kind of exercises, rituals if you will, to break down the brainwashing feminism has done on contemporary young women. Sado-masochistic revelries and deviltry; shape-shifting exercises; discipline games — women are looking for more of that sort of thing in their private lives because it's the ideal therapy. But again they must be extremely self-aware to be willing to initiate such Satanic debaucheries. If you're just one step up from the gutter, you're too afraid of going backward to participate in vile, degrading activities. But advanced women realize they will have to return to more fantasy, formality, metaphor, imagination, magic in their relationships."

Once upon a time, certain women — because they were overly attractive, promiscuous, unusual in some way — were accused of being witches and riding on their broomsticks to Sabbaths where they consorted with Satan. Before they left, older women would anoint them with a potent flying ointment laced with belladonna to prepare them for their journey. Then the girls were instructed to lay on their backs, put their broomstick between their thighs and let Satan take them.

In the movie *Svengali,* Barrymore compels Trilby to have feverish thoughts of him, his mind reaching out to her over the rooftops of London. Vampires, Svengali, Satan — whatever the metaphors used they all have a certain power. For women, fantasy is just as valid as physical contact. These are the representations, the only interpretations we have of the frightening, enticing, darkly Romantic force that contacts certain girls. Some force comes to them, speaks to them, makes love to them, overwhelms them. There's enough we don't yet understand about windows of space/time and how they can be manipulated by force of will. What better way to service many women than through long distance contact, fantasy and artifice?

The obsessions begin at a very young age then re-ignite at puberty, causing unendurable longing, and indescribable ecstasy when "touched". There's a pulsing, surging urgency and aching. Girls seek out hidden books and wicked, forbidden ideas to explore these yearnings and try to discover what is happening to them. Many of them, after much searching, come to believe they have been touched by Satan.

Lurking behind all the nasty tricks of high heels, seamed stockings, fantasies, fetishes and odors, however, is the real, and dangerous, content of

Anton LaVey's *Satanic Witch*. It's a topic that couldn't be approached direct-ly in 1970, and is still taboo today. In the guise of practical witchery, LaVey has written a handbook of eugenics, insidiously putting forth a system for applied natural selection to be implemented by any woman who reads and heeds what LaVey has written. "Because of forced egalitarianism," says LaVey, "the lost science of eugenics, the art of typing people, has been all but outlawed, and the Darwinian process of natural selection has been vir-tually reversed."

# Chapter Fifteen

# Masochistic America

A recurring theme in LaVey's writings and musings for the past dozen years is that the only motivations for most humans are pain and fear. "The more pain something gives them, the better they like it," says LaVey. Masochists have been on the rise over the past 40 years, especially since the 1960's. To explain why, LaVey links pain, overpopulation, carnival rides, jogging shoes, Christianity and Capitalism together, in ways that only he could, to show exactly what is happening to the American psyche. As with all LaVeyan world-views, this one has a disturbingly Machiavellian ring to it.

LaVey has described himself as a "very happy man in a compulsively unhappy world."[28] With the growth of our postwar consumer society, LaVey sees that Americans must be kept dissatisfied, uneducated and insecure to maintain economic stability. We must be kept in a vulnerable position, easy prey for television commercials and politicians. Self-aware, secure people don't have to buy the right underarm spray or jog an assigned number of miles a day to gain social acceptance.

The Evolution of the Drone (i.e., the ideal, malleable consumer) began during World War II, when emergency made it necessary for women to work at men's jobs and take on men's roles, in factories and on farms, while their husbands and sweethearts battled in Europe and the Pacific. With the economy in women's hands, marketing was altered to take advantage of feminine capriciousness and inherent insecurities.

"Women are better consumers than men," says LaVey, "because of their inherent masochism. Freud said it long ago — that's one of the reasons he's looked on with such disfavor in our post-feminism age. Women do have a need for increased agitation, physical activity, and high energy output. I'm talking about bottom of the clock women, and bottom of the clock men for that matter. Those physical types, what I call the pure feminine type, are inherently more insecure, and advertising plays on that insecurity. They're more malleable, they're more vulnerable. All these things are used in selling products. And it begins to feed on itself." When men returned home, the sales methods didn't change. The sexual inversion blossomed in 1955 when the first issue of *Playboy* hit the stands. What LaVey terms "top of the clock" women — tall, big-breasted women with large shoulders and slim hips — were glorified while round, Cupie-doll cute girls were soundly criticized as "fat." Men were encourage then to act out the role of women by admiring top of the clock (purely masculine) women.

Romantic idealism and the fun of prurience was smashed as the clinical, gynecological view of women began to predominate. The *film noir* period, with its loyal chorines and gangster anti-heroes, ended. Bright, splashy colorful movies of clean, wholesome women in frilly dresses became the rage. Gone were the cheaply seductive waitresses who got anything they wanted by the use of subtle exhibitionism. Women became de-sexed and men de-masculinized, with round-shouldered, Madison Avenue men in grey flannel suits held up as the ideal.

And then came the final flowering of the Drone: Hippies — the final de-evolution of man, to LaVey's mind — completely androgynous, convinced they were rebels against society (all 50,000,000 of them), and so zonked out on drugs they could no longer think for themselves or question anything that was fed to them (while they were all convinced of their individuality and uniqueness). What better way to make people vulnerable to attack than to pump mind-blowing drugs into them? "People in the 30's and 40's generally weren't as gullible. They weren't very sophisticated — they hadn't been exposed to a lot of things. Now everyone's sophisticated and smart — but much more gullible and naive than they were 40 years ago."

LaVey sees that Christianity has contributed no small part to the current consumer dependence. If a religion teaches blind faith, blind belief in authority, and ignorance, no one can think for themselves. Just as priests flogged themselves for their Lord, we are now taught "No pain, no gain," by those who sell athletic equipment. Same purpose, different sales pitch. There are only three characteristics rewarded in modern man: stupidity, irrationality, and irresponsibility.

"They're masochists," declares LaVey, "unrealized, unrecognized masochists. They live on a binary system — might as well be real machines. Love/die, hate/die, run/die. No shades of grey, no hues, no subtlety. Nothing but on/off, black/white, good/evil, act/die. They either have to kick, scratch, harass, goad or die. Nothing in between. It's part of the death wish, the Calvinist ethic of holding back. Most people have a need to be punished. Then they win either way. If they're being assertive, like all these books tell them to be, and get what they want then they win. If they get a punch in the nose then they get what they want — personal attention, pain, a feeling that they're alive. They play the odds. Say they push with ten people and one of those people gives them what they're asking for, they're ahead. It's like with salesmen — the sales start at the first 'No.'

"There are just too many people for our system to support. It's as much a law as gravity or thermodynamics — the more people there are, the stupider they'll be. To a man. The most important thing an overcrowded society must encourage and provide is an inalienable right to stupidity — as in 'life liberty and the pursuit of stupidity.' It's economically infeasible for it to be otherwise. After all, isn't that what happiness is all about? It used to be said that the only completely happy people were in the nut house."

"People we call suicidal aren't really aberrant — they're just voicing what's felt by most of society. They don't really want to live, they really want to die. It's too much work to live, to feel emotions fully, to be dedicated, to be loyal, to breathe, to reach further, fulfill your potential — it's just too much work. What they really want to do is kick around a little bit and then just roll over.

"Most people have to manufacture turmoil in their lives or have it manufactured for them. They go through life searching for distractions, escapes, to keep them from thinking about living. And an executioner to kill them. The weak see somebody that looks strong, successful, superior, and keep poking at him until he turns around and smashes them. Then, like the orgasm at the point of death, their ultimate goal is the ecstacy as their neck snaps.

"That's why you have to have parasites perish in ignominy, without being able to point and say 'Look, he's doing this to me.' That's a masochist's dream. They *want* to be victimized so they can have the identity (the only identity of their existence) of being able to destroy the strong one with their accusations. I'm not that charitable."

LaVey's unbridled misanthropy becomes frightening at times. "I go one step beyond Carl Panzram's 'I put them out of their misery' to 'I make them feel something they wouldn't have ever felt otherwise. I stimulate them — for the first time in their lives.' Even in dying, they're living.

"They *should* suffer — I have to suffer from my awareness every single day. They wake up to a new world every morning. They don't have any demons or attackers facing them. It should be a balance factor. I have the philosophy that 'I have to do it — why are they exempt? I couldn't get away with that! Satanists face a world everyday where everyone tells them they're wrong, deluded. Why shouldn't stupid people be forced into a little perspective too?"

As for the political machinery in America, LaVey has little positive to say, believing it's nothing more than a spectator sport presented to keep people occupied while the real moving and shaking goes on elsewhere. "Most people don't want to pick a leader — they want to pick an executioner. So when they 'elect a leader' they're really saying 'I want you to pull the switch, not the other one.'"

Now, says LaVey, there are too many *Gauleiter* Zombies — strawboss zombies in charge who are media slaves themselves and more than willing to take from the deserving non-zombies that are left.

The problem with a society aimed at only growing more consumers is obvious — it drags the strong down and halts, even reverses, evolution. Survival of the fittest is inverted because the weak are better consumers. Consequently all the worst elements are preserved and protected, all the best elements are discouraged. Intelligence, resourcefulness, originality, curiosity — all the elements of the human brain that made us successful animals on this planet have been bred out of us.

Are there ways for higher man to protect himself from encroaching masochistic consumerism and the stupidity it breeds? LaVey has some suggestions, ranging from the ephemeral to quite practical solutions. "In the old days, a gate, steel bars, guards were enough to protect yourself from invaders. Now there must be means of protection developed from legalistic, accredited thievery, which destroys the best, individualistic elements. There must be a plan, a format, a guideline for protection. Now attackers steal the rights of anyone with a mind, a force of will, a sense of individuality, just as they once stole stereos out of cars.

"Big business has developed tax shelters for everything. We must do the same thing, even stretching to abstract values. No one would guess that people would want to take what's in the mind — your memories, your feelings, your perceptions — but they do. They want to rob us of the most precious things we have. Satanists must utilize protective coloration and camouflage, more than we ever have before. Anything coveted, real or abstract, must probably be protected in dummy corporations — one thing pod people might be unwittingly good for. We have to develop a strawboss system of competent, perceptive people so real leaders aren't forced to waste their time. That's another rather abstract commodity the zombies would like to deprive achievers of."

Besides these precautions and protections for the higher man, LaVey proposes several means of effectively channeling people's masochism. As an example, he relates an early ceremony the Church of Satan performed called a Strengthening Ritual. LaVey selected an individual who represented that part of the world which must be hurt in order to be happy; someone whose personality contained a bit of the masochism at the heart of the devout Christians' guilt and sin complexes, but who rebelled against the kicking around he got because of his offbeat attitudes. Members scourged the person called the "Vessel of Holy Pain" who thereby absorbed their transgressions instead of ridding themselves of sins by self-flagellation as in the Christian religion. LaVey proposes a variation of this idea for society in general. According to LaVey, we can be free of discord if we have the courage to discover our own natural predispositions without blindly buying (in more ways than one) everything we're told.

First, we have to eliminate semantic traps — boss and secretary; sadist and masochist; master and slave. "People shouldn't be afraid of using words that are supposed to connote weakness or subservience," explains LaVey. "If the truth were known the master is often much more dependent on the slave than vice-versa. And how could a boss get along without an efficient secretary? She's the only one who knows where everything is. We don't need to develop a new language (as feminists have tried to do); people only resent it and resist. The easiest and most effective way is to take what's given and redefine it. When one hears the word 'slave,' the goal is to think of the truer aspects of 'facilitator, supporter.' Master is a 'motivator', a 'provider.' Very much like taking the term 'Satanist' and seeing it in a positive light. It's the whole philosophy of Satanism — taking a tabooed word or concept and using it to your advantage."

There *are* advantages to being able to enjoy pain. The best businessmen have to be a bit masochistic because they have to take incredible risks and not worry about it. An indulgent personality would defeat himself from the start because he would be too fearful of the pain of losing the entire investment. Many masochistic men are the most successful because they have learned to exercise their predilections in a controlled, contained environment that won't be deleterious to their success. Masochists are more willing to take chances and lose — they don't mind getting hurt. If a masochist wins, he wins. If he loses, he still wins.

However, LaVey defines an important difference between self-destructive masochism and self-endowing masochism. These are two distinct aspects of a person which mean the difference between failure and success. There are self-affirming masochists who want to exercise/exorcise their predispositions to gain in the world and self-destructive masochists bent on self-defeat. In LaVey's cosmology, the difference between an inferior and a superior woman lies in whether or not she can look clearly and boldly at herself and use what she has to her best advantage. A self-aware masochist can be an extremely strong individual and a potent ally.

To assist in this process of discovery and honest utilization of pain, LaVey proposes establishing clinics with attitudes like the Church of Satan, aimed at purging the guilt about enjoying pain rather than trying to "cure" anyone of masochistic tendencies. He even has ideas for machines devised to aid the therapy. He calls them "Auto-Erotic Agitation Tumblers" — big cylinders that vibrate and bounce with the woman thrown around inside. The machines would be the female equivalent of anatomically-complete artificial human companions. They would be ideal female masturbation devices for women who would finally be able to shake themselves up to release their excess energy anytime they wished. "If there was a forum, properly presented, women would be taking charge of their own lives and they wouldn't be prey to fashions anymore. They'd be taking control of their masochism and using it.

LaVey also suggests the American public exercise masochism on private as well as public levels. Mass interests (Christianity, TV, consumer society) exploit the individual need/instinct for love by placing them on a mass level. LaVey proposes a private pact between women and men to focus on the master/slave component of a successful relationship. Problems often crop up between couples because one person isn't dominating enough, fulfilling the role of master. LaVey asks, "Isn't it better to be able to choose your master rather than being forced to serve an impersonal one? There are too many mindless, useless people bred by our consumer society. Given the choice, isn't it better to be used than useless?"

LaVey sees that we are presently enmeshed in a consumerist-oriented "Invisible War," complete with technologically advanced chemical and electromagnetic weapons, crowd control, weather control and misdirection to mask the entire operation. He claims there is no need for conspiracy theories — that private interests make such theorizing unnecessary. But the results far surpass any conspiratorialists' worst nightmares of secret government agencies, CIA plots, UFO's, or MIB's. "People don't understand there are different forms of weaponry," says LaVey, who has written extensively about the subject in recent *Cloven Hoofs*. "There can be food weapons, sonic or subsonic weapons, just as there are cannons, hand grenades, and submarines. How can people be so naive to think that warfare development would have stopped with nuclear weapons?"

The invisible war's measures/methods now being applied — thought control, diseases, pseudo-sickness, demoralization, etc.— serve a two-fold function: force stratification and keep population thinned as a stop-gap until space colonies can be perfected.

Eventually, says LaVey, human drones will be sent into space. After stratification takes place and an underground of surviving sensitized people is established, space colonies will develop at an alarming rate so good consumers will be shipped out to penal camps where they can spend lots of money and not destroy what's left of a beautiful planet. Space colonies are perfect closed, controllable environments — all food has to be shipped and processed, all air, water can be treated with the proper substances and dispersed, with no wind or natural currents to worry about.

People have been softened up for the coming Space Revolution for years. Movies (a la *Star Wars*), TV *(Star Trek)*, books about cyberpunks and space rebels, cartoons, toys, politics between Russia and U.S. finally stabilizing all point toward the same goal — *space*. The ones who willingly go into space will be the adventurous, the rebels, the oppressed who can't get justice on earth but who can finally be in the forefront of new developments in the fabulous uncharted regions above. There can be plenty of jobs for everyone, in construction, maintenance, service — all the comforts of home without the muss and bother. Only those weirdos attached to the past (i.e., Satanists, freethinkers) will want to stay behind. With no major industries left on Earth, those left will have to adjust to life with minimal population.

In the meantime we'll design AET's and settle for masochism clinics. Perhaps they'll be called "Physical Therapy Centers" or "Erotic Agitation Clinics." Rather than suppressing our needs or frenetically forcing someone else to smash us, we can go to a clinic, relieve our "itch," then channel our creative energy into other, far more productive avenues. Applying Satanic perspective, masochists can be the slaves of their own, wisely-chosen masters rather than slaves to a desensitizing system.

## Chapter Sixteen

# The Humanoids Are Coming!

*"When I come home at night, she will be waiting,*
*She'll be the truest doll in all this world.*
*I'd rather have a paper doll to call my own,*
*Than have a fickle-minded real live girl."*
— "Paper Doll," words and music by Johnny S. Black, 1942

In the March - April, 1979, issue of *The Cloven Hoof,* the newsletter of the Church of Satan, Anton LaVey announced a new phase for his organization: "The development, promotion, and manufacture of artificial human companions." To those who were working closely with LaVey, this came as no surprise. Many in his immediate circle had been assisting in the manufacture of his "people" for years. But a large number of members were baffled, to say the least. What could making robots possibly have to do with practicing Satanism? Over the next few months, LaVey explained in a series of follow-up articles exactly what he had in mind, including methods of construction, and how this new phase tied directly into his vision of the growing Satanic movement around the world.

*"Man can be easily fooled. In fact, he has shown every indication that he must be fooled. If he isn't, he demands it. He complains, 'It's a Barnum and Bailey world, just as phony as it can be,' yet he won't have it any other way and seems to survive best under the most artificial conditions. Only when one can fully accept artificiality as a natural and often superior development of intelligent life, can one have and hold a powerful magical ability."*[29]

Anton LaVey believes the manufacturing of humanoids will be the next major consumer industry, and an unparalleled answer to a range of human problems, from sexual incompatibility to economic recession and violent crime.

LaVey explains: "... we find ourselves treading on theologically thin ice when we advocate humanoids. If man creates graven images in whole-sale lots which will produce ecstasies unrivaled by all the religions of the past—and those graven images are in the form of the most perfect physical specimen each human could pray up — and 'God' is supposed to carry the contract on the creation of such images — but man threatens to give 'Him' competition — doesn't this bring man a large step closer to being God?"[30]

The advantages of having an artificial human companion are seem-ingly endless and, as LaVey explains them, very compelling. The first, and most obvious use, would be sexual. Even in our post-Freudian world, mas-turbation is not the preferred method of sexual release. There is still an unspoken stigma associated with someone who is "forced" to resort to those methods alone. But, when customized humanoids become coveted status symbols (much as a teenage boy would take great pride in his custom hot rod), they will make masturbation acceptable at last.

With infinite modifications possible in body size, shape, hair color, proportions, musculature, facial features, dress, expressions, smell, voice, taste — the visual and tactile aspects of a humanoid would be exactly what the buyer has always wished for, perfect in every detail. Even those who might be considered less than attractive themselves could design an ideal-ized, willing mate incorporating his or her own particular fetishistic desires. Singles bars (along with the accompanying shallow conversation, insecuri-ties, performing, and frustrating one-night stands) would become obsolete — no need to go looking for "Mr. Right" when you can create one.

For those with less imagination, there would be many models fash-ioned after desirable movie stars and popular personalities, both living and dead, so anyone could have their idol in bed with them, acting exactly as they wanted them to act, saying what they wanted to hear. There can be only one Elvis Presley, for example, but with the help of advanced technol-ogy, there can also be thousands of Elvis "dolls" in the arms of thousands of women across America.

*"Everyone needs fantasies — I have nothing against them. I encour-*

*age and create them. My only objection is that most fantasies are passed off as reality these days — people don't have the imagination to create their own so they must believe those manufactured for them. If a person had enough fantasy in his life — fantasies he chose — he wouldn't be victimized by all these impersonal fantasies and fake conspiracies he is expected to believe."*

A humanoid always looks perfect, never has bad breath or any obnoxious habits that are suffered in human companions purely for reasons of sex or habit. "How many people enter into emotionally unsatisfying or intellectually barren relationships just for sexual reasons?" asks LaVey. "With an artificial human companion, the sexual aspect would be completely satisfied, and a prospective mate would have to come up with something more enticing than just sex."

Programmed to accept measures of beauty as communicated by television, the individual becomes desensitized, unable to experience authentic stimulation he might discover on his own. But with artificial companions in every home, the individual could exercise his own vision. Freed of societal pressure, personal fetishes could run wild — perhaps leading to prurient pleasures that would otherwise never have been explored. LaVey sees this as supremely Satanic: "It would be a case of a pre-programmed human deprogrammed by a non-human!"

*"I can afford to be gullible in the ways I choose, not in the ways advertisers and modern soothsayers would want me to be."*

Sexual psychopaths would have the chance to play God with an artificial human companion instead of a real one, perhaps defusing a volatile situation before it has a chance to build up. "Since almost all creative and/or destructive acts result from sublimation of sexual drives," LaVey writes, "the humanoid would preclude sublimation leading to non-sexual but harmful actions.

"Instead of enslavement *of* the people, it would enact slavery *for* the people. It could be the ultimate power trip: sovereignty over another 'human' being. So far, they can pay a few hundred dollars and 'command' a computer. It has made for a lot of electronic slave-drivers."

An obvious advantage to humanoids is in cutting down the number of unwanted pregnancies. In our overcrowded world, that is a major concern. LaVey, with characteristic disdain, has written, "Unfortunately, many humans' sole contribution to the world — if it can be considered as such — is the ability to produce another human being." With artificial companions, women can have all the sex they want and never fear getting pregnant, and men need never fear that a woman might have fibbed about birth control.

LaVey sees no reason to fear that, even with all the advantages he outlines, people would ever become too complacent and satisfied with their humanoids. He maintains that humans have an irrepressible drive to compete for recognition. "If everyone is sexually satisfied, obtaining his partner in the image most pleasing to his taste, his only means of recognition must come from his non-sexual accomplishments. Thus status through achievement in non-sexual pursuits can only occur in a society where sexual conquest has become as obsolete as warfare, both having been discarded as wastes of time and human energy, relative to the dubious bounties of each."

"It is up to Satanists to realize that artificial human companions are on their way," says LaVey. "We must place ourselves ahead of the pack, look beyond the immediate, and see that they are the next Satanic evolution of man."

*"Scoffers who tell me, 'Oh, these things will never be accepted' are probably slaves to their TV sets and will be the first to be affected by the humanoids. When people can stop personally interacting with a two-dimensional screen, turn their sets to the wall, and not be influenced by the images on a cathode tube, then they might honestly say that they will be immune to surrogate stimulation — but I don't think there's any danger of that happening."*

"Many things will have to be adapted when the humanoids come," says LaVey. "Advertising now is dependent on everyone being made to feel important. Everybody's a big shot. The pitch for artificial human companions will have to include that aspect, establishing them as real status symbols, much as an expensive car would improve the consumer's image. Other consumer products will take a nose-dive because the companions themselves will be more impressive than the humans they would be intended to impress. Prostitutes will be unnecessary — except as an elite class of modern courtesans to service those who desire more than sex and simple companionship."

LaVey's absorption with the concept of artificial people is one of a handful of themes which seems to have haunted him from childhood. He had been fascinated by a miniature Chicago housed in the Illinois Building at the 1939-40 World's Fair, held on San Francisco's Treasure Island. The model was so true to the map of Chicago that a visitor could ask the attendant to point out a particular address. Factories, business districts, major stores and holes-in-the-wall — Anton stood for many hours watching the city below him, formulating his own images of the interiors of the buildings and houses seemingly far below him.

This obsession led Anton to build a city of his own, on 4 x 8 plywood sheets dominating the floor of his bedroom. Using balsa wood, lichen, minutely painted vehicles and buildings, he began created his own miniature Gotham.. There was a harbor with ships of all sort, cars and trucks on the roads, modest homes, rich homes, a ghetto, rolling hills.... He experienced his first truly magical exercise, projecting himself into any building or street his city. By concentrating, he could feel the cold or heat of the place, smell and feel all that surrounded him, peer up at the buildings looming above him, peek into windows and hear the low chatter of people talking within.

Many years later, after Anton had moved into the Black House and was holding regular seminars, he had occasion to see exactly how far an artificial person could replace a real one. The lecture was on literary interpretations of "human sacrifice," complete with "demonstration." One of the female members of the Magic Circle had volunteered to assist. The attractive young girl lay on the altar stones, partially covered with a white sheet. Anton lifted a knife high above his head and plunged it deep into the girl's chest. The audience gasped as the white sheet was stained with spurting blood.

What the horrified onlookers didn't know was that Anton had just performed one of the most effective techniques of professional conjurers or spiritualists. The girl was substituted with a modified mannequin that Anton had been working on for days ahead of time. Anton altered the showroom dummy, until it looked like the "volunteer" herself — enough like her to convince the people attending the lecture that no switch had taken place. A bag filled with fake blood was concealed under the sheet, which Anton burst with the point of the knife. Similar effects were demonstrated in his lecture on "Psychic Surgery," in which Anton removed "diseased" organs from a volunteer, with healing instantly facilitated.

*"In Dariel Fitzkee's* The Trick Brain, *he categorizes applications of 'substitution' used by stage magicians. It's something the American public will have to be taught. Instead of considering the substitute to be of inferior quality, as with all the commercial propaganda urging us to 'accept no substitutes,' there will be a re-education to emphasize the attitude that the 'substitute' is often better than that which is being substituted."*

Dr. Cecil Nixon tried to interest Anton in the construction of a new violin-playing automata named Galatea, patterned after Isis, who played the zither. Instead of reclining like Isis, Galatea would stand as she played. Anton worked with Dr. Nixon on Isis, learning various techniques of construction and animation. Anton has been quoted as saying Dr. Nixon "spent a quarter of a lifetime building a woman who could not be laid."[31]

It wasn't until the 60's that Anton began in earnest to construct realistic human substititutes, testing raw materials for satisfactory look and feel, tensile strength, plasticity, and articulation. Sometimes starting with mannequin figures and modifying them far beyond their intended use, he would cut off their faces in his workshop and then build new ones using plaster, fiberglass, and various plastics. Recruiting some of his students and staff members as models, he used plaster or latex to take casts of their faces as a basic mold for subsequent modification.

Anton wrote about his humanoid experimentation in *The Cloven Hoof*, including *Popular Mechanics*-style suggestions on materials and methods. If one's need for a humanoid was purely visual, it was possible to create a satisfying model using plastic resins and fiberglass, applying appropriate dyes for the flesh tones, and finishing off the creation with suitable clothing, make-up and wig.

More tactilely-oriented Satanists were advised to put together some sort of skeletal structure using dowels, metal, or plastic tubing, fitted with ball and socket joints, and covered, perhaps, with polyurethane foam for the feeling of human flesh. Anton suggested the use of either vinyl or rubber sheeting, or dyed and stretched fabric, for the best authentic feeling of skin. Faces could be cast from real people, or from a clay model, using conventional moulage techniques. The resulting latex mask could be laced over a faceless skull-structure, with a wig to cap the top. Faces could then be easily substituted, depending on the desired effect. Making the artificial human companion "anatomically complete" would be the easiest part. Artificial sexual apparatus could be purchased at any sex shop.

It is painstaking work. Those who venture into this avenue of Satanic practice face the dubious pleasure of bending over curing sections of polyurethane, inhaling the vapors of catalysts and resins, and sawing, grinding and finishing body parts in clouds of fiberglass or plaster dust. LaVey has spent untold hours experimenting with these various materials and, despite heavy duty blowers and respirators, suffered the consequences of breathing the dangerous substances deeply into his lungs.

An interesting sidelight to to LaVey's humanoid creations is that many human replicas of his "people" have suddenly appeared, Pygmalion-like, some time after LaVey had already constructed his creation. Instead of modeling the humanoid after a person, the person seems to have been modeled after the humanoid. Anton doesn't try to explain these "conjurings" beyond referring to a method he uses in magical rituals which he terms "cosmic superimposition," a phrase borrowed from Wilhelm Reich.

Few have been privileged to see the bizarre showcase of Anton's work. A room reached by a dizzying descent down a ladder is bathed in grayish-amber light reflecting off the mirrored walls and ceiling, looking for all the world like a roadside bar in the 40's. A neon sign flashes "The Den of Iniquity." The authentic Rock-ola jukebox plays "Prisoner of Love" and "Detour, There's a Muddy Road Ahead." A pyrolene drum set and old Hammond organ sit unattended on the opposite side of the room. Behind the wet bar, rows of bottles wink below the bowling trophies. Acrid, beery, smoky bar smells affront your senses. Everything is just as it should be.

Even the people, all LaVey's creations, reflect the dress and spirit of the War years. A saucy brunette named Bonita makes time with a cab driver, gesturing rudely at another woman who watches prudishly from the end of the bar. Sylvia, a besotted lush, stares blankly at her glass, as if she's forgotten something important she was supposed to remember — her cigarette glows endlessly without burning down. With eyes half-closed, Gwen listens to the music, slumping drunkenly against the sailor behind her. Alphonse, the ever-attentive bartender, tries to ignore the fact that Gwen is almost slipping off the barstool, her dress hiked up around her waist, thighs bulging over her stocking tops, and urine pooled on the floor beneath her. At a lonely table in the corner, a sad-eyed blonde watches the entrance — waiting for someone who will never come. Sylvester, an impudent-looking boy in a Cub Scout cap, stands inside the foyer lasciviously watching the whole scene, while his mother slouches in a chair, her bag of groceries at her feet, apparently overcome by the spirit of the place. All these, among others, people LaVey's private world.

Anton LaVey includes a spot for himself in this sordid tableau, among his more stationary creations. The argon and neon lights from beneath the Hammond keyboards, blue and orange, shine softly on his face as he sets a festive mood with a chorus of "Zip-a-dee-doo-dah." The instrument is the same one that bounced over many country roads with him when he played the carnival circuit. As with any artist, LaVey loves to watch people's reactions to his creations — "I've actually seen people become nauseated when they get down here. They either love it or hate it — nothing in-between." Flecks of light from a rotating ball play slowly around the room, and as the magic of the room becomes palpable, it is all too easy for the mind to play tricks. The music, lights, and endless reflections blend diabolically to disorient the unwary visitor, adding movements and fleeting expressions to LaVey's figures. One gets the uneasy feeling one has interrupted an ongoing party. Not only has LaVey created his "people," he's created a total environment that is a savage triumph of evocation.

By the early 70's, when word had leaked out about the super-realism of LaVey's unusual figures, he was contacted by Cory Galleries in San Francisco who requested he exhibit his "people" with them. Despite Diane's and others' urging, LaVey stubbornly refused. He maintained that he had constructed his "people" as experiments, for magical purposes only — not as public displays. It was clear that some viewers found his figures extremely offensive, and any additional publicity would throw more of a spotlight on him at a time when he was trying to keep as low a profile as possible. Duane Hanson, George Segal, John DeAndrea, and others, have subsequently come on the scene with similarly realistic figures, enjoying public acceptability and critical acclaim.

Anton has kept in contact with humanoid-makers from Japan and England, among other countries around the world. After communicating with leaders in the fields of robotics, androids, and artificial intelligence, Anton has discovered that, much as he suspected, the most significant work must still be clouded and obscured. "The people creating humanoids now have to hide their ideas behind techno-speak and gobbledygook or people won't be impressed with their work. As has been true of many great discoveries in the past, the real secrets are too simple — they can't be told."

Besides resistance to artificial human companions on religious grounds, there is an innate dislike, almost fear, that LaVey describes when people are confronted with human reproductions that are too close to the real thing. Jacques Vallee, a close personal friend and associate of LaVey's, noted this phenomenon and described it in his book, *The Network Revolution*: "Several Hollywood productions of the 1970's have shown automata used as personal companions, and satanist Anton LaVey has suggested that the commercial development of such alternative beings was unavoidable.... Yet the same experts who rave about the powerful capabilities of their software creations are scared of their machines looking human. They cringe at the suggestion that the computer's ability to speak, compose poems, compute and even play music could be embodied in anything more elegant than a steel cabinet with plastic buttons, set on four casters and firmly held in place by thick black cables. This reluctance is understandable. It is the reaction of the monkey looking at himself in the mirror. It is the shudder that seizes any being when he recognizes his own self, or part of it, in the world of the others."[31]

Regardless of these native fears, LaVey feels the construction of humanoids would be a logical progression from the first anatomically correct Betsy-Wetsy dolls, and "Chatty Kathys" to more advanced talking/moving dolls. Incorporating convincing micro-chip technology, substitute pets, for example, have been programmed to "Come" or "Speak" on command, but have the advantages of being cleaner and quieter than real pets. The "Teddy Ruxpin"-type dolls who tell stories — mouths apparently forming the words, bodies and eyes moving with friendly expressions — are based on the animation techniques developed at Disney Studios. "Walt Disney certainly had the right idea for the realistic presentation of humanoids. Children appreciate that — they've been prepared for human substitutes for a long time," says Anton. Even the more recent "Cabbage Patch" doll phenomenon can be seen as evidence of the growing dependency on artificial companions. Millions of adults paid exorbitant prices for substitute "babies" that didn't talk or move but had assigned names, birth certificates and identities. Now the process of "softening up" has extended from dolls into movies, books, even television series about humanoids. Whether we recognize them or not, the humanoids seem to be seeping into our culture.

LaVey's darkest reasons behind artificial human companions are evidence of his misanthropy. "Most people have become little more than fixtures, spectators, and can be easily replaced with humanoids," says LaVey, speaking from the ultimate Satanic viewpoint. "Some people find the thought of artificial companions quite threatening. Those who are most opposed to humanoids are the ones who secretly fear themselves to be of similar substance, importance, or potential. If they are that lackluster, that unstimulating that they can so easily be replaced by a machine, then so be it. They should be replaced."

# Chapter Seventeen

# Curses and Coincidences

> "The world we live in may seem to be a rag-bag of odd, fortu-
> itously assembled bits and pieces, but magicians believe that it is
> really a whole — like a design or a machine — and that all its
> parts are necessarily connected together in a certain way.
> Human beings are wholes of this kind.... Just as all the facets of a
> man's character and behaviour are aspects of a single personali-
> ty, so all the phenomena of the universe are aspects of some one
> thing which underlies and connects them. This one thing is a
> being, a force, a substance, a principle, or something which it is
> not possible to describe in words at all."
> — Richard Cavendish, *The Black Arts* [33]

Anton LaVey embodies an uncompromising sense of justice.
Speculation concerning his powers to curse people weaves relentlessly
around him. When asked directly about the rumors, Anton rather cryptically
maintains that all magic involves a necessary "balance factor." "The universe
insists on that balance," states LaVey, "and will enforce or exact the necessary price. Perhaps I'm a catalyst for that process."

Below is a sampling of "coincidences" gleaned in conversation with
LaVey — the few incidents he's willing to talk about. The Satan-hunting
media, looking everywhere for grand conspiracies, tend to overlook these
more obvious connections that prove more potent than all the fabrications
of talk-show hosts in the midst of ratings sweeps.

1947: While in the employ of the Clyde Beatty Circus, LaVey wants to
polish his keyboard skills by practicing on the show's calliope. He asks the
veteran calliope player, a drunken lush, if he can use the instrument for a

half-hour, and the man refuses. Anton curses the drunken sot for his stubbornness. Within days, LaVey replaces him as the circus' calliope player.

1948: When LaVey is 16, he gets into a tussle with a friend over the virtue of a girl Anton is dating at the time. The boy pulls a knife on LaVey, leaving him with a livid scar that remains on his right cheek for many years. Two years later, the boy is hauled down to the police station on an unrelated charge. While in a holding cell, he hooks his belt around an overhead pipe, wraps the other end around his neck, and hangs himself.

1960: Diane snuggles close to Anton while he drives. A truculent motorcycle cop stops beside them at a traffic light, glares into their car and motions to Diane to get to her side of the seat. "Keep both hands on the wheel," he warns, roaring off. Without thinking, Anton raises his hand in the "hex" sign toward the policeman. When Anton and Diane catch up to the officer, he is sprawled across the pavement, victim of a gruesome collision.

1960: The San Francisco Fox Theater is generally conceded to be the grandest movie palace ever built, constructed to stand two thousand years. Eventually, it was decided the space could be more lucratively exploited as an office high-rise. LaVey is one of the entertainers present for a final evening of tribute, before the theatre closes its doors forever. Fingering the last organ chords that echo through the theatre, Anton curses the plot of land, vowing that any building on the site will have nothing but bad luck. The office building now occupying the site, Fox Plaza, experiences problem after problems, and is said to be cursed...

1966: Angered by plans to tear down the fabled San Francisco Sutro Baths to make the valuable oceanfront land available to developers, LaVey curses the area, stipulating that until there is a small corner of any proposed plans devoted to the Devil, nothing would ever be built on that ground. Thirty-six hours after cursing the property, the buildings burst into flames just as the wrecking ball swings.

1967: LaVey's much-publicized curse on Jayne Mansfield's overprotective attorney, Sam Brody, claims not only Brody's life, but Jayne's as well, despite LaVey's warnings to her.

1968: Togare, LaVey's beloved Nubian lion, who had been forced out of the LaVey household and into the San Francisco Zoo, becomes the recipient of the zoo director's intense disfavor, and is shipped out to Lion Country Safari in Southern California as breeding stock. Togare is spirited away in the middle of the night, without allowing LaVey to say goodbye to his friend. Anton focuses his frustration and anger onto an exquisite Egyptian baboon made of crystal in a friend's ritual chamber.

Soon afterwards, the papers tell of a strange tragedy involving the zoo director, who had gone into the apes' cage late one afternoon. No one explained what he was doing there, or why the normally docile apes rushed at him, but their attack was swift and murderous. The apes ripped and clawed and pounced. By the time help arrives, summoned by the apes' demonic screams of blood-fury, the zoo director slips into unconsciousness.

1969: On August 8th, LaVey conducts a Hippie Ritual at the Church of Satan in which he bitterly curses the "psychedelic vermin" infesting the world. He calls for a purge to relegate the slaves to the pens in which they belong, catalyzing a new era of Satanic awareness. The next day the participants of the Hippie Ritual read about the horrors discovered in the Benedict Canyon home of Sharon Tate and Roman Polanski.

1969: LaVey agrees to appear on Lou Gordon's hot-seat television show in Detroit even though it is Halloween night and Anton has other commitments. The producer promises to get Diane and Anton to the airport in time to catch their plane. The show starts late, drags on, and with their flight time growing closer and closer, Gordon ridicules LaVey's odd beliefs. Finally Diane storms onscreen, says, "Come on, we've got a plane to catch," and rushes LaVey off the set. A friend rushes through a merciless storm to get the LaVeys to the airport in time. Airline personnel are just about to pull away the boarding ramp as the LaVeys run to the plane and jump on. As the plane takes off, LaVey vents his considerable anger. The city blacks out beneath them as they lift clear of the runway. A few days later, upon returning to San Francisco, LaVey writes a formal curse on blood-red Church of Satan stationary and sends it to Mr. Gordon, who reads it on his next broadcast, laughing and scoffing. Gordon dies within the year.

1970: LaVey consents to appear on reactionary Joe Pyne's hot-seat radio show, during which LaVey is treated to Pyne's unusually caustic tongue. Pyne dies within a few months of having LaVey on his show.

1972: The city fathers decide it is time to destroy another San Francisco landmark — Playland at the Beach, an amusement park stretching along eight blocks of prime oceanfront property. It is here where LaVey met his first wife, Carole, and lived for some time on the adjacent cliff. When LaVey learns the fate of his beloved amusement park, he vows that no one will be able to make a success of anything else built on the land. As of this writing, the high-rent condominium complex constructed on the site remains largely vacant and the area is rapidly becoming too crime-ridden to warrant further development.

1984: On the afternoon of July 18th, LaVey is summoned into court to be formally criminalized for the first time in his life. A restraining order is invoked against LaVey by Diane, the woman he had lived with for 24 years. Anton sends a letter to Karla in Amsterdam before the hearing saying he wasn't going to stand for it; that he had performed his magic, that he was going to "ride on the hot Santana winds" and that "all Hell will break loose." LaVey cautions Karla to keep the letter in a safe place.

On the appointed afternoon, at the exact hour LaVey would have been standing in front of the judge (he didn't attend to contest the action), James Huberty walks into a McDonald's in San Ysidro, California on a day cursed by blistering Santana winds. Armed with a machine gun, a revolver, several rounds of ammunition and a ghetto blaster, Huberty sprays the fast food restaurant with bullets, shooting anything that moves. He had earlier kissed his wife goodbye and told her he was going off to hunt humans. It is the worst massacre of its kind in history. Diane's father's name is James Hegarty.

# Chapter Eighteen

# The Second Wave of Satanism

*"Gibble, gobble, gobble, gabble — we will make you one of us,
one of us, one of us — we will make you one of us."*
— recited by dwarf during the wedding feast scene in *Freaks*

"What I'm doing now is teaching the 'Black History' of Satanism," says LaVey, regarding his current sinister endeavors. "I'm tracing back to our Satanic roots in the philosophies of Machiavelli, Milton, Herbert Spencer, Rabelais, G. B. Shaw, Maugham, Nietzsche, *film noir*.... There has always been a genetic strain of Satanists but it's just now getting to the point where we can stand up to identify ourselves and our forebears. Young people are hungry to know the philosophy behind Satanism. Now, since 1984, it's time for the second wave to crest." Augmenting his philosophy recorded in *The Satanic Bible*, which LaVey maintains is just as valid as when it was first written, he views his current role as broadening the principles of Satanism through application. "We'll follow Huey Long's direction: 'When Fascism comes to America it will be in the form of Americanism.' I'm taking a thoroughly American thoughtform and seeing it for what it always was. When Satanism becomes the major religion in the United States, it will be complete with red, white and blue banners flying accompanied by the blaring trombones of John Phillip Sousa."

As evidence of the rising tide of Satanism, LaVey points to the cavalier, even flaunting, attitude young people have about the images of the Devil. While their horrified parents wonder what kind of heathen monster they've raised, their children idolize Satan as their Rebel King. "There are plenty of people in their teens and twenties out there saying they worship the Devil because it's cool now and a lot of their friends call themselves Satanists. A lot of them don't understand much more than what they see on MTV but the point is they are giving homage to the Devil and not to God. There's no need for human sacrifices and pacts with the Devil anymore. These kids are already aligned with Satanic forces. Now they participate in altar calls at rock concerts regardless of, or because of, their parents' outrage.

"They can take delight in wearing the Baphomet for great shock value. People who wear the symbol regularly report they get a much stronger reaction with it than they do when they wear, for instance, Nazi regalia. With a swastika, people can get righteously offended. The person wearing it wants to be labeled an Aryan Supremacist, far right-winger, something like that. Immediately pigeonholed. But the Baphomet doesn't represent a particular historical context. You can't pigeonhole the Satanic symbol, or Satanists. It just evokes dark, unexplained but intense primal fears. The reaction tends to be, 'We don't know much about it but we know we should be afraid of it.' And it's not just young people participating in mainstreaming Satanism. Halloween is now more popular and widely celebrated than Christmas. Christmas only means distress, guilts, suicides, loneliness, death. Halloween is fun, not a time for necessary family reunions but just getting together with friends for parties, drinking and playing dress-up.

There are whole systems of thought, like Neo-Tech Discovery, which offers Satanism in a grey flannel suit, promises overnight wealth, and never mentions the dreaded "S" word. *Megabrain* applies early Church of Satan-style ritual to the business world, adding meditation techniques to appeal to the softcore New Age and yuppie markets. C.A.S.H., the Continental Association of Satan's Hope (just make your checks out to CASH), based in Canada, began by reprinting sections of *The Satanic Bible* and reproducing the Baphomet before they were warned of copyright infringement. Another Canadian, a Dr. Lawrence Pazder, claimed to have never heard of the internationally famous Church of Satan before the publication of his purportedly factual *Michelle Remembers,* the Rosetta Stone of all current Satanic abuse testimonials. Dr. Pazder eventually married his subject, Michelle Smith, and they are still gathering credulous audiences for their Satanbusting seminars.

"In reality, our mainstream influence is just the tip of the iceberg. For every one of those kids you see at rock concerts holding up the sign of the horns and not knowing anything about it, there are maybe five more kids who have read *The Satanic Bible,* know what Satanism is, and are growing up to the stage now where they are gaining positions of power and having a real effect in the world around us. In the motion picture industry, the arts, business, academia, politics — they don't wear it on their sleeves so you probably wouldn't even know they were Satanists. But you figure those who were born in 1955 or 1960, who have grown up living most of their lives in a post-1966 Satanic Age, are now reaching 27, 29, 32 years old. They're getting established in their chosen fields and their philosophy is bound to have an effect on the way they operate. They're getting tired of the bullshit. Now we're getting what I call second-generation Satanists; the Church of Satan has been in existence for most of their lives and they take the effects of Satanism as the rule rather than the exception — sexual freedom, not believing in God, independence of mind. They are choosing Satanism as a way of life because it was never shoved down their throats like Christian parents do with their religion."

*"The infant is learning to walk, and by the first Working Year of his age — that is to say 1984 — he will have steadied his steps, and by the next — 2002 — he will have attained maturity, and his reign will be filled with wisdom, reason and delight."* — last sentence in *The Satanic Rituals.*

LaVey describes Satanism as a secular philosophy of rationalism and self-preservation (natural law, animal state), giftwrapping these ideas in religious trappings to add to their appeal. A Satanist enters the supernatural realm by choice, with eyes open and hearts clear rather than taking a supernatural belief as a starting point, like superstitious primitives trying to explain lightning, or Christians explaining the Virgin Birth. "Satanists must have a firm grounding in rational methods of thinking as a foundation to stand on. Without it, you're trying to reach the sky, or even stand on the sky, with no ladder beneath you. Christians consider logic a non-option, something that is treated as if it were dangerous.

"Under the Christian pastoral system, you have to keep paying to keep sinless. If you stop paying, then you won't get to heaven. You have to go to big buildings to pray. If we have altars set up in our own homes, they can't be legislated; money can't be collected on them. Satanism takes religion beyond the realm of consumerism. If the truth were known, one of the major threats of reports of devil-worshipping sabbaths is that they are independent, not tightly organized into a strict structure. Trying to discover Satanists, real Satanists, is like nailing custard to the wall. You'd have to break into everyone's home and see if they had a Satanic altar. And even if they didn't have an altar, they might *still* be Satanists!

"People send letters to the Church, frantically asking, 'What can I do to become an active member?' 'What do I do to become a Satanic priest?' Of course, what they're really asking is 'Where do I go to meet other Satanists? — give me an address to meet other people.' 'How to I get to be an official?' My attitude would be, 'If you have to ask, you ain't one.' It's like the joke about the price of the yacht — if you have to ask, you can't afford it. If you're a priest or priestess in the outside world already, we'll know. The five degrees of Satanism are still valid, but in a much more practical way, based on the Satanist's level of participation in the outside world. What I call 'Mainstream' or 'First-level' Satanists are the equivalent to what we used to call 'Apprentices'. They go to a nine to five job, earn good money, wear acceptable clothes, have formal rituals, drive cars that look basically the same as everyone else's, watch television, yet agree with and apply Satanism in a positive way in their lives. At the other end of the spectrum, we still have practicing Magisters and Magistras who divorce themselves from the mainstream as much as possible and arrange their lives to earn money at things that entail a minimal amount of contact with the herd — artists, directors, writers, performers, entrepreneurs of various kinds.... If you want to get titles and wear robes, this is not the organization for you. We want to apply Satanism for our own good, not use it as a crutch to convey false achievement.

As a rule, LaVey doesn't disclose membership figures. "If it's too low, we would be perceived as insignificant, and if it was too high we'd be considered too much of a threat and there would be reason to destroy us. If you can be quantified, then you can be expendable, then you can be disposed of. Besides, after 25 years, it would be very difficult to calculate our membership. Members are lifetime members; they don't have to pay any renewal fees every year so we have had a cumulative increase since 1966." Tom Wedge explains this phenomenon in his 1987 book, *The Satan Hunter*: "However, it must be realized that the great preponderance of the followers of the Church of Satan have never formally made an effort to actually 'join' the church. The thousands who follow portions of the teachings of Anton

LaVey and others of his like are not those who [...] become contributing members. The majority of the followers of the precepts of the Church of Satan are those teenagers who pay the $3.95 purchase price for a copy of the paperback edition of *The Satanic Bible*."[34]

LaVey feels that's the way it should be. As for actual members, "Either they're with us or they're not. It won't change ten or twenty years later. The idea is to mold people's minds and send them out among men, not to keep them milling around the same corral like sheep. If their eyes are opened there is no turning back — nothing will ever be the same for them. These are people who don't need to go to group rituals to feel connected to the source — a truly secret society for magicians who are working advanced Black Magic and influencing the outside world. What's the advantage in being a big fish in a little pond when you can be a big fish in a big pond? When you're a somebody 'out there,' you don't need to advertise your affiliations. That's fine for people who are just starting out — it's fun and indulgent and if they want to get together with a few friends to use my books to perform rituals, that's great. But eventually they want to apply their magic in a way that will get them ahead in the real world."

Just as there has been a new breed of Satanist surfacing, there's a new breed of "experts" in Satanism to round out the field. LaVey is disdainful of these self-appointed "occult investigators." "They obviously don't know the first thing about what I've written or what I advocate. If they'd read my books instead of just wave them in the air, they might know something about Satanism. But they seem to prefer making it up as they go along. There was more factual, more informed reporting going on in 1975 than there is now. Of course, there's more money and attention in being a professional hysteric now, making a living telling your masturbatory fantasies on nationwide TV. There are people on the talk show circuit who claim to be ex-members or ex-priests in a Satanic organization who can't even show they read the same book I wrote, let alone give an accurate rendition of our practices and philosophy. It's funny that they're always 'High Priests,' there are never any 'Low Priests' or just plain 'Priests.' There were no 'High Priests' until I came along except in Puccini operas.

"In Chicago, there's a Center for Multiple Personalities studying 'adult survivors of Satanic child abuse.' Now what's that supposed to mean? There was no modern, organized Satanic movement before I came along, and here are all these middle-aged women telling how they were raped and tortured as children, when their parents belonged to a Satanic cult? That would have been in the 1940's. There were none! Lord knows, I looked. Producers don't send camera crews out to track down these women's parents and get their stories; no one looks up the women's psychological histories. If there were any Freudians left they'd see what's going on.

"But the din of sensationalism muffles the sound of falling ratings. When it's ratings time, it's a good time to talk about Satanism. What unfortunately happens is they want to talk about Satanism, but it's too dangerous to talk about *real* Satanic ideas."

Since the airing of a 1985 *20/20* episode,[35] a renewed mythology has formed around Satanism. The catalogue of blood-curdling and spine-chilling "true stories" about Satanists hark back in style and in content to Julius Streicher's anti-Jewish propaganda — sucking the blood from Christian children with a straw.

LaVey answers his accusers concerning dark Satanic doings:

*"There's no possible way to get out of a Satanic cult — only through death."*

"All anyone has to do is write a letter to get out. No one's kicked out unless they do something that is blatantly against our tenets or unless they request to have their names taken from our lists."

*There are three categories of Satanists: 1) Traditional Satanists, 2) Religious Satanists, and 3) Freestyle Satanists."*

"There are no categories of Satanists — there are Satanists, and then there are nuts. The Satanic know-it-alls try to fabricate a division just so they won't get sued. By saying there are different categories, they can say, 'Oh, we didn't mean you, of course. We meant these other guys (that really don't exist). You're good Satanists!' There's no such thing as a 'good Satanist'. Actually, I would divide Satanic poseurs into three groups — Satanists, Christian Satanists, and nuts. I'd define Christian Satanists as those who are attracted to Satanism but can't seem to break away from Christianity altogether. They continue to work within a primitive framework of Good vs.

Evil, taking the part of Evil instead of Good. Whenever you get an inkling of the Dungeons and Dragons, Good/Evil mythos, you know they don't know much about true evil. You have to take Satan within yourself to smash that Christian orientation."

*"You have to sell your soul to Satan and sign a pact in blood."*

"Come on — souls come very cheap these days. This myth is perpetuated by Christian Satanists who are following the lead of medieval witch-hunters. Satan demands a much harder task than signing over your soul in blood. He demands that you live your life as fully as you can, prosper by your own wits and avoid misery. You wouldn't believe what a tall order that is for most people!"

*"You have to believe in God to believe in Satan. Satan is a myth designed by Christians so you can't believe in one without the other."*

"People, even those who call themselves 'practitioners of the Old Religion,' can't conceive of a philosophy beyond Christianity, beyond good against evil. It's like 'worshipping the Devil.' We don't worship Satan, we worship ourselves using the metaphorical representation of the qualities of Satan. Satan *is* the name used by Judeo-Christians for that force of individuality and pride within us. But the force itself has been called by many names. We embrace Christian myths of Satan and Lucifer, along with Satanic renderings in Greek, Roman, Islamic, Sumerian, Syrian, Phrygian, Egyptian, Chinese, or Hindu mythologies, to name but a few. We are not limited to one deity, but encompass all the expressions of the accuser or the one who advocates free thought and rational alternatives by whatever name he is called in a particular time and land. It so happens that we are living in a culture that is predominantly Judeo-Christian, so we emphasize Satan. If we were living in Roman times, the central figure, perhaps the title of our religion, would be different. But the name would be expressing and communicating the same thing. It's all context."

\*\*\*

The more harmful accusations levelled against Satanism of ritual human and animal sacrifice, kidnapping, child abuse, torture, rape... These go beyond theology into the realm of criminal activities. LaVey remains unruffled. "When a Christian commits a crime it's not dubbed a 'Christian cult murder'. As more *Satanic Bibles* are sold, there are more chances one will be found at a murder site, or among a murderer's personal effects. It's inevitable, with so many members, that some time soon a criminal or victim's going to have an actual Church of Satan membership card on their person. And won't that be exciting!

"It doesn't make it a 'ritual' murder. It makes juicy copy. I'd like to see the day when headlines read 'Slasher reported to be involved in Christian group' with the accompanying article outlining the incriminating evidence found in the killer's apartment — pictures of saints on the wall, the Holy Bible and other Christian books found in shelves, various crosses in small jewelry boxes. With these supposed Satanic crimes, 'evidence of Satanic involvement' doesn't have anything to do with the crime itself, might not even have anything to do with Satanism!, but is picked out because it piques people's prurient interests."

Police officials from the beginning have tried to quell the hysteria for the most part, quickly modifying their earliest flyers and guidelines on the subject, which listed ceramic cats, stained glass, and circles as Satanic symbols to watch for at crime sites. While a few are still trying to make a name for themselves as "Cops for Christ," most of the many articles in police magazines take a fairly even view. There are still Satanic task forces in every town, and costly seminars on occult crimes abound, but LaVey has always been on friendly terms with police and investigators, continuing to help when asked.

San Francisco Police Inspector Sandi Gallant, one of the foremost authorities on occult crimes, instructs fellow investigators to focus on the framework of "ritualistic crimes or abuse" rather than singling out any one religion. "Someone involved in a crime might use certain elements of a particular religious orientation to justify their crime, whether it's Christianity, Catholicism, Rastafarianism, Santeria, Satanism, or any combination of these things. You can't just look at a room, see what looks like a upside-down star or an Ozzy Osbourne poster and say, 'This is a Satanic crime.'

"When looking at a crime now, investigators have to put it into one of two categories — is the crime a *demand* of the particular religion (like animal sacrifices in Santeria or Voodoo), or is the religion being used as a justification for their crimes that, because of their own psychological makeup, would be happening anyway?"

Over the last few years, things have gotten silly. A brief review of "expert" vocabulary shows not everyone who hangs out her shingle as an occult investigator is as well-grounded as Ms. Gallant. Talk show hosts across America have insisted we concern ourselves over the Feast of the Beast, the WICCA Letter, breeders, altar babies, Dabblers, Stoners, Traditional Satanists, Orthodox Satanists, Freestyle Satanists, Religious Satanists, ritual abuse, Satanic survivors, the Black Hole ritual, acid pits and portable crematoriums (used to get rid of the bodies of sacrificial victims, often brought up in answer to the question, "Where are the bodies?"), Spotters (those who act as look-outs, usually gardeners or trashmen, at day-care centers where Satanists are ensconced), ritualers (pronounced "RIT-chal-erz"), grimoires (pronounced "grim-OR-eez"), trainers, recruiters and Devil dances (what preschoolers do when they've been ritually abused).

Indicators your child might be getting into Satanism have been listed as wanting to spend time alone, wearing incriminating t-shirts, requesting black sheets or black curtains, wanting a snake as a pet ... all are sure signs of the Devil at work. When Pope John Paul toured the United States and spoke at the University of Arizona auditorium, the Red Devil mascots painted on the walls were covered up so as not to offend His Holiness. High school teams across the country that called themselves some kind of "Devils" changed their names to something less Satanic-sounding. House numbers, license plates and telephone prefixes that contained the sinister "666" were finally seen for the demonic influence they are and were immediately altered — including the number of the house the Reagans moved into after they vacated the White House. A senate Bill number had to be changed from Bill 666 to Bill 649 in February of 1986 because it was feared the legislators would be unduly influenced by the original number.

All of it would be pretty funny except for those losing their jobs, homes, positions in the community or parents' trust because of irrational, unfounded fears and accusations. Using Satanism as a justification, too, have been the righteous teachers and school administrators who have searched high school children's lockers for signs of diabolical dabblings. Any kid with a pentagram can be hauled into the principal's office for a thorough talking-to by the local priest. Articles report that school librarians are reviewing check-out records to track down anyone checking out dangerous (read: "subversive") books from the school library.

"It all works eventually in our favor, though," says LaVey. "All these Pray TV evangelists have had their last gasp. They're hurting. So who else do they turn to but the Devil? He's always been their real Savior. People are tired of the noise. They grow tired of the hysteria. We couldn't have planned it any better. When the Satanic hysteria gets to the point of absurdity, people start questioning the whole line of crap. It will eventually get so no one believes anything Christian ministers say anymore. When they hear about the Devil and how rotten he is, it just makes them curious about what the Satanic viewpoint might be.

There are many who are already questioning the wild claims. Arthur Lyons' *Satan Wants You* (Warner, 1988) challenged the accusers' stories after finding they could produce no hard evidence. In October, 1989, the Committee for the Scientific Examination of Religion issued a report on the claims of various "breeders" and "Satanic survivors." After a thorough investigation, the report concluded that, "The most shocking claims, those involving the abductions and ritual murder of children, are easily shown to be false. The allegations of large scale Satanic conspiracies are totally without foundation. In fact, the available evidence leaves only one reasonable conclusion: *they do not exist!*" [Their italics.][36] Various magazines, including *The Skeptical Inquirer,* have since devoted cover stories to the debunking of Satanic hysteria.

"There's no propaganda necessary. Just let Satanists speak for themselves — there doesn't have to be a bias one way or another. What irritates me is that, even if the producers of a television show make a concession by having a bona fide Satanist on their show, not just some pseudo-Satanist, they give more time to the self-appointed 'experts' than they do to the real Satanists. How can they have more authority about Satanism than the adherents themselves? You don't ask Hitler about the joys of Passover. All that needs to be said about Satanism is the truth and it can't help but alter people's way of thinking. If they ever get a dose of what real Satanism is, Lord help them."

# Chapter Nineteen

# The Invisible Revolution

> *"Do you know one thing, though? I am certain that under-ground people like me must be kept in check. Though we may be capable of sitting underground for forty years without saying a word, if we do come out into the world and burst out, we will talk and talk and talk..."*
> — Dostoevsky, *Notes From Underground*

In 1967, Anton LaVey worked up "Eleven Rules of the Earth" to augment the "Nine Satanic Statements" he had already devised and published among his followers. LaVey long considered the Rules to be too brutal for the uninitiated, prefacing *The Satanic Bible* with the Statements alone. Now he feels the time is right to publish them. They are edicts designed for the human animal, laying out the law of the jungle, "Lex Talionis." LaVey specifically *prohibits:* harming children; killing non-human animals except for food or in self-defense; telling your troubles or giving opinions unasked; and making sexual advances toward someone who may not appreciate it. The two Rules that will raise eyebrows among the non-Satanically-oriented are: "If a guest in your lair annoys you, treat him cruelly and without mercy," and "When walking in open territory, bother no one. If someone bothers you, ask him to stop. If he does not stop, destroy him."

LaVey stands by these sometimes violent edicts all the more in the 1990's. "If people simply had to face up to their own actions, their own evolution, and make adjustments for their own progress, the population would be cut in half in one generation. Instead we've devised laws and lawsuits to protect people from themselves. If these feeble, modern, inbred creatures had to live by their wits and take care of themselves, they'd be too scared to go out of their houses. They'd be dead. They wouldn't be able to move fast enough or think fast enough and they'd be eliminated.

"Any creature, human or otherwise, is only as important as they make themselves to other creatures. What would happen if, in the wild, one aberrant monkey kept shrieking, or tearing up other monkeys' beds, or scratching and attacking the others in the tribe? They would get bit back, gnawed on. If they kept it up, they'd be chased away or ripped apart. That's what our instincts tell us should happen. Up until now we've been instilled with the attitude that we're supposed to allow for others' ineptitude — drive for everyone else on the road, place warning signs out for people not to fall into ditches or walk where it's wet; that it's our responsibility if they fall. Everything now is people-proofed. What would happen if one day they woke up and found they were expected to pay the consequences of their own ineptitude, or hooliganism, or boorishness?"

One of LaVey's pet peeves is the inequity he sees in America — but not the kind of inequity most might spout about. "People get rewarded in our society for what they can't do, not what they can. That's a terrible inequity to me. It seems everything — laws, schools, economics, jobs — is calculated to encourage the lowest elements, not the highest."

To counteract this inequality LaVey proposes a few Satanic solutions. In 1988, Anton published a *Cloven Hoof* essay entitled "Pentagonal Revisionism: A Five-Point Program," which outlines "the current thrust of Satanic advocacy." The platform prioritizes stratification, strict taxation of churches, re-establishing a "Lex Talionis" attitude in the legal and judiciary arenas, development and production of androids, and the opportunity for "total environments." While most of these points have already been discussed at greater length elsewhere in the book, *stratification* should be understood to be LaVey's cornerstone of contemporary Satanic activity.

"Stratification is the point on which all the others ultimately rest. There can be no more myth of 'equality' for all — it only translates to 'mediocrity' and supports the weak at the expense of the strong. Water must be allowed to seek its own level without interference from apologists. No one should be protected from the effects of his own stupidity." Later in the same issue, LaVey writes, "The current Third World War — human locusts overrunning the world, necessitating the thinning out of populations because the Rule of the Fool has, for the first time in history, threatened to destroy civilization and evolution. *This* must never happen again! Technology has left human awareness in the dust. Surely, it would be simpler and more economically practical to continue the propagation of consumers, at the cost of evolution. But the Earth could not survive. How to isolate and evolve genetically superior humans is the great task of stratification."

"I'm saying there's an unrecognized war going on in this country right now," declares LaVey, "an economic war. War will not come from without, it will come from the people who have the most money to gain right here in this country. The Great Consumer wars. All the other 'causes' are just misdirection devices. Any supposed protesting going on is carefully contained rebellion. Otherwise people would be rioting in the street when they have to pay $30,000 for a three-day stay in the hospital. But the warfare now going on is much more sophisticated than science fiction writers ever imagined. It's absurd to think that research in chemical, sonic or bioelectric weaponry has been abandoned. I realize certain things have to be done for the good of society, to keep the economy afloat or the population down, but I don't like to be played for a fool."

For now, isolation, abdication and stratification are LaVey's proposed Satanic weapons against the ongoing Invisible War. LaVey has already given a name, Satanism, for the small percentage of the population that he feels are chromosomally different, and perhaps chromosomally resistant to the effects of control. Stratification is a magical process of purification — subtractive rather than additive. Says LaVey, "As the war progresses, and as population increases to an even more intolerable level stretching resources to impossible lengths, the strong will begin fighting for their very survival. That's what we're seeing right now. Society will become more and more stratified into the people who aren't buying the bullshit in society and those who blindly follow where they are led. Satanists, freethinkers, are a burgeoning minority cause. We have an illness that needs to be recognized just like alcoholism, handicaps, addictive behaviors and AIDS. We suffer from a disease called independence — a pathological aversion to regimentation and institutionalism — which prevents us from getting 'regular' jobs and living a 'normal' life.

Instead of encouraging "proliferation of the weak," LaVey feels it's imperative to isolate and foster the emerging new genetic strain of Satanists. With the debut of *The Compleat Witch* in 1970 (later *The Satanic Witch*), LaVey presented his guide for selective breeding. In an August 16, 1971 article, "Evil Anyone?," *Newsweek* captioned a picture of LaVey baptizing his daughter, Zeena, "...Building 'a better race,'" and quotes Anton describing his Satanic goal as "the creation of a police state in which the weak are weeded out and the 'achievement-oriented leadership' is permitted to pursue the mysteries of black magic."

Later, in *The Satanic Rituals,* LaVey included this directive to his followers: "Now it is the higher man's role to produce the children of the future. Quality is now more important that quantity. One cherished child who can *create* will be more important than ten who can produce — or fifty who can *believe!*" [37] In an interview for *Fling,* Anton vows that he would "enhance the growth of new, more intelligent generations, if I had the chance, by selective breeding. But this is so terrifyingly related to Hitlerism that usually I can't even talk about it."[38]

When asked exactly what kind of Master Race he envisions, LaVey explains that the Satanic stratification and segregation he advocates is based on "ethics rather than ethnics." "As I've said, I wish to identify, isolate and breed a new ethnic — one that's been there all along, unrecognized, from the beginning of man's existence. There have always been leaders, innovators, risk-takers among all cultures. These are the few, perhaps one-tenth of one percent, that lead nations forward, lead evolution forward. Satanism is the first time in history where a master race can be built of genetically predisposed, like-minded people — not based on the genes that make them white, black, blue, brown or purple — but the genes that make them Satanists. We need a forum from which to assert our culture. Any person I've ever met who's accomplished anything in his life had a real disdain for his own 'people'. Not that they hate Jews or Germans or Irish or Italians per se — just that they hate stupidity and herd mentality. They hate the idea of using any ethnicity as an identity. Some people that come from Jewish backgrounds, where Judaic traditions were really emphasized in the home, are the most rabid anti-Semitic people I know. And I don't blame them. If they grew up in a stifling environment with professional Jews for parents or professional Catholics, I don't blame them for running away, changing their names, completely inverting their lives and never wanting to see their parents again! That's often how leaders are born.

"You have to be a sociopath to be in my position. Look at all the depictions of Satan throughout history, his Satanic sadness and dismay at the unhappy world people seem compelled to make for themselves. As a Satanist, of course I'm a sociopath. I love life and am honestly dismayed. That's why, when people are supportive of me, I'm suspicious — it's hard for me to accept, because that pall, that death is ever-present.

"People looking at Satanism from the outside, with all its black-draped chambers and sinister trappings, might think that we advocate death. Christians are supposed to be the life-loving ones, striving for happiness and good. In reality, a true curse comes from 'God' when he answers their prayers. They don't want their prayers answered. They don't really want contentment. That's why they pray to a god that isn't there. The truth is that those who surround themselves and speak most of death are probably the most life-loving of all, and truly like Satan — they find themselves dismayed that things can't be pure and complete, the way they should be. If Satanists didn't care, they wouldn't be so dark and pessimistic. You can find plenty of optimists in lunatic asylums — only fools are ever truly content."

Along with most contemporary soothsayers, LaVey perceives momentous changes as we approach the millennium. "People are now making important decisions. We've evolved to the point where all the information from our history is there for anyone to examine. All the methods have been written about. It's now a volitional, well-informed choice whether you want to accept Satanism or not. Whether you choose death over life. Christians have conjured their apocalypse and we certainly wouldn't want to disappoint them. The end of the millennium is coming fast."

Selective breeding, elitist stratification, advocacy of polygamous relationships for breeding purposes, and eventually building communities of like-minded individuals are Satanic programs antithetical to the cherished egalitarian ideal. Since 1966, these subjects have become the *zeitgeist* for any number of extremist offshoots, and it has finally become apparent that LaVey and the Church of Satan should be recognized as their progenitor.

"Extremism in whatever form, forces the card," says LaVey. "That's all the American public seems to understand. They can't see shades of grey. Extremism causes the changes to occur more quickly and more completely. Satanism is not just an atheistic stance but a anti-theistic stance. We prefer destruction of mystically-oriented religions through active opposition rather than simple non-participation."

Because his picture hanging in Moscow's Museum of Atheism, his long-time use of authentic Nazi black magic ceremonies and symbols, and his early association with Zionist terrorists, LaVey has inevitably been linked with extremist groups of all kinds. "There's a difference between stalking someone who's made trouble for you and bothering someone who's minding his own business. It's all too easy to hassle people just because of the color of their skin. Why not do something really productive with that same energy and throw a scare into a person who's obviously out selling drugs, pimping, raping, killing, looting, robbing — not the race of people but the individuals, or the type of individuals. There's a magically valid technique of seeking out surrogates for your tormentors, or would-be tormentors, and venting your wrath on them to superimpose it on your actual tormentor. If you took out your rage and frustration on the person you'd like to, the connection might be so obvious it would be laid directly at your doorstep. As a substitute, a sacrifice of sorts, you look for someone who might not have done anything to you directly but you can tell he's the type who has probably screwed up other people like you. But these are very fine points of magic I can't in good conscience recommend to most people.

"That's the strength of a forum like Satanism. We aren't against Jews, Blacks, Whites ... We refuse to continue to compromise our standards to allow for stupidity and laziness! They have to be expected to come up to our standards rather than us lowering hurdles to suit them. If they can't, they should be told, probably for the first time in their lives, 'You know what? You're stupid! You're inferior!' instead of being protected from the effects of their incompetence. If a person is ethical, productive, sensitive, and knows how to conduct himself among human beings, fine; if he's an amoral parasite, he should be dealt with quickly and cruelly."

LaVey denies the existence, or need, for anything quite so obvious as a grand Satanic conspiracy. "The kind of changes I envision don't require skirmishes on the street or a revolution, merely a cabal. A conspiracy implies a carefully delineated plan of attack, all neatly mapped out for all participants. A cabal is a group of loosely connected people who have deep, unswerving loyalty and allegiance to the same ends and who do what comes naturally. They have the unlisted phone numbers; they'll know, in their respective positions, what to do when the time comes 'round. Oh, we do have goals. We all know what they are. I believe in all forms of stealth, cunning and guile to achieve our ends."

Instead of revolution, LaVey proposes a Satanic revisionism. "Maybe evolution has brought enough of us out of our cocoon so we can surround ourselves with true aesthetics rather than standards based on economic imperatives. Satanism is bringing back is discipline in all forms of art and expression. We emphasize a return to classical grounding in music, painting, sculpture, writing, poetry — re-establishing a common body of knowledge and expression so there are some constants of beauty and form. Satanic thought doesn't encourage the 'splash and smear' school of unbridled 'artistic expression.'

"A Satanist understands why and how certain economic and political imperatives most be answered to in a Machiavellian sense, but he doesn't want to be played for a chump. As we grow in numbers, we will have more say in the economy. Productive consumerism is necessary and preferable, when tempered by the awareness of population limitations on the planet. But not this rampant, unorganized, money-hungry, destructive consumerism derived directly from the Judeo-Christian 'more Christians equals more money' attitude.

"People still have a primordial fear of the night. But Satanists should soon be a strong enough economic force to keep our own stores and businesses open all night, at our hours. Not only will we become a major voting block and economic demographic to be catered to, but we've worked ourselves into places where we pull the strings ourselves."

LaVey has begun to enforce changes on a personal level that reflect on a national and international level. "At this stage of the game, I don't have the time for patience and tolerance. Ten years ago, even five years ago, I would have listened to people ask their questions, explained to them, mollified them. No more. That time is past. Now, as Norman Mailer said in *Naked and the Dead,* 'I hate everything which is not in myself.' If it doesn't have a direct bearing on what I'm advocating, if it doesn't augment or stimulate my life and thinking, I don't want to hear it. It has to add something to my life. There's no more time for explaining and being ecumenical anymore. No more time.

"That's a characteristic I share with the new generation of Satanists, which might best be termed, and has labeled itself in many ways, an 'Apocalypse culture.' Not that they believe in the biblical Apocalypse — the ultimate war between good and evil. Quite the contrary. But that there is an urgency, a need to get on with things and stop wailing and if it ends tomorrow, at least we'll know we've lived today. It's a 'fiddle while Rome burns' philosophy. It's the Satanic philosophy. If the generation born in the 50's grew up in the shadow of The Bomb and had to assimilate the possibility of imminent self-destruction of the entire planet at any time, those born in the 60's have had to reconcile the inevitability of our own destruction, not through the bomb but through mindless, uncontrolled overpopulation. And somehow resolve in themselves, looking at what history has taught us, that no amount of yelling, protesting, placard waving, marching, wailing — or even more constructive avenues like running for government office or trying to write books to wake people up — is going to do a damn bit of good. The majority of humans have an inborn death wish — they want to destroy themselves and everything beautiful. To finally realize that we're living in a world after the zenith of creativity, and that we can see so clearly the mechanics of our own destruction, is a terrible realization. Most people can't face it. They'd rather retreat to the comfort of New Age mysticism. That's all right. All we want, those few of us who have the strength to realize what's going on, is the freedom to create and entertain and share with each other, to preserve and cherish what we can while we can, and to build our own little citadels away from the insensitivity of the rest of the world."

Reacting, perhaps, to millennial pressures, certain people are doing more than building protective citadels. Some, it seems more all the time, are taking guns and killing innocent people. Investigators, no matter how objective they may be, become disturbed by the increasing number of *Satanic Bibles* found at crime sites or in the personal effects of mass murderers. It may be that LaVey's Satanic thought can release forces within unstable people that they are not able to control.

LaVey insists we'll never really know how much influence Satanism has on the nut cases. "Frankly, so little factual information is leaked out through the media. I'm in a prime position to know that first-hand! The media will only look at Satanism from a firmly prescribed perspective. "Like that kid in New Jersey [Tommy Sullivan] who supposedly killed his mother with a Boy Scout knife as a result of his growing involvement with Satanism. He was a good kid from a Catholic family and suddenly he 'snapped' because of Satanism. Bullshit! A few of the stories leaked the truth, if you can read between the lines. The kid was a bright. He wanted to explore, he wanted to stretch his mind and imagination to examine ideas his parents, particularly his mother, couldn't tolerate. He became confused, then increasingly hostile as she continued stifling him and holding him down. This went on for months, probably preluded by years of over-mothering in the guise of protecting him. Then, finally, after an intensive session of anti-Satanic counseling and praying at their Catholic church, the kid got fed up. Maybe everything went blank all of a sudden. Maybe he was a good kid who couldn't take any more of the bullshit and had to impose the justice he perceived to be lacking. He knew he was being treated unjustly, felt there was no way out and took the only action immediately available — slashing his mother's throat then doing the same to himself. What a needless tragedy. If only he'd been allowed to freely explore the avenues he'd wanted to perhaps it never would have happened."

Second-wave Satanists have definite visions of right and wrong, and use *The Satanic Bible* as a guide to impose demonic justice. Sean Sellers, as quoted by Tom Wedge, translated what he believed to be qualifications for an appropriate human sacrifice. "Sacrificed people are those people who beat their wives, molest children, kick their dogs, etc. We do the world a favor by getting rid of them. After all, people like this have no right to live, anyway."[39] Sellers was eventually sentenced to death for the murder of his mother, stepfather and a convenience store clerk in 1985 and '86. Sellers has since recanted his Satanic beliefs and is now hailed by Christians for his youth ministry from Oklahoma's Death Row. David St. Clair in his book, *Say You Love Satan,* aptly describes through a teenager's eyes what freedom *The Satanic Bible* might offer: "If what this book said was true, if what this book promised could be realized, then nothing was impossible. Nobody should have to put up with the shit they were born into. If the guy that wrote this really knew what he was talking about, then Satan was the way to go. The devil had the answers for life on earth. The devil was the one to contact, the one who would do things for human beings who wanted to achieve."[40] The subject of St. Clair's book, Ricky Kasso, killed one of his classmates and later killed himself.

Anton LaVey maintains that he isn't really concerned about accusations of people killing other people in the name of Satan. He swears that each time he reads of a new killing spree, his only reaction is, "What, 22 people? Is that all?" Anton is more concerned about those nobodies he's bestowed godhood on with his philosophy. "Certain people like to take up the trappings, methods and hardboiled philosophy of Satanism but aren't willing to adopt my imposition of 'responsibility for the responsible.' They just pick out what they want, change it around to justify what they want to do, invent it if it's not there and ignore what they find too difficult to adhere to. As a mass-market book, *The Satanic Bible* breeds pretentiousness in the inferior — everyone believes he is a superman. Of course it bothers me. It's antithetical to the essence of Satanism to puff up undeserving people. But in reality, I have to admit it's an effective shortcut to stratification. I'd rather be grouped in the company of killers than in the company of wimps. I don't think you'd find the pretentiousness in people like Ramirez, or Stanley Dean Baker, or Huberty, or Manson — I don't think you'd find the noise that all these puffed-up, empty barrel, supposed-Satanists make." In a 1986 article regarding accused "Night Stalker" killer, Richard Ramirez, convicted of 13 murders in California, LaVey said, "When I met Richard Ramirez, he was the nicest, most polite young man you'd ever want to meet ... a model of deportment."

LaVey remembers the incident clearly and regrets giving the young Ramirez such an abrupt meeting. "He stopped me on the street and said, 'Excuse me, Mr. LaVey, could I talk to you a few moments?' Well, I don't generally like people coming up to me like that so I just brushed him off: 'I don't do business on the sidewalk. You can write to the post office box.' He backed away and apologized for bothering me, said he just wanted to ask me a couple of questions but he can see I'm busy — so he wished me a happy Solstice and walked on down the street with his friend, the one from Texas, I guess. I watched him walk away and when he was almost to the corner, I almost called for him to come back and I'd talk to him. After thinking about it, I felt really badly. He seemed like such a polite kid."

LaVey doesn't shirk responsibility for what his writings may catalyze. "If *The Satanic Bible* is spurring a changed perspective to unleash certain demons, certain elementals into the world, so be it. We will evoke many, many centuries of bloodshed before we approach the terror that Christianity has loosed on humanity. There will undoubtedly be more Satanically-motivated murders and crimes in the sense that *The Satanic Bible* tells you 'You don't have to take any more shit.' But if Judeo-Christian society hadn't encouraged this immoral succoring of the weak, and made it laudable to buoy up the useless, then there wouldn't be this intensive need for a reaction against it. Of course, this extreme counter-swing of the pendulum, this vigilantism, will be interpreted as 'mere anarchy loosed on the world,' but in reality it will be, for the first time since cave days, justice.

LaVey points to James Huberty's case as a textbook example of anti-Christian abreaction. Early San Diego reports leaked that *The Second Coming,* Arthur Lyons' definitive work on Satanism, was found among Huberty's books when police searched his home after the McDonald's shooting. "James Huberty was laid off from a high paying job because of our undeclared economic depression. Trying to get work, he traveled down the coast of California, ending up in a little Mexico where he hardly heard a word of English spoken. Huberty knew he was under a lot of pressure. He contacted a mental health clinic. Because of the crackdown on Valium at the time, only street-people and pushers could get it. Those who used Valium in moderation were completely cut off, so Huberty wasn't able to get the one chemical that had leveled him out. And to top it all off, the crew at McDonald's couldn't get the fucking ice cream machine fixed for two weeks! He was tired of incompetence, he was tired of foreign inundation; he was tired of being treated like a second-class citizen in his own country; he was tired of the weak getting everything for free and those who are trying to stand up on their own two feet getting nothing. He was just tired. After awhile these things get frustrating and something's got to give. And I'll tell you a secret. There's going to be a lot more Hubertys reaching a breaking point in the next few years. We've got a long way to go.

"By the same token, if a kid is dragged to church against his will, if his parents tear up his *Satanic Bible* — the one book he sees as containing some truth beyond the narrow framework of Christian belief—an 'antisocial, psychopathic' kid might be provoked. *The Satanic Bible* tells him, 'I will create justice in my own way. I feel an injustice has to be righted and I feel the strength to carry it out.' It imbues him with the ideal that if he wants justice he will have to *take* justice in his own way, it won't be given to him.

"Satanists are *true* reformers, as we are true ecologists. We believe in the preeminence of the laws of Nature. The epitome of the *film noir* anti-hero — the Green Hornet, the Shadow, the Avenger, Batman — is the perfect manifestation of the Satanic ethic. These are the heroes who work in the shadows, doing what officials cannot do or will not do. *The Satanic Bible* doesn't say, 'Vengeance is mine sayeth the Lord.' It teaches you to not wait around for outside intervention from God or the state on your behalf. There is no protectionism, no over-legislation. Satanism advocates personal justice, personally administered.

"The Satanic Master Plan is worse than any fictions the Church could possibly dream up over the past 500 years. All our lives, seem to have been diabolically guided from birth. All it takes is a handful of people in the right places. 23 people led the Russian Revolution."

Listening to LaVey, the impossible becomes the probable. In his Satanic anthem, the "Hymn of the Satanic Empire," LaVey makes his intentions clear: "Once there was a need for simple minds, once there was a need to save men's souls. Fools had to be forced to stay in line, preachers and bibles could serve those goals. With their holy writ and their card'nal sin they could force their paper demons into a cardboard prison, a paper cell — they can't do that anymore!.. With our morning star from the deepest night smash the crumbling cross, for Might is Right. Let the shuffling zombies grope for light — and we'll reign forevermore!"

# Chapter Twenty

# The Evilest Man in the World

*"I was only trying to cheat death. I was only trying to surmount for a little while the darkness that all my life I surely knew was going to come rolling in on me some day and obliterate me. I was only trying to stay alive a little brief while longer, after I was already gone. To stay in the light, to be with the living a little while past my time."*
— Cornell Woolrich, frontispiece for *Nightwebs* [41]

"When I look in the mirror I see this haunted, hunted look that was in Traven's eyes, or Woolrich's, or Gresham's. A look that is predatory and hunted at once. You can analyze such characteristics better in others than in yourself."

If LaVey can see things better in others' faces than he can in his own, the reverse is also true. Anton Szandor LaVey is not the one to ask about his own talents. The advantages of Satanism, yes; the merits of his diabolical forebears, certainly; what distinct qualities make Anton LaVey tick.... "I try not to think about it. I can't think of myself as performing uniquely, as others apparently think of me, or I'd probably fall under a sudden overwhelming self-consciousness. Unless I think of myself only in a grand overview perspective, I'm dangerously stifled. I'd either become an insufferable megalomaniac and lose credibility or implode and become paralyzed, unable to act at all. It's safest, most productive, for me to see myself as if in a dream, acting and watching the action from the outside at the same time. When I think of things like being in the big cage when I was so young, it seems unreal. I know I did these things but it's almost as if it was another person. I have to distance myself. It's like playing keyboards — I can do it as long as I don't have to think about it."

LaVey depends, consequently, on other people to provide perspective or recognition he won't/can't/isn't able to experience by himself. Two of LaVey's most outspoken supporters are his own daughters, Karla and Zeena. Karla, a svelte, raven-haired stunner, has been lecturing professionally on Satanism since the early 1970's, becoming a subject of photos, fantasy and fixation around the world. Zeena, now a tantalizingly curvaceous blonde, has taken over much of the publicity responsibilities for the Church, representing the organization on a number of national television and radio shows over the past few years. As an accomplished enchantress, Zeena wrote the introduction to LaVey's *The Satanic Witch*. Both Karla and Zeena utilize their own unique charms to expand LaVey's sphere of influence among both dynamic young innovators and established powerbrokers. Zeena's son, Stanton Zaharoff, appropriately born in 1978 during one of the most violent thunderstorms in San Francisco history, is already exhibiting a decidedly independent spirit — reading *The Satanic Bible* on his own and taking advantage of his grandfather's personal tutelage whenever possible. All three share the characteristic LaVey eyes, and the cynical LaVey mind as well. Though the High Priest appreciates recognition and support, his caution concerning overly-adulatory types is typified by a sign on LaVey's desk: "Beware of those that fall at your feet, they may be reaching for the corner of the rug." But he attacks most savagely those who ride on his coattails, or who steal his ideas, all the while pretending at originality or innovation — with, at best, a begrudging acknowledgement of their inspiration's very existence.

In the last few years, LaVey has been accused of being impossible to reach, hardly ever granting interviews, even when the payment offers for new footage run into the six-figure range. Networks have offered $10,000 bounties for contacts leading to any kind of videotaped interview with LaVey. In light of LaVey's steadfast refusals, rumors of ill-health, death or passing the reins of the Church of Satan to his daughters haven't surprised him. "When I think of how I've flirted with death so many times, I must have been crazy. I could've hurt myself. When I was 16 I never expected to see 21. Then I figured I'd surely never make it to 30. There's always been this feeling of mortality right around the corner with me.

"Rumblings about my early departure don't surprise me. From the time I was 45 years old, I've gotten reports. But as Mark Twain said, 'Rumors of my death are greatly exaggerated.' There are people even inside the organization wondering idly what's going to happen to the Church of Satan when I'm gone, who's going to take over — very supportive types, hah, practically rubbing their hands together in anticipation. I don't worry about that — Satanism is here to stay and the Church of Satan will take care of itself. I'm amused by the progression of dismal tales about me. First they said, 'He died young' or 'He compromised his vision and gave up on the whole idea.' Then, since they've found out I'm still around, it's been, 'Well, he's not in the best of health, you know.' I suppose as I get older and am still around they'll have to say something like, "Well, he's crazy, you know. He doesn't remember so good and has been off his rocker for years.' It gets comical. Certain people would really rather be basking in the glory of my demise."

LaVey says he has distilled his life to include only a handful of people who are willing to commit themselves fully to LaVey's demonic directions. LaVey jokes that those closest to him call him "Dr. LaVey," "Doc," or "Herr Doktor" as a term of respect, while people he hardly knows, and probably wouldn't want to know, make it "Anton" from the start. For those who enter his immediate circle of associates, LaVey makes a demanding taskmaster. It seems his own personal demons are even more merciless. There's always too little time for a man like LaVey, who finds he can usually only sleep in four hour stretches. There are so many books to get out, recordings to do, music to play and listen to. LaVey recognizes his audience will always be limited and says he wouldn't have it any other way. He laughingly recalls that some of his well-meaning friends and relatives could never quite appreciate LaVey's Satanic endeavors, commenting that it was, "Such a shame Anton turned out the way he did. He could have been such a brilliant (painter, musician, organ repairman — among the alternatives that have been suggested) if he'd only applied himself."

"I don't try to please anyone but myself any more. Maybe when I was younger it was different but now I'm getting fed up with what people think. I've been accused of contriving my appearance for dramatic effect, wearing my beard and shaving my head. I shaved off my beard once just to see what it looked like. I upset people more without the beard — less approachable.

The consensus seemed to be that I looked more diabolical with the beard but more intrinsically evil without it. You can't win. I wear the beard and the shaven head because I think I look best that way. People expect certain things of you and will rip you to shreds if you don't give them what they expect."

What we expect of LaVey, what we project on him, is fed by a blend of LaVey's native attributes and his own early identification with the ultimate outcast-rebel, Satan. It isn't so far-fetched that LaVey would match our vision of that legendary figure. If we apply the principle of Socratic ideals, the stronger the thought wave, or the more waves there are directed at a consistent image of an ideal, the stronger the archetype becomes. The archetype of Satan has been created and developed in one name or another since the beginning of time. Anton LaVey taps into so much of what that archetype encompasses that he has grown into the role, the ideal, the metaphor of Satan. Could LaVey be so attuned that he taps into the metaphysical powers assigned to that archetype as well? Certain powers may be at LaVey's disposal, but to satisfy the natural balance, something is also demanded in return: the sorrows of Satan.

As LaVey predicted in his *Satanic Rituals,* 1984 was a significant year for him both personally and organizationally. Despite increased avenues to express his views with its resultant reactionary feedback, LaVey experienced terrible emotional upheaval. "If contentment leads to soft wits, and pain and increased cynicism is what it takes to sharpen verbal and mental skills, mine have certainly been sharpened over the past few years." It seems LaVey, irrevocably true to his Satanic archetype, is destined to remain eternally alone, unable to share his memories or past with any woman. Marilyn and Jayne are gone. LaVey's first wife, Carole, died in 1975. In 1984, after 24 eventful years together, Diane decided she no longer wanted to be part of LaVey's world. Amid accusations of physical violence against her and attempts to force the sale and division of all LaVey's property, Diane has gone on to fill a range of office administrative positions, changing her name and attempting to divorce herself completely from her past with LaVey.

LaVey has been haunted by a recurring nightmare of searching and searching in a crowded immense movie palace or a frenetic Mardi Gras for the woman he's with — and not being able find her. His dream conveys an almost child-like fear of being alone. Yet LaVey makes the strong distinction between wanting to be around people and wanting to be with carefully selected persons. In actuality, he has a strong need to be alone, to feel alone, set apart from the mainstream. "I never minded the vision of myself as an old man wandering alone through a large old house or castle, strolling down long dark hallways, with only my echoing footsteps as company. I guess maybe it's been a secret dream of mine from the time I was a boy."

LaVey's world is self-indulgent, hedonistic, elitist ... yet also brutal, opinionated, extreme. He needs no other humans to populate it, so any who come into his immediate circle, enter understanding LaVey's emotional/psychological inaccessibility and distance. LaVey has little faith in the value of hyacinths, seldom tolerating any wool-gathering among his ranks. It has been said LaVey has a tendency to universalize his own experiences, his own beliefs, his own fetishes and project them onto the world around him, but he expects these attitudes to be catered to among his intimates. While he is generally extremely supportive of those around him, he can become pathologically critical over what others might see as inconsequential. Before one knows it, LaVey becomes almost brutally puritanical in his purism. He gives strict, detailed directives and expects his orders to be followed to the letter, even at the expense of the person's own physical, psychological or financial health. Though LaVey places back-breaking (and ego-breaking) demands on his students and volunteers, demanding more and more output with each task completed, he recognizes that "if I don't do it, someone, probably far less qualified, will." But, as LaVey is quick to add, no one puts a gun to anyone's head. If LaVey's people stay with him, and he maintains many relationships stretching back several decades, it's because of the loyalty and allegiance he evokes in them. LaVey recognizes that perhaps his true strength, that people seek from him to add to their own lives, is exactly that — his strength, mastery and discipline. "I've never been sorry because I was too mean to someone. Only for being too nice."

As he grows older, LaVey allows himself the luxury of being harsher and more demanding of people, and more selective. "Every day I think less and less of what others are going to think. I don't care what people say about me. What are they going to say? That I'm mad? That I'm wrong about the way the world really is? That I'm an evil, murderous mastermind? That I'm too extreme? That I'm a greasy, slimy, Jew-Gypsy roustabout who looks at the world through a carny's eyes? They can think what they like. At least I'm not pretentious and I'm not stupid. And when someone comes along who can play the kind of music I play in the style I play it, they can come see me after supper and we'll talk about it. As for all those other things, I've made it a policy never to deny anything. I'm people's worst nightmares ... and more. I don't want to give anyone the satisfaction that they have me all figured out; that they know everything about me and have all the answers. If people only knew. I've always loved that ubiquitous Johnson-Smith Company ad copy, 'Imagine the expression on their faces...!' That's a kind of leitmotif that has tempted me into most of the heinous, evil, or disreputable things I've ever done. Just imagine people's reaction if they ever found out. But they won't. It began in mystery; I want it to end that way."

No one ever "gets to know" Anton LaVey. If you're lucky, you glimpse enough to know that you don't know much about him. If you're unlucky, judged untrustworthy in his eyes, you'll be unfortunate enough to walk away smugly thinking you've plumbed the depths. In either case, you walk away from meeting Anton Szandor LaVey knowing you've had a unique experience — floating out of his presence, usually just as the sun is rising, heady with the speculation he has invited into your life by immersing you in his world. Your mind lingers on special secrets he has shared with you alone because he knows you can understand. But, when all is said and done, one only knows about LaVey what he chooses to reveal. He is the last mystery man, in the tradition of Howard Hughes, B. Traven, Basil Zaharoff — at the same time, a paradox and a reconciliation, a puzzle and an answer. A man you know you should hate but somehow meeting him, listening to him play, crack jokes and voice ideas that you yourself have felt for so long, you'd feel ridiculous calling LaVey an evil monster. And each step you take away from him into the cold dawn leaves you more comfortable, yet more empty inside.

More than ruling the world, gaining credit for what he's done, or rallying followers to his cause, Anton LaVey wants to be left alone. That's all he's ever wanted. As you walk, you realize he's not a rabble-rouser, not a shit-disturber, not a speech-maker. He wants to write, play and create as he wishes; to enjoy the few people and unique material pleasures he has gathered around him over the years of his life. Simple desires which would find sympathy in any human heart. And then you stop in mid-stride, suddenly recalling with crystal-clarity an ancient Eastern proverb, apocryphally credited to the nine unknown men:

"Lie to a liar for lies are his coin;
Steal from a thief, 'tis easy you'll find;
Trick a trickster and win the first time —
But beware of the man who has no axe to grind."

# LaVeyan Glossary of Terms

**Artificial Human Companions** — The next major industry in America; humanoids designed for personal, sexual, and emotionally gratifying use by a mass-market audience.

**Auto-Erotic Agitation Tumblers** — Enclosures, inside of which a person can be harmlessly tossed and spun, thus releasing excess energy and relaxing tensions resulting from pent-up sexual impulses.

**Black Mass** — This ritual, as employed by the Church of Satan, is performed to blaspheme and free the participants from the hold of anything widely accepted as sacred, not just organized religion, as in the traditional Black Mass which is meant as a blasphemy against Catholicism.

**Command to Look, The** — The title of a photographic treatise by William Mortensen published in 1937. Also the methods used in Lesser Magic to enchant your chosen quarry by using certain techniques to arrest their gaze, commanding attention and compliance.

**Council of Nine** — Ruling body of the Church of Satan.

**Cui Bono?** — "Who gains?" (Latin); What's in it for whom?, the assumption being that no one does anything except that which is in his/her best interest.

**Demonic Personality** — The type of person directly opposite you on the Synthesizer Clock, a type you are most likely to attract and be attracted to.

**Dominant Mass** — Hulking visual (and therefore magical) power which overwhelms and eclipses all surrounding elements.

**ECI (Erotic or Emotional Crystallization Inertia)** — The point in time and experience in which a person's emotional/sexual fetishes are established.

**Frustration Music** —Music that is often frenetic and/or dissonant, lacking in Ur Song form and resolution.

**Greater Magic** — Ceremonial or Ritual magic, performed under specific conditions with certain implements to achieve a directed goal. As opposed to Lesser Magic or Stage Magic.

**INKT Syndrome** — The acronym stands for "I never knew that!" Used to describe the pose of ignorance regarding certain skills or talents, which go unnoticed and unacknowledged until faced with overwhelming exposure.

**Is, Not Does** — The preeminence of dramatic, timeless, archetypically sound imagery over action for visual impact. (Distilled from *The Command to Look.)*

**KISS** — Not the rock group, but rather "Keep it simple, stupid!" A useful dictum with wide application.

**Law of Invisibility** — A trick of the brain that allows for something or someone to be overlooked, regardless of visual cues, if the viewer doesn't expect to see such a thing in that particular setting.

**Law of the Forbidden** — That which is not meant to be seen or experienced holds the most fascination.

**Law of the Trapezoid** — A recurring magical formation (looking like a pyramid with the top chopped off—called the "frustrum") which, because of its inherent dominant mass, acts as a lodestone for overwhelming, sometimes devastating, phenomena. LaVey wrote in 1976: "Angles and space-planes that provoke anxiety — that is, those not harmonious with the visual orientation — will engender aberrant behavior, translate: change."

**Lesser Magic** — Applied psychology and everyday enchantments used to achieve desired goals.

**Lex Satanicus** — Law of the Satanist, as described in the Eleven Rules of the Earth, inclusive of Lex Talionis and "Do unto others as they do unto you."

**Lex Talionis** — Law of the Jungle (lit. "Law of the Talon"); the natural order in which the weak are allowed to perish, the strong thrive. Described in Judeo-Christian Old Testament mythology as "an eye for an eye." Described by Charles Darwin as "survival of the fittest," on which he based his theories of evolution.

**More of the Same** — A useful rule of thumb for devising a suitable archetype, and in dealing with others, providing them with exactly what they expect — often more than they bargained for.

**Nine Unknown** — Many writers have referred obliquely to this mysterious cabal — Shakespeare, John Dryden, Talbot Mundy, Richard Johnson — which is an archetypal cell formation reflected today in the Council of Nine and the nine members appointed to sit in positions of absolute authority on the United States Supreme Court.

**No Bullshit Music** — Music with form, lyricism, and dynamics which produces Ur Song emotional responses. The melodies and harmonies are usually predictable, and hence, dismissed or denigrated by many musical pseudo-sophisticates.

**Order of the Trapezoid** — Inner Circle of the Church of Satan referred to in the Sixth Enochian Key from The Satanic Bible which grew from LaVey's original Magic Circle of the late-50's before the formation of the Church of Satan. In accordance with LaVey's explorations of demonic geometry (see Law of the Trapezoid), the informal magical workshop took to wearing a trapezoidal black and red medallion LaVey designed, adorned with a bat winged demon that could be removed to reveal the inverted pentagram/666 design underneath. As their magical experiments took shape, the group dubbed themselves the "Order of the Trapezoid" and eventually became the founding members of the Church of Satan. The Order of the Trapezoid continues today as the directing force within the organization.

**Psychic Vampire** — Term coined by LaVey and now widely used to describe manipulative individuals who drain others of their vital energy, impose guilts and feelings of responsibility, yet fulfill no apparent purpose.

**Sex, Sentiment and Wonder** — Identified in *The Command to Look* as the three general categories into which all archetypal images can be divided; later described both in *The Satanic Bible* and *The Satanic Witch*.

**Shibboleth Ritual** — Psychodramatic ritual performed in the early days of the Church of Satan in which the participants take on the personas of those they most despise or who cause them problems, thereby exorcizing them.

**Silver-headed Cane Principle** — From carnival methods; a principle of giving someone a title, job or physical representation that looks fancy but that actually communicates incompetence or pretentiousness on the part of the bearer. It's a variation on pumping someone up so you can see where the leaks are.

**Stage Magic** — Prestidigitation, sleight of hand performed for an audience with no claims of supernatural ability. Stage Magic can be used quite effectively in concert with Greater and Lesser Magic to achieve a convincing atmosphere conducive to accomplishing magical goals.

**Suspend Disbelief** — A willingness to temporarily set aside expectations in order to establish a more conducive atmosphere for magical experimentation.

**Synthesizer Clock** — A method of typing people defined in LaVey's *Satanic Witch*. According to their position on the clock, i.e., a "9 o'clock type," "3 o'clock type," a person can be identified as having certain personality traits which match their physical appearance.

**Total Environments** — Privately owned, operated and controlled environments designed to replicate a particular place or time in history, with all participants or visitors conforming to strictly enforced visual and behavioral illusions characteristic of that world.

**Transmogrification** — To change in physical shape and appearance, either through one's own endeavors or through the influence of another powerful magician.

**Ur Song** — A set of archetypal vibrations and resonances that, since the primal beginnings of music, produce overt, often dormant, emotional responses—excitement, sorrow, despair, enthusiasm, etc.

**Whipping Music** — Music in which the beat is heard/felt above lyricism or melody, replicating the incessant, hypnotic drumbeats once used to drive galley slaves to power Viking ships.

# Notes

1. Burton H. Wolfe, *The Devil's Avenger* (New York: Pyramid Books, 1974), p. 35.

2. Don Boles, *The Midway Showman* (Atlanta: Pinchpenny Press, 1967), p. 24.

3. Ibid, p. 30.

4. Lenni Brenner, *Zionism in the Age of the Dictators* (Westport, CT: Lawrence Hill and Co., 1983).

5. Wolfe, *The Devil's Avenger*, p. 52.

6. Ibid, p. 98.

7. Ibid, pp. 186-7.

8. Shana Alexander, "The Ping is the Thing," *Life* (February, 1967), p. 31.

9. Arthur Lyons, *The Second Coming: Satanism in America* (New York: Dodd, Mead and Co., 1970), p. 192.

10. "Evil, Anyone?," *Newsweek* (August 16, 1971), p. 56.

11. Wolfe, *The Devil's Avenger*, p. 216.

12. Ibid., pp. 215-6.

13. Ibid., p. 216.

14. Ibid., p. 96.

15. Dick Russell, "Anton LaVey: The Satanist Who Wants to Rule the World," *Argosy*, p. 43, p. 59.

16. Fred Harden, "Anton LaVey: Disciple of the Devil," *Hustler*, (December, 1979), p. 102.

17. Anton LaVey, "Misanthropia," *The Cloven Hoof*, May - June, 1977.

18. Arthur Lyons, *Satan Wants You: The Cult of Devil Worship in America* (New York: Mysterious Press, 1988), p. 183.

19. Charles G. Finney, *The Circus of Dr. Lao* (New York: Vintage Books, 1983), pp. 61-62.

20. Peter Heiss, "Draculas Zartliche Kinder," *Tempo* (May, 1988), p. 74.

21. Charles Higham and Joel Greenberg, *Hollywood in the Forties* (New York: Paperback Library, 1970), pp. 19-20.

22. Gabe Essoe, *The Book of Movie Lists* (Westport, CT: Arlington House, 1981), pp. 156-7.

23. Ibid., p. 156.

24. LaVey, *The Satanic Rituals*, pp. 122-3.

25. LaVey, *The Satanic Bible*, p. 155.

26. William Mortensen, *The Command to Look* (San Francisco: Camera Craft Publishing Co., 1937), p. 24. p. 54.

27. LaVey, "The Law of the Trapezoid," *The Cloven Hoof*, November-December, 1976.

28. LaVey, "We're All Going Calling on the Kaiser," *The Cloven Hoof*, March-June, 1980.

29. LaVey, *The Satanic Bible*, p. 105.

30. LaVey, "On Androids," *The Cloven Hoof*, July-August, 1979.

31. Wolfe, *The Devil's Avenger*, p. 70.

32. Jacques Vallee, *The Network Revolution: Confessions of a Computer Scientist* (Berkeley, CA: And/Or Press, 1982), pp. 190-91.

33. Richard Cavendish, *The Black Arts* (New York: Capricorn Books, 1968), pp. 5-6.

34. Tom Wedge and Robert Powers, *The Satan Hunter* (Canton, OH: Daring Books, 1987), p. 127.

35. *20/20*, "The Devil Worshippers," American Broadcasting Co., May 16, 1985.

36. Shawn Carlson, Ph.D., and Gerald Larue, Ph.D., *Satanism in America: How the Devil Got Much More Than His Due* (Buffalo, NY: Committee for the Scientific Examination of Religion, 1989), p. *v*.

37. LaVey, *The Satanic Rituals*, p. 12.

38. Burton H. Wolfe, "Interview with Anton LaVey," *Fling* (July, 1978), p. 60.

39. Wedge and Powers, *The Satan Hunter*, p. 22.

40. David St. Clair, Say You Love Satan (New York: Dell Publishing Co., 1987), p. 51.

41. Cornell Woolrich, *Nightwebs: A Collection of Stories by Cornell Woolrich* (New York: Harper and Row, 1971), p. *vi*.

# Bibliography

This is a limited list of material about LaVey and the Church of Satan including books, magazine or newspaper articles which the author felt were particularly insightful or otherwise remarkable. Foreign papers and magazines are not covered, nor are most newspaper items, since an exhaustive listing would be ... exhausting. The years from 1967-1970 were a blur of media coverage on the Church of Satan, as a visit to the microfiche files of any major library will show. To cite subsequent creative echoes over the last two decades in fiction, films and recordings would require another book altogether. I have chosen not to include the innumerable books and articles written on the subject since c. 1986 from a decidedly Christian viewpoint, since most, if not all, of these authors do not attempt to provide original or accurate information on LaVey' and his philosophy.

Adams, Gerald, "Confessions of a Ghost Chaser," *People* (Sunday section of the *San Francisco Examiner),* March 7, 1965.

Adler, Margot, *Drawing Down the Moon.* Boston, MA: Beacon Press, revised and expanded edition, 1986.

Alexander, Shana, "The Ping is the Thing," *Life,* February, 1967.

Allen, Steve, *Curses! or How Never to be Foiled Again.* Los Angeles, CA: J.P. Tarcher, Inc., 1973.

Atkins, Susan (with Bob Slosser), *Child of Satan, Child of God.* Plainfield, NJ: Logos International, 1977.

Bensen, Carle, "A Call to the Church of Satan," in Doug Warren's *Demonic Possession.* New York: Pyramid Books, 1975.

Blackman, Jim, "Satan in Person," *Modern Man,* January, 1968.

Boeth, Richard, "Hoodoo, Voodoo and You!," *Cosmopolitan,* July, 1970.

Bronte, Louisa, *Lord Satan*. New York: Avon Books, 1972 (fiction).

Buckland, Raymond, *Here Is the Occult*. New York: House of Collectibles, Inc., 1974.

Caen, Herb. Long-time San Francisco Chronicle columnist and myth-maker. Included column drops about LaVey's doings from the early 50's on.

Carlson, Shawn, Ph.D., and Larue, Gerald, Ph.D., *Satanism in America: How the Devil Got Much More Than His Due*. El Cerrito, CA: Gaia Press, 1989.

Case, Judith (as told to Rose Perlberg), "We Were Married by the Devil," *True Confessions*, June, 1967.

Cohen, Daniel, *The New Believers*. New York: Ballantine Books, 1975.

Davis, Lisa, "Please Allow Me to Introduce Myself...," *Prism* (San Francisco State literary magazine), May, 1990 (cover story).

Davis, Sammy, Jr., with Boyar, Jane and Burt, *Why Me?*. New York: Farrar, Straus and Giroux, 1989. (Brief explanation of his Satanic dabbling — p. 209.)

Diggs, Jeff, "Black Magic is Big Business," *Companion*, September, 1967.

Drury, William. Mr. Drury had a column in the *San Francisco News-Call Bulletin* in which he wrote a number of delightful articles about LaVey ("Dracula, I Presume?" August 20, 1964; "Nice Kitty ... Ouch!" October 7, 1964; "A Lion o' Type or Two" January 6, 1965) when LaVey was getting press on his ghost-chasing, sorcery and his lion, Togare.

Elwood, Roger, *Strange Things Are Happening: Satanism, Witchcraft and God*. New York: Family Library, 1973.

Essoe, Gabe, *The Book of Movie Lists*. Westport, CT: Arlington House, 1981.
— *The Book of TV Lists*. Westport, CT: Arlington House, 1981.

Farren, David, *The Return of Magic*. New York: Harper and Row, 1972.

Fitzgerald, Arlene J., *Everything You Always Wanted to Know About Sorcery ... But Were Afraid to Ask*. New York: Manor Books, Inc., 1973.

Freedland, Nat, *The Occult Explosion*. New York. G. P. Putnam's Sons, 1972.
— "Anton LaVey and the Church of Satan," *Jaybird Journal,* March, 1968. (Cover story.)

Fritscher, John, *Popular Witchcraft: Straight From the Witch's Mouth*. Bowling Green, OH: Bowling Green University Popular Press, 1972. (Some 16 tightly-spaced pages of straight monologue from LaVey in the last chapter.)

Furth, Jane, with Murphy, Mimi, and bureaus, "Satan," *Life,* June, 1989.

Gardner, Helena, *Witchcraft: The Path to Power For Those Who Dare to Use It*. Chatsworth, CA: Brandon Books, 1974.

Godwin, John, *Occult America*. New York: Doubleday and Co., Inc., 1972.

Goeringer, Conrad F., "Bimbos For Satan", "The New Witch-hunt," and "Drug Killings Fuel Hysteria," *American Atheist,* May, 1989.

Haining, Peter, *The Anatomy of Witchcraft*. New York: Taplinger Publishing Co., 1972.
— *Witchcraft and Black Magic,* New York: Grosset and Dunlap, 1972.

Harden, Grant, "The Devil's Advocate," *California Today* (magazine of the *San Jose Mercury-News),* August 19, 1979. (Cover story.)
— under "Fred" Harden, "Anton LaVey: Disciple of the Devil," *Hustler,* December, 1979.

Harrington, Walt, "The Devil in Anton LaVey," *The Washington Post Magazine,* February 23, 1986. (Cover story.)

Hedren, Tippi, and Taylor, Theodore, *The Cats of Shambala*. New York: Simon and Schuster, 1985. (Includes photos of LaVey's lion, Togare, who spent his last years on Miss Hedren's lion preserve.)

Hershman, Florence, *Witchcraft U.S.A*. New York: Tower Publications, Inc., 1971.

Hilton, Thomas H., *Exorcism, Sex and the Black Arts*. Los Angeles: Eagle Publishing Co., 1974.
— *Sex and the Occult,* Vol 2. Los Angeles, CA: Centurion Press, 1974.

Holt, Simma, "Simma Holt Finds 'The Black Pope' A Gentleman of Integrity, Rare Wisdom," *The Vancouver Sun,* June 28, 1972.

Jeschke, Paul R., "Speak of the Devil", *Fate,* September, 1967.
— "Satan, 1968 Style," *Adam,* Vol. 12, No. 4.

Kamp, I.M., "The Devil's Wedding," *Uncensored,* August, 1967.

Kanderson, "Anton LaVey: Sorcerer of San Francisco," *Stanford Chaparral,* April, 1967.

King, Francis, *Sexuality, Magic and Perversion.* Secaucus, NJ: Citadel Press, Inc., 1971.
— *The Rebirth of Magic,* London: Corgi Books, 1982 (w/Isabel Sutherland).
— *Satan and Swastika,* Herts, England: Mayflower Books, Ltd., 1976.

Krassner, Paul, "Paul Krassner's Flicks and Kicks: Rosemary's Baby," *Cavalier,* October, 1968.

LaVey, Anton Szandor, *The Satanic Bible.* New York: Avon Books, 1969.
— *The Satanic Rituals,* New York: Avon Books, 1972
— *The Compleat Witch, or What To Do When Virtue Fails,* New York: Dodd, Mead and Co., 1970.
— *The Satanic Witch* (a re-release of *The Compleat Witch,* incorporating an introduction by Zeena LaVey), Los Angeles: Feral House, 1989.
— "Misanthropia," *Rants and Incendiary Tracts,* Bob Black and Adam Parfrey, eds., New York: Amok Press and Port Townsend: Loompanics Unlimited (co-publishers), 1989.

Lefebure, Charles, *Witness to Witchcraft.* New York: Ace Publishing Corp., 1970.

Lyons, Arthur, *The Second Coming: Satanism in America.* New York: Dodd, Mead and Co., 1970.
— *Satan Wants You: The Cult of Devil Worship in America,* New York: Mysterious Press, 1988; Warner Books, 1989.

Mann, May, *Jayne Mansfield: A Biography.* New York: Drake Publishers., Inc., 1973.

— "Did Jayne Mansfield Know She Was Going to Die?," *Motion Picture,* October, 1967.

Mannix, Daniel P., *We Who Are Not As Others.* New York: Pocket Books, 1976. Re-released by Re/Search Publications, 1990. (LaVey's reminiscences of special people he has known throughout book.)

Mather, Bobby, "Witchcraft and Satanism Are Alive and Living in Michigan; Meet Bill, Who Believes," *Detroit* (magazine section of *The Detroit Free Press),* June 15, 1969.

Melton, J. Gordon, Ph.D., *The Encyclopedic Handbook of Cults.* New York: Garland, 1986.

Michaels, Jason, *The Devil is Alive and Well and Living in America Today.* New York: Award Books, 1973.

Milward, Doris, "Witchcraft and Sex — 1968," *Sexology,* May, 1968.

Molina, Jean, "Anton LaVey: San Francisco Satanist," *Witchcraft Today,* Martin Ebon, ed. New York: Signet Books, 1971.

Moody, Edward J., "Magical Therapy: An Anthropological Investigation of Contemporary Satanism," *Religious Movements in Contemporary America,* Irving I. Zaretsky and Mark P. Leone, eds. Princeton: Princeton University Press, 1974.

Morrill, Sibley S., "How Belief in Magic Grows in the Bay Area," *Alameda County Weekender* (magazine section of *Alameda Times-Star),* February 12, 1966. (Mr. Morrill did a whole series of fascinating, in-depth reports on esoteric subjects for his Weekender section, among them a pre-Church of Satan profile of LaVey, replete with photos, including the bat-demon symbol covering the Order of the Trapezoid sigil and LaVey's 1937 Cord.)

Mulshine, Paul, "The Dark Side," *New Jersey Monthly,* October, 1989.

Painter, Hal, "What's Happening to That Nice, Devil-May-Care Family Next Door?," *Pageant,* August, 1967. (Extensive layout of unusual photos of LaVey and his family.)

Parfrey, Adam, "Anton LaVey: Satan's Pope," *Chic,* October, 1989.
— "Geek Thrills," Screw, October 30, 1989.

Petersen, William J., *Those Curious New Cults,* New Canaan, CT: Keats Publishing, Inc., 1973.

Phillips, Tom, "The Satanic Church," *Monsieur: The Swinger,* January, 1968.

Prelutsky, Burt, "West/View: Satan's Local Rep," *West* (magazine of *Los Angeles Times),* October 8, 1967.

Rascoe, Judith, "Church of Satan," *McCall's,* March, 1970. (Cover story.)

"Religious Requirements and Practices of Certain Selected Groups, A Handbook For Chaplains", Department of the Army pamphlet, #165-13, April, 1978.

Resnick, Mike, "Inside the Church of Satan," *The National Insider,* 6-week series, from October 27, 1968 to December 1, 1968.

Riese, Randall, and Hitchens, Neal, *The Unabridged Marilyn.* New York: Congdon and Weed, Inc., 1987.

Roberts, Susan, *Witches U.S.A.* New York: Dell Publishing Co., Inc., 1971.

Robinson, Eugene, "Anton LaVey/The Church of Satan," *The Birth of Tragedy* (Stanford, CA), God Issue, 1987. (Cover story.)

Russell, Dick, "Anton LaVey: The Satanist Who Wants to Rule the World," *Argosy,* June, 1975.

Schurmacher, Emile C., *Witchcraft in America Today.* New York: Paperback Library, 1970.

Shadowitz, Albert and Walsh, Peter, *The Dark Side of Knowledge: Exploring the Occult.* Reading, MA: Addison-Wesley Publishing Co., 1976.

Smith, Dave, "The Devil, You Say?," *Midwest Magazine* (of the Sunday *Chicago Sun-Times),* August 30, 1970.

Smith, Susy, *Today's Witches.* New York: Award Books, 1975.

Spiegleman, Art, "Vampirism For Fun and Profit," *Chic*, October, 1989. (LaVey on vampires; also good interview with Zeena LaVey.)

Staff, "High Priest of the Devil," *Sepia*, October, 1967.
— "Seventh Annual Dubious Achievement Awards for 1967," *Esquire*, January, 1968. (Zeena LaVey's baptism is cited with the caption, "One reason why God did not descend in the form of a dove during 1967.")

St. Clair, David, *The Psychic World of California*. New York: Doubleday and Co., Inc., 1972.
— *Say You Love Satan*, New York: Dell Publishing Co., Inc., 1987.

Steiger, Brad, *Sex and the Supernatural*. New York: Lancer Books, 1968.
— with Warren Smith, *Satan's Assassins*. New York: Lancer Books, 1971.

Stoker, Bram, *The Annotated Dracula* (special ed., with an introduction, notes and bibliography by Leonard Wolf). NewYork: Clarkson N. Potter.

Stone, Gail, "Swingers Turn to Satan," *Confidential Flash*, December 9, 1967.

Truzzi, Marcello, Ph.D., "Towards a Sociology of the Occult: Notes on Modern Witchcraft," *Religious Movements in Contemporary America*, Irving I. Zaretsky and Mark P. Leone, eds. Princeton: Princeton University Press, 1974.

Vale, V., and Juno, Andrea, interview with Anton LaVey included in Re/Search #12: *Modern Primitives*. San Francisco: Re/Search Publications, 1989.

Vachon, Brian, "Witches Are Rising," *Look*, August 24, 1971. (Cover story.)

Wallace, C.H., *Witchcraft in the World Today*. New York: Award Books, 1967.

Wallace, Irving, et al., *The Intimate Sex Lives of Famous People*. New York: Dell Publishing Co., 1982.

Wilson, Colin, *Witches*. New York: A & W Publishers, 1981.

Winer, Richard and Ishmael, Nancy Osborn, *More Haunted Houses*. New York: Bantam Books, 1981.

Wolfe, Burton H., *The Devil's Avenger.* New York: Pyramid Books, 1974.
— "The Church That Worships Satan," *Knight,* Vol. 6, No. 8. (1968)
— "The Church of Satan," *Inside the Cults,* Tracy Cabot, ed. Los Angeles: Holloway House Publishing Co., 1970.
— "Interview with Anton LaVey," *Fling,* July, 1978.
— "Meet the Devil," *Fling,* May, 1978.
— "The Devil and Jayne Mansfield," *Fling,* November, 1978.

Woods, Richard, *The Occult Revolution: A Christian Meditation.* New York: Herder and Herder, 1971.

Zellerbach, Merla, "My Fair City: A Charm Course for Witches," *San Francisco Chronicle,* July 19, 1967.

# The Nine Satanic Statements

1. Satan represents indulgence instead of abstinence.

2. Satan represents vital existence instead of spiritual pipe dreams.

3. Satan represents undefiled wisdom instead of hypocritical self-deceit.

4. Satan represents kindness to those who deserve it instead of love wasted on ingrates.

5. Satan represents vengeance instead of turning the other cheek.

6. Satan represents responsibility to the responsible instead of concern for psychic vampires.

7. Satan represents man as just another animal — sometimes better, more often worse than those that walk on all-fours — who, because of his "divine spiritual and intellectual development," has become the most vicious animal of all.

8. Satan represents all of the so-called sins, as they all lead to physical, mental, or emotional gratification.

9. Satan has been the best friend the Church has ever had, as he has kept it in business all these years.

# The Eleven Satanic Rules of the Earth

1. Do not give opinions or advice unless you are asked.

2. Do not tell your troubles to others unless you are sure that they want to hear them.

3. When in another's lair, show him respect or else do not go there.

4. If a guest in your lair annoys you, treat him cruelly and without mercy.

5. Do not make sexual advances unless you are given the mating signal.

6. Do not take that which does not belong to you unless it is a burden to the other person and he cries out to be relieved.

7. Acknowledge the power of magic if you have employed it successfully to obtain your desires. If you deny the power of magic after having called upon it with success, you will lose all you have obtained.

8. Do not complain about anything to which you need not subject yourself.

9. Do not harm little children.

10. Do not kill non-human animals unless attacked or for your food.

11. When walking in open territory, bother no one. If someone bothers you, ask him to stop. If he does not stop, destroy him.

# The Nine Satanic Sins

For years, people have asked Church of Satan representatives, "Well, okay — your philosophy is based on indulgence of human instincts but do you have any sins like other religions?" Our answer has always been "No." But the time has come to amend that response. We have grown steadily over the past 21 years and find that it is appropriate to have some clearer guidelines on, not only what we strive for, but also what we work to avoid — what we disapprove of. The difference is where other religions develop sins that people can't avoid, we consider a number of things "sinful" that people could avoid if they worked a little.

1.) **Stupidity** — The top of the list for Satanic Sins. The Cardinal Sin of Satanism. It's too bad that stupidity isn't painful. Ignorance is one thing, but our society thrives increasingly on stupidity. It depends on people going along with whatever they are told. The media promotes a *cultivated* stupidity as a posture that is not only acceptable but laudable. Satanists must learn to see through the tricks and cannot afford to be stupid.

2.) **Pretentiousness** — Empty posturing can be most irritating and isn't applying the cardinal rules of Lesser Magic. On equal footing with stupidity for what keeps the money in circulation these days. Everyone's made to feel like a big shot, whether they can come up with the goods or not.

3.) **Solipsism** — can be very dangerous for Satanists. Projecting your reactions, responses, and sensibilities onto someone else who is probably *far* less attuned than you are. It is the mistake of expecting people to give you the same consideration, courtesy, and respect that you naturally give them. They won't. Instead, Satanists must strive to apply the dictum of "Do unto others as they do unto you." It's work for most of us and requires constant vigilance lest you slip into a comfortable illusion of everyone being like you. As has been said, certain utopias would be ideal in a nation of philosophers, but unfortunately (or perhaps fortunately, from a Machiavellian viewpoint) we are far from that point.

4.) **Self-Deceit** — It's in the Nine Satanic Statements but deserves to be repeated here. Another Cardinal Sin. We must not pay homage to any of the sacred cows presented to us, including the roles we are expected to play ourselves. The only time self-deceit should be entered into is when it's fun, and with awareness. But then, it's not self-deceit!

5.) **Herd Conformity** — That's obvious from a Satanic stance. It's all right to conform to a person's wishes, *if it ultimately benefits you*. But only fools follow along with the herd, letting an impersonal entity dictate to you. The key is to choose a master wisely instead of being enslaved by the whims of the many.

6.) **Lack of Perspective** — Again, this one can lead to a lot of pain for a Satanist. You must never lose sight of who and what you are, and what a threat you can be, by your very existence. We are making history right now, every day. Always keep the wider historical and social picture in mind. That is an important key to both Lesser and Greater Magic. See the patterns and fit things together as you want the pieces to fall into place. Do not be swayed by herd constraints — know that you are working on another level entirely from the rest of the world.

7.) **Forgetfulness of Past Orthodoxies** — Be aware that this is one of the keys to brainwashing people into accepting something as "new" and "different," when in reality it's something that was once widely accepted but is now presented in a new package. We are expected to rave about the genius of the "creator" and forget the original. This makes for a disposable society.

8.) **Counterproductive Pride** — That first word is important. Pride is great up to the point you begin to throw out the baby with the bathwater. The rule of Satanism is: if it works for you, great. When it stops working for you, when you've painted yourself into a corner and the only way out is to say, "I'm sorry, I made a mistake, I wish we could compromise somehow," then *do it*.

9.) **Lack of Aesthetics** — This is the physical application of the Balance Factor. It is important in Lesser Magic and should be cultivated. It is obvious that no one can collect any money off it most of the time so it is discouraged in a consumer society, but it is an essential satanic tool and must be applied for magical effectiveness. It's not what's *supposed* to be pleasing — it's what *is*. Aesthetics is a highly personal thing, reflective of one's own nature, but there are universally pleasing and harmonious configurations that should not be denied.

This is the first doctrinal.proclamation in over a decade and outlines some important rules for Satanic practices. It should be understood that this in no way supersedes the Nine Satanic Statements or the Eleven Rules of the Earth, but is intended to augment these principles even further.

# The Church of Satan, Cosmic Joy Buzzer

In 1966 the Church of Satan was born, a witch named Sybil leaked on America, and a placental membrane began thickening over the land which was to be called "the occult movement." Sure, there had been those who sent to a Rosicrucian scribe on the back of a magazine cover for the secrets of man's destiny, attended flying saucer conventions, held hands at spiritualists' "closed circles," and read their daily horoscopes. Dennis Wheatley was a blighty hack who shuddered pudding-faced Englishwomen to sleep in their flats. A renegade named Seabrook wrote about strange doings among were-wolves and lady vampires (and, incidentally, whose *Asylum* was the original *Cuckoo's Nest)*, and two guys named Symonds and Mannix chronicled, respectively, the exploits of "the wickedest man in the world" and the Hell Fire Club. One could obtain the *Sixth and Seventh Books of Moses* and the *Albertus Magnus* in paper before they were called paperbacks. An old man named Roy Heist made good copy selling "mummy's dust" to witch doctors. Sure, there was an occult movement before the Year One — a movement like a slumbering wino shifting position in a doorway.

No detailed chronology is required to illustrate the events of the past ten years. Concurrent with the increasingly liberal social climate of the 60's, many former taboos became relaxed. The Dark Side displayed itself flagrantly in polite society and where beatnik poets and bongo drummers had recently flourished, witches and tarot readers held court. To most theologians only a single entity was responsible for everything from prophecy to meditation. No matter how innocuous an esoteric act or voluble its practitioner's disclaimer, the Devil was to blame. "Satan" headed more copy concerning the occult than any other teaser. TV-movie adaptations of classic Gothic ghost stories were pushed as "Satanic." Despite indignant attempts to differentiate witchcraft from Satanism, the public insisted on lumping them together in a willing and eager suspension of disbelief.

Despite *curanderas'* murmurings of "God-given powers," fundamentalists still denounce them as part of the occult movement and minions of Satan.

The lack of imagination and staying power of the occult movement is showing through the veneer of the incompetents who filled its ranks. As the varnish peels away, the occultist's image has become almost as ridiculous as the bible-thumping evangelist's. Now, the Church of Satan could easily become a psychical Ellis Island of refugees and emigres from the occult scene. Displaced persons who have left their covens, 90-day Magi weary of pondering the Enochian Keys and Crowleyanity, chasuble queens who couldn't make it in the Catholic Church, woebegone wiccans who find that the Goddess's bosom has run dry, Egyptoids who'd be better off as Shriners or in Laurel and Hardy's *Sons of the Desert*, pyramid sitters who've gained nothing but claustrophobia, Atlanteans who get seasick, UFO-ites who've redefined gravitational law but can't chin themselves, witless wizards, sex-starved witches, destitute diviners, pshort-psighted psychics — all the growing residue of a phenomenon that, *because of its very popularity, HAD to lose the magic it purported to have.*

Satan translates to mean "opposite," lest the *Satanic Bible* be forgotten. The essence of Satanism is what tips the balance and starts the pendulum swinging in the other direction. That is why the facts of Satanism are so often harsher than the most Gothic melodrama or speculative science-horror fiction. This actual harshness is registered in the dismay of some new applicants who had been enmeshed in the waning occult scene. Interest in the Church of Satan has never been greater, but I don't kid myself into thinking it's because people are more enlightened than ever before — only more disillusioned and/or bored. Nonetheless, I realize that with the decline in the occult movement as a credible identity factor, we have been blessed with an influx of salvageable human potential from the aforementioned categories, as well as "non-joiners" who had been waiting until the dust settled. Thus, the elitism I envisioned in the beginning has materialized fourfold.

In ten years of existence, the Church of Satan has fueled a philosophical counterculture which could have, if unchecked, thrown the baby out with the bathwater. It invoked imaginative permissiveness, rational self-interest, and forced a dying theology into ludicrous last ditch behavior (witchmobiles, papal pronouncements, etc.) or running-scared reinterpretation (suddenly "keeping up with social changes"). It also pumped hordes of creeps up till their newly-discovered godheads developed leaks or just plain busted. The ad sections of *Fate* magazine contain as prolific a source of gifted psychics, institutes of cosmic consciousness, and pushers of awareness as can be found in the contact columns of swingers tabloids or underground newspapers. Add the parasitic fringe: the "*ex's*" who seek recognition as *ex*-witches, *ex*-Satanists, *ex*-orcised, or any other wish-they-could-have-but-couldn't-cut-it types. Yes, the occult movement has provided countless persons with delusions of adequacy.

Why has Satanism succeeded? Because from our earliest literature, through the *Satanic Bible*, we have made no grandiose promises of infallible enlightenment and emphasized that each must be his or her own redeemer. That the extent of one's superiority (if any) is governed by one's human potential. That "Satan" is a representational concept, accepted by each according to his or her needs. That's the way it was in the beginning; that's the way it is now. We have rejected that which becomes faddish while championing the unfashionable. When the "monkey see, monkey do" syndrome appears, even on the Left Hand Path, then we *don't*. We have utilized the best from the worst and discerned the worst in the best and gained through each. We have defied categorization, confounding labellers, knowing that the one label we bear — *Satan* — is controversy in itself.

In looking back over the decade, it is easy to isolate each phase of our development. It has been not only a rewarding lesson in behavioral psychology, but has inadvertently served as what sociologists refer to as an "unfunded research project."

The First Phase, *Emergence*, crystallized the *zeitgeist* into reality — let loose the knowledge of a Satanic body politic into a ready but dumfounded social climate.

The Second Phase, *Development*, saw an organizational and institutional expansion as a result of carefully stimulated exploitation, attracting a variety of human types from which to distill a Satanic "ideal."

The Third Phase, *Qualification*, provided sufficient elucidation to establish the tenets of contemporary Satanism, contrary to prior or current misinterpretation. *The Satanic Bible, Satanic Rituals* and *Satanic Witch* might have been conveniently overlooked, but were readily obtainable to any who chose to gain knowledge of our doctrine and methodology. An aura of respectability prevailed — often to a point of overcompensation — to counterbalance inaccurate presumptions by the outside world.

The Fourth Phase, *Control*, encouraged dispersion and the Peter Principle as means of isolating the "ideal" evaluated from Phase Two. De-institutionalism separated the builders from the dwellers, thus filtering and stratifying what began as an initiatory organization — or persuasion — into a definite social structure.

The Fifth Phase, *Application*, establishes tangible fruition — the beginning of the harvest, so to speak. Techniques, having been developed, can be employed. The Myths of the Twentieth Century are recognizable and exploitable as essential stimuli. Human foibles may be viewed with an understanding towards radical embellishment.

The Ides of March had spent its madness and the equinox had produced its climactic. At dusk on the eve of the new Satanic Age, I immersed my razor in the waters of Zamzam and embarked upon a new role. I sometimes wonder, would things have been any different without the ceremony? Did a ritualistic catalyst help to convince this Pyrrhonic devil that his destiny was being properly exercised?

Symbolism, ritual, ceremony, totem and taboo will always exist and develop or wane as conditions dictate. As Satanists you must perceive such things and having perceived, select or reject in accordance with your needs. Countercultures invariably wind up as dominant cultures. When the occult (hidden) becomes fashionable, it is no longer occult. Yet there will always be a Dark Side. It is the natural Satanist who will be drawn to the abyss of *difference*, whether it be abstract or concrete. Those who have tarried these past short years in fixed abstractions can feel the warmth provided by their temporal identities cooling. Frightened, they know not what icons to take up, and are befuddled with devaluated doctrines and constrained by programmed hypotheses. Many will become "Satanists," who would once have shunned the name. Others will continue to eschew the name, yet survive on the by-products of Satanism, as they have unwittingly (or unadmittedly) done in the past. For those who are the lost, the disenfranchised, the bored, the ambivalent, we have prepared a place.

The past decade has been gratifying. I thank all of those who have remained loyal to me through the years and given me the feedback any symbolic leader requires. To those of you who were with me in the beginning when the show got on the road, and to you who have since become a part of us in mind, body or act of just plain orneriness, I am grateful for your support. "Evil" is still "Live" spelled backwards, and if evil we be *live* we will. Living well is still the best revenge against all adversity. Love, laugh, fancy, create, innovate, reap and revel —as Satanists — in this best of all worlds, World without end. Remember, the first 99 years are always the toughest.

*Rege Satanas!*

# How to Become a Werewolf;
## The Fundamentals of Lycanthropic Metamorphosis; Their Principles and Their Application

Anyone is a potential werewolf. Under emotional stress civilized human qualities regress to basic animal reaction, and a threshold of potential physical change is reached.

**Temperament**

People who normally behave in a coarse and boorish manner would be thought to be bordering on an animal state, hence making a complete transition relatively effortless. This is a fallacy, for churls consider themselves as humans the highest and most noble form of life. They are *almost* animals *all* of the time, so they dare not "go over the brink," for that would be abhorrent.

One who has only risen to the curbstone dares not return to the gutter. Only the higher man can metamorphose, as his ego will allow him to go all the way. He knows he is circumspect and cultured the greater part of his life. So a transition to animalism can be entertained without compunction. Manifestations of this phenomenon are abundant. The most polished individuals become the most degraded when the proper opportunity presents itself. There is no drunk quite so sloppy as a rich drunk. Analogies of such polarities are endless: drunk as a lord, Dr. Jekyll and Mr. Hyde, Count Dracula, Jack London, etc. In virtually every literary, stage or motion picture treatment, the lycanthrope is in his normal state depicted as a human of warmth, understanding, sensitivity and intelligence.

The three principal emotions of sex, sentiment and wonder may be considered as triggering mechanisms, as will be shown by the following formula by which one can effect the change from man into beast.

## Environment

Everyone has at some time or other wandered into an area of such foreboding that it is felt that someone or something is lurking in the shadows, watching, ready to spring and devour. Perhaps it was a deserted house, perhaps a lonely path through the trees, possibly an abandoned quarry. In many cases it is known or discovered that such areas have witnessed death of an unexpected or unusual nature, or perhaps mayhem, rape, or other violence. All actions involving intense or increased production of adrenaline on the part of either victim or perpetrator (lust, terror, aggression, defense, etc.) is followed by detumescence in the form of varying degrees of receptivity (shock, total submission, unconsciousness, death, etc.).

The polarity that such an atmosphere has undergone can be likened to an area where heavy concentrations of electricity have accumulated and discharged repeatedly, thereby recycling the ionization of the atmosphere in a chaotic and disturbing manner. The initial "charge" and attraction of such an area proceeds from its spatial and geometric pattern. This can be likened to an existing feeding trough to which animals come from miles around and dine on the carcasses of their predecessors.

The sado-masochistic dichotomy, with its needs for expression, keeps such an area well-stocked with both hunters and hunted. The hunted are *drawn* to such a spot because of the frightening yet submissive thrill obtained from the environment. Predators then come forth, drawn by the *ideal hunting conditions* and abundance of game. Often, however, the hunters have not originally entered the preserve as hunters, but as fear-inspired searchers after thrills.

If this appears far-fetched, consider a phenomenon common to children on Halloween or on any other night where the setting is right. The child deliberately goes out expecting to be scared, succeeds in being scared, then considers how much fun it might be to scare others, once he has been purged of his fear-needs. He then becomes the hunter and the next child who comes along is his quarry. The entire phenomenon is akin to a recognized psychological manifestation who outwardly fear a situation while at the same time doing all in their power to encourage its occurrence.

## Preparation

This children's Halloween game gives us the clue to the role-change necessary in lycanthropic metamorphosis. Briefly, it is thus: Enter the area you know to be trauma-producing with the fullest intention of being frightened. Allow yourself to be frightened. If necessary wear articles of clothing conducive to the most submissive or vulnerable image. "Accidental" victims are always thus attired. Get the feel of the place as a victim, allowing yourself to be frightened as much as you can. If you can supplement your fear with a sexually stimulating feeling, so much the better. Allow yourself to virtually shake apart with fear and if possible attain an orgasm by whatever means may be necessary, for this will make your subsequent lycanthropic change-over easier.

After you have released all fear and fled the scene of your terror/ecstasy, go home and ruminate over what you felt. You will soon discover that a sort of magnetic pull will manifest itself, beckoning you back to the blighted spot. This uneasy attraction will increase with each succeeding day, ideally bordering on compulsion. When you find yourself unable to resist the temptation to return to your danger spot, repeat the first incident in much the same manner. You will find the second foray into the area even more profound than the first, due to the anxiety and anticipation that has developed over the past days.

In the truest sense, you have been performing a ritual of sending forth your energy into a living, breathing environment. That environment, *because of continual taxation upon its vitality*, acts as a vampire, absorbing energy from those it attracts and, once having attracted, contagiously ensnares for future sustenance. Wilhelm Reich called such areas DOR, indicating a persistent starvation of orgone or enervation of the atmosphere. Such areas are atmospherically hungry and in their barrenness cry out to be fed. All alleged haunted house and terror spots are reinforced by the accumulation of energy supplied them by the anxieties of occupants and anticipation of visitors to return, i.e., the obsessive thoughts of those who have been affected.

The second time you enter your chosen area, you may not be able to spend as much time as first, owing to your increased fear and subsequent need to quickly exercise/exorcise it and move yourself. At this point you are prepared for the metamorphosis — unless you find the second time a "charm," and crave to entertain your fears to greater and more ecstatic heights, in which case you either haven't scared yourself enough, or else there is little chance for role-change. In other words, before you can become the hunter, you must first have aroused and then exorcised a need to be the victim.

If you are a habitual "victim" it is wise to proceed with caution. Your desire to be frightened and its ensuing manifestations could impel you into a situtation whereby you could be severely injured or killed. If, however, you are able to meet your fright-needs and exorcise them, them go on to the next step:

## Metamorphosis

Attire yourself in a manner conducive to the change that is to be effected. Legends of Berserkers donning the skins of wolves and bears hold substantial meaning, in view of the importance of costume in ritual. Dress in the most stereotyped, "corny" manner, as the second skin that you wear is a potent element in complete transmogrification. This is hermetic or sympathetic magic exemplified (as above, so below). If you wear the mask of a wolf or the skin of a beast, it is preferable if it is *not* genuine, as you can better infuse a *facsimile* of the chosen animal with your *own* personality, while drawing from the known attributes of the species represented. The skin or mask will serve as a catalyst, a blueprint, for what you will become as you merge with it.

Enter the blighted area with eager anticipation. When you approach the spots where you would have previously been the most frightened, allow yourself to revel in the thought of how terrifying it would be to another if they were to feel the same fear you had felt, plus the added terror with an actual manifestation of an unfamiliar and grotesque creature. In short, it is now your role to contribute to the fearsomness of the place.

The stage has been set and all necessary components have been activated. You have experienced intense fear; now it is your turn to manifest intense fearsomness in the form of beastiality. Allow yourself to slouch, almost dropping down on all-fours at times. Children are quite proficient in their approximations of animals. Remember when? You've also romped on all-fours with a dog or cat, no doubt. Did you ever consider the implications?

Sniff the air, savoring it and the smells of the environment in which you stand. If there are trees around, get close to them, touching them, pawing them, climbing and shaking them. Do everything possible to emulate an animal. If you are in a building, urinate against a wall or on the floor. Remember, wild creatures are not housebroken! Snort, snarl, roar, grunt — make all the unsavory sounds you want.

As you progressively become more imbued with the sensation of being an animal, you will actually feel certain areas of your body responding in a manner alien to the human anatomy. Your legs will become haunches. Your arms will become forelimbs for claws or paws that crave to grasp at the nearest thing. Your countenance will change. Your facial muscles will begin to twitch in beastial grimaces. All of your senses will become more acute. You will feel the need to urinate more frequently. You will become fascinated with the moon, especially if it is full. If you are indoors, you will seek to explore behind things, into cracks, below boards. You will feel a desire to snuffle into closed areas, burrowing your head and body.

If you feel sexual desire, it will be in a rapacious manner, and if you should perceive another person who might not normally appear sexually to you, the nature of your transformation will make up for their lacking attributes. The impulse to attack will be present, but your *higher* mind must refrain, taking over and holding you in your spot, while still allowing you sufficient impetus to release yourself. This is the stage of transformation where control is essential, unless one is with a willing partner who can enter the Game as the hunted and revel in their roles. If this is the case, then complete sexual assault can be manifested. If not, sufficient restraint to attain sexual release *without* an attack upon the "victim" must be exercised.

At the moment of orgasm, a complete and irrevocable encompassing of the animal within must occur, with whatever abandon to this level may ensue. It is at this time that the change will take place, and if one should be unfortunate (or fortunate?) enough to witness your metamorphosis, you may be assured they will never forget it.

This entire principle, carried out in a ritualistic exercise between pre-cast hunter and hunted is, of course, the basis of such children's games as hide and seek, where one child revels in being frightened while the other delights in terrifying, often with both roles interchanged within a single episode of the game. As children are naturally closer to an animal state, so they are well qualified to teach us means by which we might bring ourselves closer. It is the transitional nature of children that makes them ideal teachers.

Once your transformation has been effected (remember, the most profound manifestation can only occur after sufficient build-up), allow yourself to "come down," having retreated if necessary to a place where you can unconcernedly drop to the ground or floor. If you have done your exercise well, you should, upon returning to your normal state, feel the desire to partake of nourishment.

The tremendous build-up and discharge of energy in reaching this state will have consumed a vast amount of calories. So the obvious epilogue to your ritual, and completion of the animal cycle, is to eat your fill and go to sleep.

# 𝔓entagonal 𝔑evisionism: 𝔄 𝔉ive-𝔓oint 𝔓rogram

In recent years, we've wasted far too much time explaining that Satanism has nothing to do with kidnapping, drug abuse, child molestation, animal or child sacrifice, or any number of other acts that idiots, hysterics or opportunists would like to credit us with. Satanism is a life-loving, rational philosophy that millions of people adhere to. Now we're ready for something that goes quite a few steps beyond just explaining our principles. Every revisionist movement needs a set of goals — guidelines that are clear, concrete, and that will effect significant changes.

The following Five-Point Program reflects attitudes which allow others to decide whether they wish to align themselves with Satanism or not. Each is necessary for Satanic change to take place. When asked what we're "doing," here's the answer:

1.) **Stratification** — The point on which all the others ultimately rest. There can be no more myth of "equality" for all — it only translates to "mediocrity" and supports the weak at the expense of the strong. Water must be allowed to seek its own level without interference from apologists for incompetence. No one should be protected from the effects of his own stupidity.

2.) **Strict Taxation of All Churches** — If churches were taxed for all their income and property, they'd crumble overnight of their own obsolescence, and the National Debt would be wiped out as quickly. The productive, the creative, the resourceful should be subsidized. So long as the useless and incompetent are getting paid, they should be heavily taxed.

3.) **No Tolerance for Religious Beliefs Secularized and Incorporated into Law and Order Issues** — To re-establish "Lex Talionis" would require a complete overturning of the present *in*-justice system based on Judeo-Christian ideals, where the victim/defender has been made the criminal. Amnesty should be considered for anyone in prison because of his alleged "influence" upon the *actual* perpetrator of the crime. *Everyone* is influenced in what he or she does. Scapegoating has become a way of life, a means of survival for the unfit. As an extension of the Judeo-Christian cop-out of blaming the Devil for everything, criminals can gain leniency, even praise, by placing the blame on a convenient villain. Following the Satanic creed of "Responsibility to the responsible," in a Satanic society, everyone must experience the consequences of his own actions — for good or ill.

4.) **Development and Production of Artificial Human Companions** — The forbidden industry. An economic "godsend" which will allow everyone "power" over someone else. Polite, sophisticated, technologically feasible slavery. And the most profitable industry since TV and the computer.

5.) **The Opportunity for Anyone to Live within a Total Environment of His or Her Choice, with Mandatory Adherence to the Aesthetic and Behavioral Standards of Same** — Privately owned, operated and controlled environments as an alternative to homogenized and polyglot ones. The freedom to insularize oneself within a social milieu of personal well-being. An opportunity to feel, see and hear that which is most aesthetically pleasing, without interference from those who would pollute or detract from that option.

# Hymn of the Satanic Empire

*or*

# The Battle Hymn of the Apocalypse

Drums out of the darkness, listen well.
Drums beating like thunder straight from Hell.
Trumpets are blaring, the time's come 'round —
Satan is here to claim his ground!

*Chorus:*
There's an earth that's green, there's an earth that's free,
There's a place for you and a place for me.
But the bleeding hearts wouldn't let it be,
We don't need them any more!

Let the lions and tigers rip them up.
The arena shouts for Christian blood.
Let them chew them up and spit them out —
We don't need them any more!

Once, there was a need for simple minds.
Once, there was a need to save men's souls.
Fools had to be forced to stay in line,
Preachers and bibles could serve those goals.

*Chorus:*
With their holy writ and their card'nal sin
They could force their paper demons in —
To a cardboard prison, a paper cell —
They can't do that any more!

Furies from Hell are diving down!
"Lex Talionis" is their cry!
Even though tricksters make the law,
Justice is served by fang and claw!

*Chorus:*
With their beaks of steel, see them slash askew
Righteous Christian, Buddhist, Moslem, Jew;
They've become a plague, so let's start anew —
We don't need them any more!

Drums out of the darkness, listen well.
Drums beating like thunder, straight from Hell.
"Rege Satanas!" — the time's come 'round —
Satan is here to claim His ground!

*Final Chorus:*
With our morning star from the deepest night
Smash the crumbling cross, for Might is Right.
Let the shuffling zombies grope for light —
And we'll reign forevermore!

© Anton Szandor LaVey
11/18-19, 1988